Global Corporate Social Responsibility Initiatives for Reluctant Businesses

Syed Abdul Rehman Khan
School of Management and Engineering, Xuzhou University of Technology, Xuzhou, China & Department of Business Administration, ILMA University, Karachi, Pakistan & Beijing Key Laboratory of Urban Spatial Engineering, Beijing, China

Zhang Yu
Chang'an University, China

Mirela Panait
Petroleum-Gas University of Ploiesti, Romania & Institute of National Economy, Bucharest, Romania

Laeeq Razzak Janjua
Poznan University of Economics and Business, Poland

Adeel Shah
Institute of Business Management, Pakistan

IGI Global
PUBLISHER of TIMELY KNOWLEDGE

A volume in the Advances in Business Strategy and Competitive Advantage (ABSCA) Book Series

Published in the United States of America by
IGI Global
Business Science Reference (an imprint of IGI Global)
701 E. Chocolate Avenue
Hershey PA, USA 17033
Tel: 717-533-8845
Fax: 717-533-8661
E-mail: cust@igi-global.com
Web site: http://www.igi-global.com

Library of Congress Cataloging-in-Publication Data

Names: Khan, Syed Abdul Rehman, 1987- author.
Title: Global corporate social responsibility initiatives for reluctant businesses / by Syed Abdul Rehman Khan, Zhang Yu, Mirela Panait, Laeeq Janjua, and Adeel Shah.
Description: Hershey, PA : Business Science Reference, 2021. | Includes bibliographical references and index. | Summary: "This book covers the emerging trends and best practices in the context of corporate social responsibility by providing the best practices, techniques, and empirical studies conducted around the globe from both developed and developing countries perspectives"-- Provided by publisher.
Identifiers: LCCN 2021009393 (print) | LCCN 2021009394 (ebook) | ISBN 9781799839880 (hardcover) | ISBN 9781799881308 (paperback) | ISBN 9781799839897 (ebook)
Subjects: LCSH: Social responsibility of business. | Sustainable development. | Poverty. | Corporate governance.
Classification: LCC HD60 .K4835 2021 (print) | LCC HD60 (ebook) | DDC 658.4/08--dc23
LC record available at https://lccn.loc.gov/2021009393
LC ebook record available at https://lccn.loc.gov/2021009394

This book is published in the IGI Global book series Advances in Business Strategy and Competitive Advantage (ABSCA) (ISSN: 2327-3429; eISSN: 2327-3437)

British Cataloguing in Publication Data
A Cataloguing in Publication record for this book is available from the British Library.

All work contributed to this book is new, previously-unpublished material.
The views expressed in this book are those of the authors, but not necessarily of the publisher.

For electronic access to this publication, please contact: eresources@igi-global.com.

Advances in Business Strategy and Competitive Advantage (ABSCA) Book Series

ISSN:2327-3429
EISSN:2327-3437

Editor-in-Chief: Patricia Ordóñez de Pablos Universidad de Oviedo, Spain

MISSION

Business entities are constantly seeking new ways through which to gain advantage over their competitors and strengthen their position within the business environment. With competition at an all-time high due to technological advancements allowing for competition on a global scale, firms continue to seek new ways through which to improve and strengthen their business processes, procedures, and profitability.

The **Advances in Business Strategy and Competitive Advantage (ABSCA) Book Series** is a timely series responding to the high demand for state-of-the-art research on how business strategies are created, implemented and re-designed to meet the demands of globalized competitive markets. With a focus on local and global challenges, business opportunities and the needs of society, the **ABSCA** encourages scientific discourse on doing business and managing information technologies for the creation of sustainable competitive advantage.

COVERAGE

- Business Models
- Balanced Scorecard
- Co-operative Strategies
- Strategy Performance Management
- Resource-Based Competition
- Customer-Orientation Strategy
- Foreign Investment Decision Process
- International Business Strategy
- Globalization
- Value Creation

The Advances in Business Strategy and Competitive Advantage (ABSCA) Book Series (ISSN 2327-3429) is published by IGI Global, 701 E. Chocolate Avenue, Hershey, PA 17033-1240, USA, www.igi-global.com. This series is composed of titles available for purchase individually; each title is edited to be contextually exclusive from any other title within the series. For pricing and ordering information please visit http://www.igi-global.com/book-series/advances-business-strategy-competitive-advantage/73672. Postmaster: Send all address changes to above address.

Titles in this Series

For a list of additional titles in this series, please visit:
http://www.igi-global.com/book-series/advances-business-strategy-competitive-advantage/73672

Handbook of Research on Entrepreneurship, Innovation, Sustainability, and ICTs in the Post-COVID-19 Era
Luisa Cagica Carvalho (Polytechnic Institute of Setubal, Portugal & CEFAGE, University of Évora, Portugal) Leonilde Reis (Polytechnic Institute of Setubal, Portugal) and Clara Silveira (Polytechnic Institute of Guarda, Portugal)
Business Science Reference • © 2021 • 451pp • H/C (ISBN: 9781799867760) • US $295.00

Disruptive Technologies and Innovative Strategies for Organizational Success
Nilsa I. Elias (Western Governors University, USA) Terry M. Walker (University of Louisiana, USA) and Robin Walker (Metropolitan State University, USA)
Business Science Reference • © 2021 • 315pp • H/C (ISBN: 9781799837909) • US $225.00

Cases on Digital Strategies and Management Issues in Modern Organizations
José Duarte Santos (Instituto Superior Politecnico, Spain)
Business Science Reference • © 2021 • 300pp • H/C (ISBN: 9781799816300) • US $195.00

Advanced Perspectives on Global Industry Transitions and Business Opportunities
Fanny Saruchera (University of the Witwatersrand, South Africa)
Business Science Reference • © 2021 • 352pp • H/C (ISBN: 9781799843030) • US $225.00

Competitive Drivers for Improving Future Business Performance
Carlos Martins (Lusíada University of Porto, Portugal) and Paula Rodrigues (Lusíada University of Porto, Portugal)
Business Science Reference • © 2021 • 267pp • H/C (ISBN: 9781799818434) • US $225.00

Entrepreneurial Innovation for Securing Long-Term Growth in a Short-Term Economy
Jorge Gamez-Gutierrez (Universidad de la Costa, Colombia) and Jose Manuel Saiz-Alvarez (Universidad Católica de Santiago de Guayaquil, Ecuador & Universidad Autónoma de Manizales, Colombia & CEIEF-Universidad de Santiago de Chile, Chile)
Business Science Reference • © 2021 • 256pp • H/C (ISBN: 9781799835684) • US $215.00

For an entire list of titles in this series, please visit:
http://www.igi-global.com/book-series/advances-business-strategy-competitive-advantage/73672

IGI Global
PUBLISHER of TIMELY KNOWLEDGE

701 East Chocolate Avenue, Hershey, PA 17033, USA
Tel: 717-533-8845 x100 • Fax: 717-533-8661
E-Mail: cust@igi-global.com • www.igi-global.com

Table of Contents

Preface

Writing this book is primarily to provide an up-to-date text at a reasonable cost. The scope of corporate social responsibility (CSR) has continued to grow with a rapid speed, which is reflected in the content of this book. This book has included core aspects of CSR philosophy and practice.

ORGANIZATION OF THE BOOK

There are 14 chapters in the book. A brief description of each of the chapters follows:

Chapter 1 aims to explain the phenomenon of internationalization of firms and companies in the current world. Furthermore, this chapter also explains the importance of the international process and its theoretical background. The chapter concludes that CSR is an essential pillar for economic growth and helps companies achieve overall economic profits.

Chapter 2 highlights the problems of poverty and the sustainable policies for its reduction. The aim of writing this chapter is to explain the significant causes of poverty around the world. Furthermore, this chapter also describes how the private and, more specifically, the corporate sector can influence overall poverty reduction.

Chapter 3 discusses and explores the basics of Islamic Corporate practices in the Muslim world. The chapter reveals that Islamic corporate social responsibility provides a systemic framework of CSR practice, which is beneficial for everyone. By applying the framework, companies in Muslim countries can achieve sustainability as this in the form of social, economic, and environmental sustainability.

Chapter 4 describes the nexus between emerging technology in terms of the fourth industrial revolution and corporate social responsibility in the presence of driven challenges and opportunities. This chapter also explains the current implications of the fourth industrial revolution to understand the current challenges and address and find opportunities to increase sustainable development.

Chapter 5 explores how Financial institutions can make a substantial contribution to promoting the principles of sustainable development among their primary stakeholders, namely portfolio investors and financial consumers. The chapter highlights how climate change has led to the intensification of the financial innovation process and new financial instruments such as green bonds or sustainability indices.

Chapter 6 signifies the importance of fintech. The chapter discusses how financial education can benefit the consumer in making intelligent buying decisions. The chapter concludes how fintech impacts financial markets to improve sustainability.

Chapter 7 reflects on the exploitation of foreign direct investment by translations in developing countries. The chapter aims to highlight International organizations like the United Nations or the Organisation for Economic Co-operation and Development to promote corporate social responsibility.

Chapter 8 discusses the involvement of different stakeholders to promote corporate social responsibilities. It elaborates the behavior of such stakeholders for CSR promotion and tools used to promote the United Nations' seventeen sustainable development goals.

Chapter 9 focuses on the analysis of the efforts made by the European Union authorities to encourage companies in the process of promoting sustainable development and involvement in various CSR actions.

Chapter 10 highlights corporate social responsibility in companies throughout developing countries in Asia. The chapter brings forward practices by companies in Pakistan, India, Bangladesh, and China.

Chapter 11 discusses CSR practices in the western world. Examples of companies practices from the USA and United Kingdom have been highlighted for readers to better understand the advantages in society and how it helps them increase market share.

Chapter 12 reveals the social and economic benefits of implementing corporate social responsibility. The chapter portrays the human side of the corporation by discussing its practices and services that affect communities.

Chapter 13 explicitly targets the involvement of Europe and how it helped in developing the CSR concept. The chapter discusses relevant history revolving around CSR practices started by Europeans. It concludes by discussing some of the CSR practices implemented by European companies and how they are closer to achieving the United Nations seventeen sustainable development goals.

Chapter 14 talks about the future CSR challenges for businesses in developing and underdeveloped countries. The chapters highlight the correct degree of trade offs the three capital (planet, people, and profit) in the same context. It lists and discusses critical future challenges, which are crucial for corporate social responsibilities.

Syed Abdul Rehman Khan
School of Management and Engineering, Xuzhou University of Technology, Xuzhou, China & Department of Business Administration, ILMA University, Karachi, Pakistan & Beijing Key Laboratory of Urban Spatial Engineering, Beijing, China

Zhang Yu
Chang'an University, China

Mirela Panait
Petroleum-Gas University of Ploiesti, Romania & Institute of National Economy, Bucharest, Romania

Laeeq Razzak Janjua
Poznan University of Economics and Business, Poland

Adeel Shah
Institute of Business Management, Pakistan

Acknowledgment

This book is partially supported by the Beijing Key Laboratory of Urban Spatial Information Engineering (NO. 20210218) and the National Natural Science Foundation of China (No. 202202457).

Chapter 1
Firm Internationalization and Essence of CSR

ABSTRACT

This chapter aims to explain the phenomenon of internationalization of firms and companies in the current world. Furthermore, this chapter also explains the importance of the international process and its theoretical background. Furthermore, this chapter also discusses the nexus between corporate social responsibilities with internationalization and its overall essence. The chapter concludes that CSR is an essential pillar for the economic growth and expansion of every firm. The more CSR policies adopted by the companies, the more will be the companies' overall economic profits by directly or indirectly helping society.

INTRODUCTION

In the recent era, the factor of globalization increases the overall world polarization. More significantly, after the recession in 2008-2009, the world is transformed from a unipolar to a multipolar state. The factor which contributes to this transformation is the stable economy, which is led by international trade. International trade always acts as a catalyst for economic growth. It generates local employment, induces domestic investment, and a great source of foreign earning. One of the essential benefits obtained from international trade is raising individual income. Thus, it accelerates the residents' per capita income, and per capita income positively increases residents' social

DOI: 10.4018/978-1-7998-3988-0.ch001

lives, thus enhancing the country's human development index. It has also been observed in developing countries that international trade and export significantly impact local communities' lives and significantly reduce income inequalities. The role of information and technology in the economic growth process cannot be ignored. Thus international trade is an essential factor in technological advancement, as Coe and Helpman (1995) conduct an empirical analysis of 21 OECE states, covering the period of 1971 to 1990, and conclude that International trade is a crucial technological channel advancement and transformation. Besides trade (import or export) of a physical good, the recent period service sector also plays a vital role in the economic growth process, especially the banking sector's cross-border expansions, insurance sector, and IT services.

Similarly, International trade, more specifically export, is the outcome of higher production; therefore, Kavoussi (1984) surveyed 73 developing countries that were further divided into middle and low-income countries. In his concluding remarks, he mentions that all these countries' higher economic growth was highly correlated with the country's high export growth. The global trade is now in USD trillions and continuously growing, table 1 exhibit value for global export and import in USD Trillion.

Table 1. Export and Import all around the world (US$ Trillion)

Year	Export of Goods and Services	Import of Goods and Services
2005	13.00	12.8
2010	18.9	18.3
2015	21.3	20.7
2018	25.1	24.5
2019	25.4	24.8

Source: World Bank Development Indicators

In the recent period, international labour migration and movement have also become push factors of international trade activities. In high-populated countries such as China and India, once their immigrants moved to other countries, they usually import religion, taste, and culture in receipt country. All these factors then future becomes the primary cause of international trade. The mentioned table 1 and figure 1 indicate the current level of import and export worldwide, thus indicating the volume of trade worldwide.

Figure 1. Worldwide Export and Import (US$ Trillion)

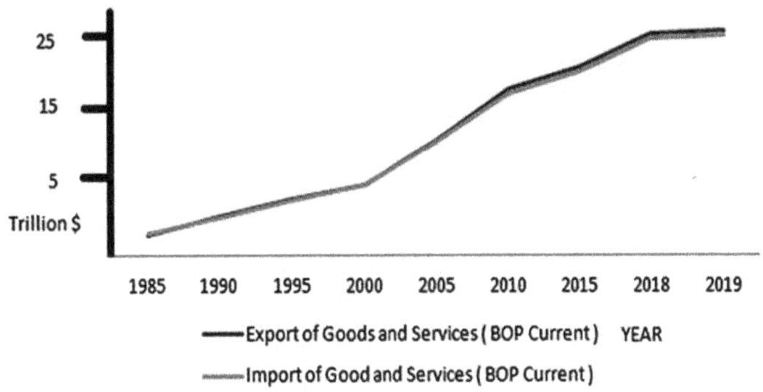

THEORETICAL DEBATE OF INTERNATIONALIZATION PROCESS

This section is composed of various theories of international trade. Trade theories generally explain the various factors and patterns of international trade. Besides, it is also true; the globalization factor also expands the process of internationalization. Therefore various economists stress a particular dimension of internationalization. Below are some of the integral theories discussed.

The Classical Theory of International Trade

As (Mill Schumacher 2012) mentions in his work that "classical theories put forward by classical economists, Adam Smith, David Ricardo, and John Stuart." The main postulates or assumptions which the classical economist explained, can be divided into three types, first illustrating the condition of a trade by which two countries can initiate a trade with each other, second demonstrating the general commodities of trade, so what things should be exported or imported? Moreover, in the last, it provides evaluation, which also describes the conditions of international trade hence the cost of goods at which the international trade exchange should be carried out. Moreover, the classical economist's primary focus is growth-oriented, so their primary concern has been to evolve around the nation's wealth and then increase it further. Classical theories of international trade are sub-divided into two major categories:

Absolute Cost Advantage

Adam Smith put forward this theory. The main factor mentioned in his work Wealth of Nations (1776) is creating wealth via international trade. He also mentions that bilateral trade's mutual benefit is generally based on the absolute advantage principle. However, Adam smith's theoretical hypothesis based on (2x2x1) is two nations, two commodities, and one output factor indicated as labor; hence his argument is grounded on labor force value. Similarly, assuming absolute cost advantage implies the country should usually specialize and only export certain goods in which they have an absolute cost advantage.

Comparative Cost Advantage

In 1917, David Ricardo, an English economist in his book Political Economic and Taxation, proposes this theory. This theory assumes that countries generate those commodities with the most significant comparative advantage or the minor comparative disadvantages. A country will also export those products where its comparative advantage is the highest and import those commodities where its comparative disadvantage is low-level Leamer and Levinsohn (1995).

Export Behaviour Theory and Motives

The theory of export behaviour originally introduced by (1968 by Kenneth Simmonds and Helen Smith) scientifically demonstrates in their research work the importance of innovation through export promotions in internationalization. Their analysis's primary postulates are that export-led promotional strategies may be more effective in the process of internationalization rather than appealing to national interest motives. The critical driver of export is to boost sales rather than build market awareness of Thomas Araujo (1985).

The Factor Proportion Theory

In economic literature, factor proportion theory is named as H-O (Heckscher-Ohlin) model, which Eli Heckscher put forward (1919) and Bertil Ohin (1933). Initially, Eli Heckscher explains one country's comparative advantage over its relative abundance of production factors such as land, labor, and capital. On the other hand, Bertil Ohlin describes the notion of output factor into a concept and then describes it further with the phenomenon of foreign trade Heckscher and Ohin (1991). This theory is used with reference 2x2x2 (country, factor, and commodity) for trade evaluation. Similarly, this theory also suggests trade equilibrium among two nations regarding heterogeneous specialties and natural resources Bajon and Kehoe (2010). Typically, as a country that consists of a large population, it often has a large labor force, so therefore these countries, it is possible to manufacture goods at a lower cost using the labor-intensive mode of production. Then a country that has high resources generally goes to capital-intensive means of production for its products.

The Product Life Cycle Theory of International Trade

The theory of product life cycle was developed by Raymond Vernon (which further turns into a model named International Product Life Cycle Model (IPLC) model, which is recognized as a mainstream internationalization model. According to Vernon's hypotheses, "product development activities are carried out at the introductory stage of the product in developed countries, while goods are exported at the growth level while the export activities and at the product maturity level the production activities are shifted to the less developing countries in order to lower the cost," indicated by Urhan (2017).

Moreover, as Mercer (1993) stated in his work, "the transition of developing production countries is generally due to the saturation of the product on the market and also to the achievement of the degree of product standardization. In the initial stage of the product life cycle (an introductory stage), the product is developed in most advanced countries, together with innovation, already possesses advantages in research and development". In most cases, due to the high societal acceptance of innovation in-country products, the local market is quickly famous, and higher demand also decreases its risk and uncertainty. Till massive production, the products are usually only available for local customers at this stage. The second phase is the growth stage, as it occurs right after the initial stage; products are also starting to grow in the international market at this stage. Foreign investors generally start investing in the product and contribute to the management and, consequently bringing in new market research strategies and techniques, thus usually reducing the cost, then the product is also internationalized worldwide. The 3rd stage of the product life cycle is known as maturity. The country typically innovates the product at this point, losing its competitive advantage as the product is worldwide famous, and new investors are starting to manufacture that specific product in developing countries. Investors will thrive on the foreign market in developing countries, owing to low labor and raw material costs. The fourth stage is known to decline; further progress can be made in the product, which will increase its sales, and there is generally little demand for the product on the market at this point. Below, figure 2 explains Vernon's product life cycle and its stages.

Figure 2. Product life Cycle

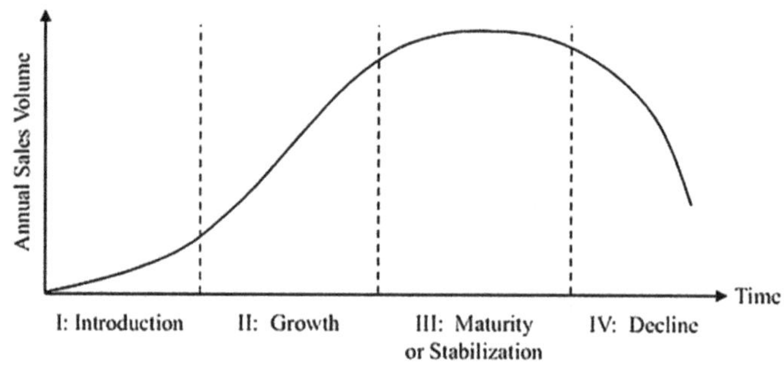

Internalization Theory

The Internalization theory explained by Buckley & Casson (1976) suggested that MNCs internalize their resources to distribute them between different product categories and target markets. To minimize costs, firms select the best structures based on the assessment of the costs related to each phase of production. Furthermore, in general, based on the internalization theory, markets are usually imperfect. In host markets, MNCs avoid market imperfections through internalizing their operations regarding tacit knowledge, raw materials, intermediate products, and perishable goods. On the other hand, Verbeke & Brugman (2009) stated that internalization theory has two essential assumptions. First of all, economic activities are only carried out inside the firm when they are more cost-efficient and effective than collaborative transactions. It is valid for both domestic and foreign projects as well, and side by side, Secondly firms will only participate in FDI projects if the expected performance is higher than that of domestic investment.

Firms also compare the expected performance with the potential returns from contractual modes, such as licensing. Internalization theory also has some limitations, and it is also criticized in various aspects; first of all, this theory does not show the effect of location advantages on the choice of entry mode. Moreover, the theory assumes that competition in the host country involves a monopolistic firm with inferior technology inactive in dealing with the entrant. In today's markets, the nature of competition is dissimilar and dynamic, which is valid due to globalization nowadays. Furthermore, in the recent ear, the theory does not explain the uncertainty caused by local partners' behavior in a joint venture or major problems regarding mergers and acquisitions, criticized by Fisch (2008). It is also true, as nowadays is a lot of MNC, faced trouble in carrying out their business operations in other countries due to local laws and unstable environments.

On the other hand, the major drawback of internationalization theory is that it cannot compare FDI with exporting, and as it assumes conditions that result in FDI as argued by Ekeledo & Sivakumar (2004). The literature, therefore, concentrated primarily on the growth and advantages of retail companies in international markets. International activity growth by retailers based in Europe emerged in the 1980s and was the precursor to significant academic interest and activity (Myers & Alexander: 1995). Furthermore, as in recent periods due to the common EU market, this particular interest researchers get more research interest. In terms of describing nexus among retail and international business, Dawson (1994) and Pellegrini (1994) conducted a research work to illustrate retail internationalization study; In the broader study of the internationalization of companies and, in particular, the necessity not only to describe the global activity but to analyze the fundamental process. Similarly, Vida and Fairhurst (1998) have suggested a model for the process of retail internationalization, which would provide a basis for further research into international retail expansion.

FACTORS OF INTERNATIONALIZATION

There are numerous factors that all multinational companies must consider before proceeding toward internationalization. These factors have a direct or indirect influence on every multinational company's day to day operation. The most common factors are mention in diagram 3 below.

Political

These are the overall governing factor of individual countries, and these factors also indirectly describe the government's response toward overall economic activities. Effect economic policies of any individual country can enhance its overall economic situation, which directly or indirectly stabilizes all other sectors of the country. These policies include internal tax and government subsidies. Furthermore, in developing countries, political stability is an essential factor for sustainable economic growth.

Economic

These factors include all the micro and macroeconomic factor on which the economic base of any individual country exists. In macro-economic factors, banks' discount rate, level of employment, exchange rate, government budget (i-e government revenue and government spending). However, all these macroeconomic factors directly affect individual firm activities at are micro-level. Efficient economic policies at the macro level could quickly increase individual firm production, efficiency, and profit, which induce them to enter the international market. The most common factors are mentioned in Figure 3.

Social

Social factors include living standard, literacy rate, culture, religious lifestyle, and then the various level of behaviours for using and purchasing any product. All these factors are considered are essential attribute which every multinational company always considers before internationalization process. Furthermore, one of the most important factors is the level of immigrants in a particular society and the level of integration with the local inhabitants.

Technological

It includes acceptability and way of dealing with technological changes internally or externally in the country or any individual society. Furthermore, these factors also include the technological transition in every sector of society. Similarly, on the other hand, usually developing is not so much advanced, so internationalization for high industries is always risky.

Figure 3. Factors of Internationalization

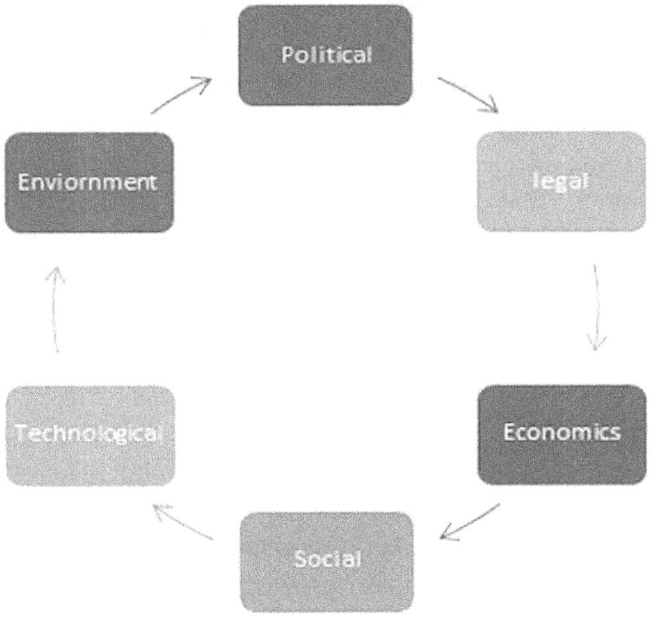

Environment

Environment includes the average temperature around the year, climate change, and the weather of any country. These entire factors together determine the level of demand of supply for any multinational company performing business activities in any foreign country. Furthermore, it has also been observed that mostly Multinational companies from developed countries usually moved their production to underdeveloped countries where environmental laws are not so strict.

Legal

Legal factors include local laws of any individual country. These laws include the law of employment, working hours, employer responsibility toward employee health, wages rates, maternity leave for women, employer or company responsibility in case of accident extra. Furthermore, that factor also includes the response of and pattern of dispute solving, and time is taken by the court of law to solve or pass any judgment.

ESSENCE OF CSR

It is the era of globalization; every day, new inventions and innovations in science bring revolution to the world. These revolutions become the grassroots for economic activities; moreover, business organizations are formed for carrying out these economic activities. These organizations consist of several resources that drive the wheel of economic activities. Moreover, these economic activities, active like fertilizer, increase societies' healthiness, where these business activities need to be done. In the past recent years, business activities' social context is the favorite hot subject for discussion in the business world. The social aspect of these activities is practiced for more than 4000 years. For example, if we study the ancient Vedic and Sutra texts of Hinduism and the Jatakas of Buddhism include ethical admonitions on usury (the charging of excessive interest), and Islam has long advocated Zakat, or a wealth tax(Pohl and Tolhurst: 2010). Nowadays, the social aspect of business also works like marketing strategy; however, it has become an integral part of every corporation for growing healthy in recent years. In the recent era, business organization activities toward society exist as the name of corporate social responsibility (CSR). The concept of CSR is not that much old, the tree of CSR start growing from last 50 years, consist of three phases Pre CSR phase, which starts from 1960 to 1990 named as phase 1 and moves towards phase 2, named CSR initiation phase, from 1990 to 2000 and finally arrived at phase3 the early CSR mainstreaming which start from 2000 to till now, see figure 4, which shows the evolution map of CSR (CSR Quest sustainability framework: 2004).

CSR is one of the earliest and most powerful frameworks in business and society sciences, stated by (Windsor 2001). In 1980, we can also found the roots of CSR in actual business practice. A notable example is Cadbury chocolate company. In 1879 they moved to greenfield sites, which came to call the Bourneville, some miles from Birmingham, where the actual factory was situated. The primary purpose of opening the Cadbury "factory in a garden" heralded a new era of industrialization and joined welfare of the employee after being in-depth consultation of Cadbury brothers. By 1899 the Cadbury factory was expanded a lot with more than 2600 employees and managed scientifically with analytical laboratory, advertising and cost office, sales department, work committee, pension department, education, and employee training. In 1900 the George Cadbury established the Bourneville village to promote the housing reforms and gave the new dimension to business with the message "successful business in thriving communities."Another example we can found in J & J Company's business strategies, six decay ago, published its credo, which states the primary shareholder were its customer, employee, and communities which they opened. New equipment has to be acquired, new services have been given, and fresh goods have been introduced.

Figure 4. The Evolution Map of CSR
(A Historical perspective of the CSR movement 2004 p 19)

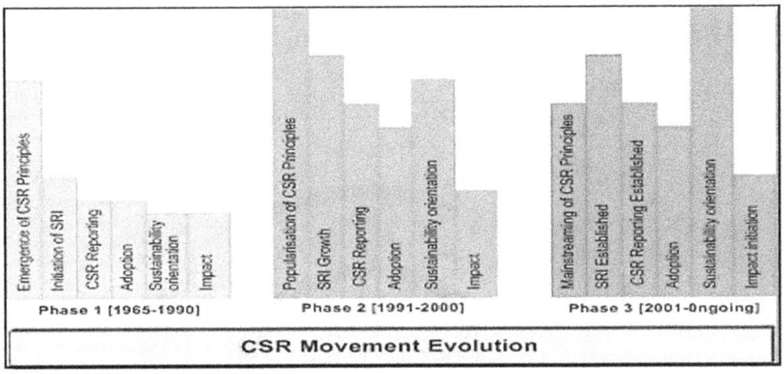

Figure 5. CSR as a core strategy
(Hadi et al.: 2013)

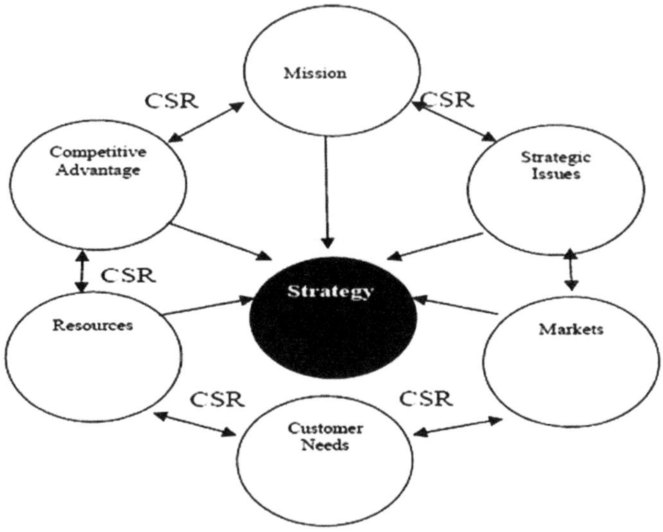

Figure 5 (Hadi et al.: 2013) illustrates the phenomenon of CSR as a core strategy, the journey of CSR now a day started from missionary statement, and on the way, with best practice, it becomes an integral part of every organization, more broadly CSR explains how an organization combines social, environmental and economic issues in a transparent and accountable way in its principles, culture, decision-making, policy, and operations, thereby establishing good practice in the business, building wealth, and improving society.

Figure 6. The business in society

As we can see, figure 6 (the business in society) illustrates that an organization is surrounded by the impact of general people, which can be employees and customers, moreover also the governmental officials, the organization's every step can influence every person who is directly or indirectly associated with the organization. In the modern era, every organization defines a different reason for adopting corporate social responsibility. Certain businesses regard CSR as a method to strengthen relationships with stakeholders (customers, regulatory agencies, local communities, NGOs). Others see CSR as a way of improving operating efficiency and lowering costs. Market opportunities influence others because it has a reputation as a good business citizen. Furthermore, some organizations may assume that the CSR commitment is moral. (Rahbek Pedersen and Neergaard: 2009).

DIMENSIONS OF CSR

Who and what is a company to us cannot avoid the basic question? The response once seemed obvious, but it did not. The corporate terms have changed, ownership has been replaced by investment, and a corporation's assets are largely contained in its workers, not in its buildings and machinery. With this transition in mind, we need to focus on business meaning (Handy, 2002). Why does the business exist? Of course, for earning some profit, the economic responsibility focuses on the maximum profit earning and attaining a competitive advantage in the market. The legal and economic responsibilities usually depend on all the activities concerning its success for attaining the highest profit by using the traditional methods. Stating the corporation's flow towards these responsibilities (Carroll, 1991) shed light on the concept of the corporation's social responsibilities. In a simple form, corporate social responsibility can be the aggregate effect of economic responsibilities and legal and ethical approaches also under the light of philanthropic responsibilities. Corporations that wish to be an ethical must at first be responsible economically and legally. (Jamali & Mirshak:2006). Although (Carroll: 1991, p. 43).In short, the CSR Business should pursue a profit, follow the law, be ethical, and be a good corporate citizen in terms of the model. Besides, economic and legal obligations are socially necessary, ethical responsibility is socially required, and philanthropy is socially desired (Windsor:2001).

Figure 7. Pyramid of CSR
(Windsor 2001; Carroll 1991)

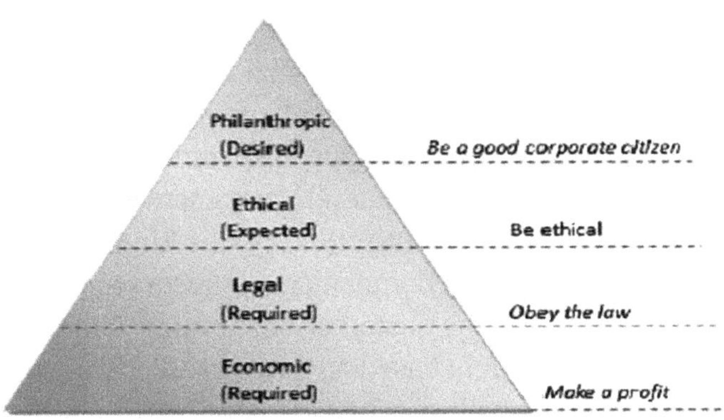

In general, (Carroll:1991) states the relationship between business and society. In contrast, he missed to state the recent trends that integrate the social, economic, and environmental aspects of corporate responsibility; moreover, nowadays the managers are likely to use the banner of sustainability within and outside the corporation (Visser, 2006).

In globalization, every organization must act according to rules and regulations set by the government and law making agencies for attaining maximum profit. We have to eat to live; food is an essential state of life. Nevertheless, if we primarily lived to feed, making food an adequate or particular reason for life would be gross. In other words, the aim of a company is not to make maximum profit. It is to make a profit so that the organization can do something or something. This "anything" is the real reason for the enterprise.

In this situation "CSR Three-domain Model" is developed to provide an additional CSR explanation. The economic domain focuses on all practices, which directly or indirectly have a positive economic effect on companies. Ethical obligations should be taken into account in the application of economic policies concerning the positive legal element. The ethical domain means that the company's ethical obligations meet society's expectations and all stakeholders (Schwartz & Carroll, 2003).

The standard and norms set regarding consumers, stakeholders, and shareholders, which help keep the organization respect, regard, and care, are considered ethical responsibilities. In recent days, technological advancement has brought a revolutionary change in legal and ethical responsibilities very vastly concerning social situation variation like human rights and standard environmental extra. Based on the legal viewpoint, the society hopes that companies will achieve their economic mission within the context of legal demands (Jamali & Mirshak,2006). Given below figure 8, illustrate these responsibilities as domains of corporate social responsibility.

In the recent era, measuring performance becomes an integral part of every business strategy; without appropriate gain, no business can exist, these gains can be objective and subjective. In general, customers are the business king, and no business can survive without servicing this king at the best level. In a free economy market, only that company gets success and become popular among the people who adopt the customer-first policy. Client satisfaction is described as a global assessment based on the consumer's overall experience in purchasing and consuming a product or service over time. (Anderson, Fornell and Mazvancheryl, 2004).

Figure 8. The three-domain model of CSR
(Schwartz & Carroll: 2003)

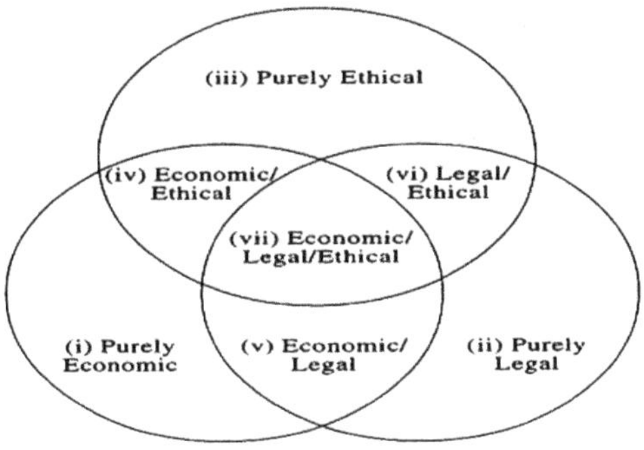

Moreover, in the current period, only those companies or business organizations can get success who believes in every long-lasting relationship with the customer by providing all their wants with superior quality, reliability, and service. If we analyze this concept under discussion for the last fifty years, it became a real competitive advantage today. However, now a day's customer always demands a great degree of ethical and spiritual behavior from the organizations in every aspect of their business dealings, and Customers are always looking for those organizations that are friendly with society. A business partnership with a non-profit organization, regardless of whether the cause was familiar or unknown, strengthened brand attitudes (Lafferty and Goldsmith: 2005). Further, those who heard of an actual corporate philanthropy program had more favorable attitudes to the organization and greater identification with it, more intentions to buy and invest better intentions to find a job with the company than those without any program. (Sen: 2006).

In general, we spend most of our time earning money, whether directly or indirectly we are associated with business enterprises, we spend most of our time at work. Our working experience strongly affects our attitudes as well as our psychology. In general, it means humans always want relaxing time and want to have relaxed life by applying the minor forces. The force directly affects our family and us, whereas it indirectly affects the community in which we live. Socially conscious organizations do more to provide meaningful work that encourages workers to grow and achieve their potential.

CSR is a form of corporate investment with a dual emphasis on social welfare and stakeholder relationships (Barnett, 2007). Employees are the most significant stakeholder for any business organization; with any motion of business organization, employees are effect directly or indirectly. In most cases, workers may serve as agents of social change when they encourage businesses to adopt socially accountable actions (Aguilera et al:2007). Employees work for the organization, and in a general way, they act as a bridge between the consumer and business organization. Employees can easily read the people's perception regarding the organization, and in the meanwhile, employees also help the organization adopt the practice for a friendly business environment. As a stakeholder group, employees perceive, evaluate, judge, and react to CSR programs and actions (Rupp et al, 2006). Nowadays, women have become an essential part of the business; business organizations are rapidly increasing policies for making work and work places more family friendly.

In addition to these strategies and procedures, leading organizations often find that they can reap substantial benefits in efficiency, employee engagement, creativity, lower turnover, and higher results through a change in work procedures, job processes, and work culture to enhance the integration of work and family members. In other words, convergence between work and family may become a competitive advantage.

Stakeholders can be divided into different categories. NGOs and other social stakeholders need to justify their involvement in the organization to be accepted as a stakeholder. The organization's cooperation is not always welcome, but often it may be the only solution to tackle a complicated issue. (Roloff,2007). The most significant benefits the organization can by collaborating with the nongovernmental or non-profit organization are reducing the cost. Interaction with the environment of the company is defined as an inclusive network definition. The inclusive network consists of interactions between businesses, organizations, and communities to establish predictability and economic activities in a non-stable environment. The organizations become stronger together with other organizations and actors than if they work individually (Reficco and Marquez: 2009).

Every business exists with different modes and different intentions with different directions as CSR's concept is not too old, so the management scientist figures out the Social performance model for companies (CSPM), which assesses the performance of every organization's social obligation. Therefore, the response model provides more theoretical integration and a greater focus on strategic and processing factors but little guidance on how adequate strategies and resources for achieving its specified goals can be established. Thus CSPM is used to measure the degree of responsiveness of the company towards CSR. Every business exists with different intentions and different work levels, some are concerned with manufacturing, and some provide services to the peoples. However, for exiting healthy in the business world, it is the duty to perform some social social-envoi mental step to gain a significant comparative advantage. CSPM deals with various CSR parameters, i-e, social aspect, philosophy aspect, and stakeholder aspects. Moreover, all these parameters are described in three different modes, which explain clearly the CSR consent in the business.

INTERNATIONALIZATION IMPACT OF CSR

The world is moving so fast; international integration brings revolutions in this world. Now a day's no organization or manufacturing body cannot work without the concern of globalization. Thus their every step or strategy has a direct impact on society. For every organization, if they wanted to get good responsiveness from their employee, customers, and other third parties, they should be more socially responsible for everyone associated with them. Corporations can only get growth through proper means of internationalization or globalization, but on the other hand, they should encounter new challenges that limited their growth and potential profits. Earning big profits by spending less cost is a fundamental principle of every corporation, but on the other hand, due to the effect of global integration, tariffs, local and international laws, culture, and also can increase the hurdle in the growth of the business. Corporate social responsibility today goes beyond the ancient philanthropy of the past – donating money to good causes at the end of the financial year – and now, it is a year-round responsibility for the world around them, best working practices, dedication to their local communities, and the awareness that brand names are based not just on them. Now we have to proceed to a daunting measure of corporate responsibility, where we judge not only by the feedback but also by the results: the difference we bring to the environment we live in and the commitment we bring to reducing poverty. (Mr. Gordon Brown 2001).

The effect of globalization just increases communication and reduces the distance gap between businesses to business. The stronger the relationship between the suppliers, joint venture, and alliance partners in every business sector, the stronger the competitive success. If business organizations can make a good network regarding business partners to reduce complexity and reduce cost, increase quality which directly benefits the consumer.

Every organization needs to build a strong relationship among its stakeholders, which is explained as its networks. The multi-stakeholder network will help establish legitimate policies for the relationship between business and society (Roloff 2008). With these network connections, the organization can get long-term benefits such as marketing or demographic clusters.

In this new era of the globalization era, and according to the current situation of the market, every multinational company or organization must create a strong bridge with non-profit organizations, which further help them in entering the new international market with a positive approach, with the help of these non-profit organizations the companies able to get vital general information which help them to penetrate or create deep roots in the local markets. Looking at domains, environmental efficiency, community relations, and labor relations are the most frequently measured dimensions of CSR (Muller and Kolk 2010), and the process of internationalization increases the importance of all domains, so for performing well and being more successful in global scenario every organization should maintain some standard according to these domains.

In the internationalization process, the multinational corporations are very actively transferred or trying to penetrate their home or origin country's corporate social responsibility practice throughout their global integration. Moreover, these companies get a high level of competitive profit or benefits, while after adopting the corporate social responsibility practice see a positive change in sales and profit. Meanwhile, buyers and consumers are also influenced by CSR because they have a right to choose goods that are manufactured in an environmentally sustainable way and whose manufacturers have taken social responsibility carefully. (Mirvins & Googins: 2006). Corporate social responsibility may be implemented as a first stage approach in the internationalization process, but the methods can take time, which can contribute to the organization's long-term benefits. As, (Udayasankar, 2008) continued to note, MNCs can be involved in a bad situation if they ignore CSR or do so inadequately. If an organization or firm can connect with the relevant network, it will eventually be more accessible for any organization to integrate into any new market. New markets are not the only advantage and strength in collective behavior that can lead to protection in harmful environments. However, (Mirvins and Googins, 2006) and (Hallbäck:2011) stated the importance of internal factors, which play a more critical role, since they are more predictive of the company's sustained success and suggested a critical internal aspect, known as the values and traditions of companies.

On the other hand (Laudal: 2011) stated that two barriers, the cost-benefit ratio, internal and external monitoring, have been completed. While multinational companies may have enough finishing capital to conduct CSR, they will still face the challenge when profits and social, ethical activities are reconciled. In a recent time in general perspective, some companies use corporate social responsibility as strategic activities to gain the best public support, which helps them stay in global and in the local market in the long-run process. In most cases, the companies adopt corporate social responsibility as their advertisement tool. See Figure 9 (O Miluwi D: 2013 and John Wei: 2011) illustrate the international process of corporate social responsibility as the cyclic process in which cooperate social responsibility initiatives start from the organization and distribute toward all the stakeholder which are spread all over the world by the medium of society.

Figure 9. International process of CSR
(Yunbu and Yuqi, 2012)

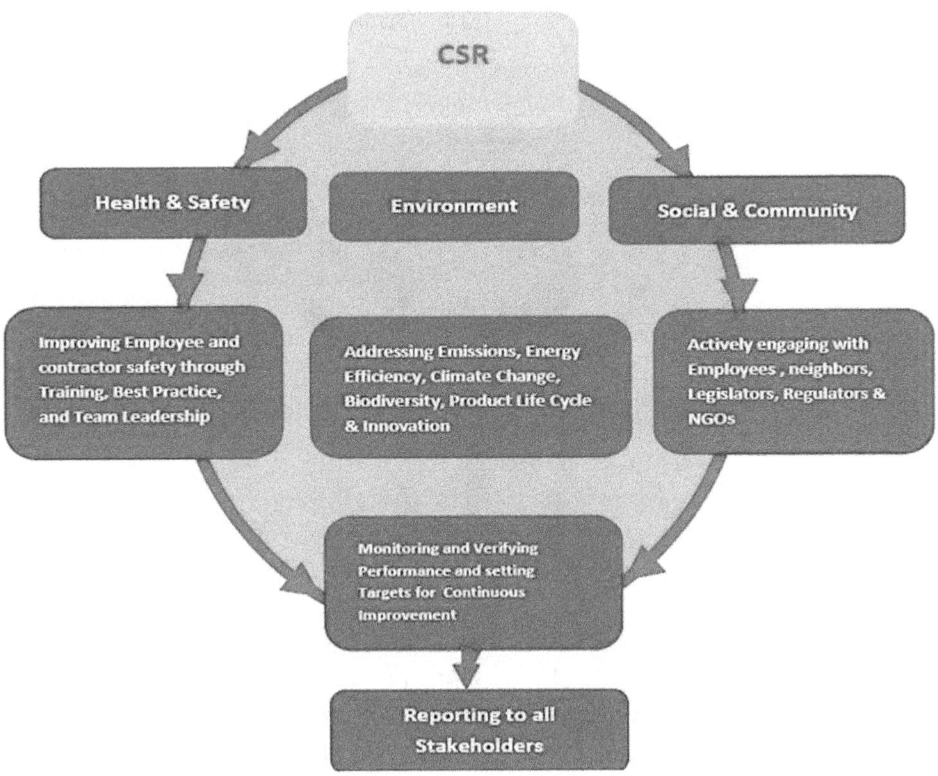

When analyzing the internationalization process, multinational businesses would be strongly affected by the local political and legal climate beyond their control and cannot alter local community perceptions. (Laudal, 2011). On the other hand (Barin Cruz and Avila Pedrozo, 2009) proposed local and global levels on various CSR aspects, including the CSR framework, stakeholder dialogues. They claimed that multinational companies' significant challenge to undertake CSR effectively is to find the balance between the local and global levels. Moreover, in developing countries, the high level of corruption and political instability creates a hurdle in multinational corporations' corporate social responsibility practice. Correct human issues, unhealthy and unsafe food technology, and an unfriendly environment make the situation more serious. As figure 10 describes, in the global world, with motivation, every multinational organization should keep an eye on sustainable development while considering the economic, environmental, and social factors, with the consultation of all direct or indirect stakeholders.

Figure 10. Internationalization process of CSR
(Yunbu and Yuqi 2012)

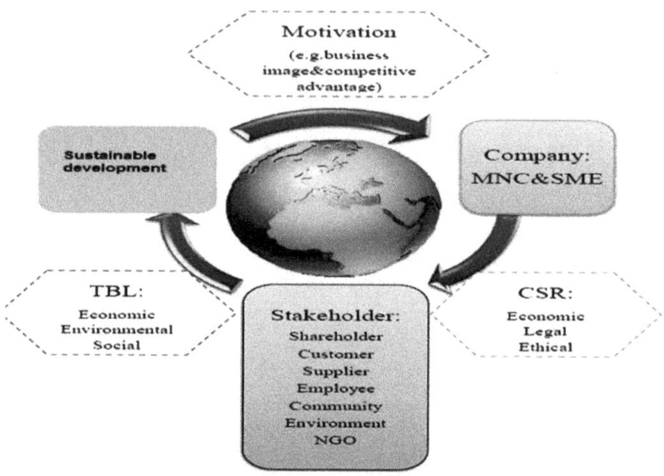

As given in figure 11, explain the phenomenon of how international strategies of CSR can enhance the performance of any organization.

Many companies negatively affect their stakeholders although, researchers have labelled this behaviour as corporate social irresponsibility (CSiR), (Strike, Gao, and Bansal, 2006) define CSiR, a series of corporate activities adversely affecting (in the longer term) legible statements of the social stakeholder. It might also say that, in the case of properly placed and marketing CSR programs, there is no net negative effect on shareholders and investors of a company, with the consequence that revenue and profits are higher even though profit merges are lowered marginally.

Figure 11. International strategies of CSR
(Bhattacharya et al. 2008)

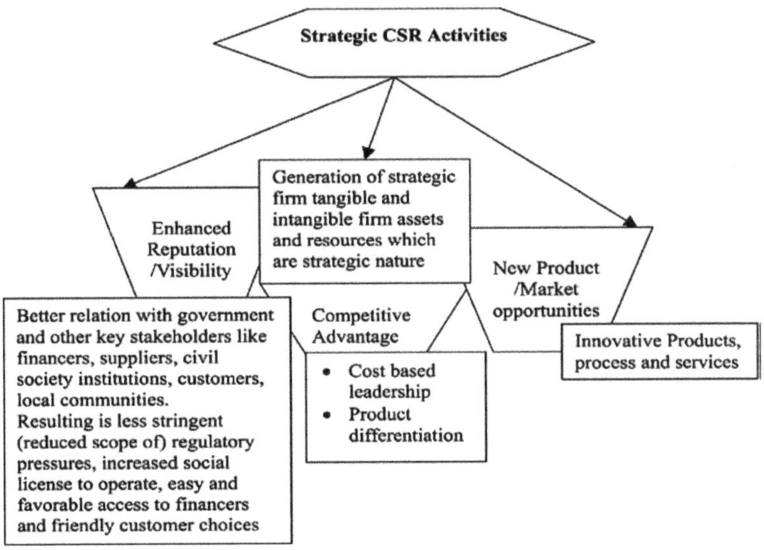

CONCLUSION

During internationalization, most businesses face a vital option to conform to local norms and to "do as Romans do" even if norms are not favourable for their country of origin, or to apply the same corporate standards internationally. However, to achieve growth, it is the firm's responsibility to adopt efficient CSR policies. Therefore, they can stay in the business world for a long time.

REFERENCES

Aguilera, R., Rupp, D., Williams, C., & Ganapathi, J. (2007). Putting the s back in corporate social responsibility: A multilevel theory of social change in organizations. *Academy of Management Review*, *32*(3), 836–863. doi:10.5465/amr.2007.25275678

Anderson, E., Fornell, C., & Mazvancheryl, S. (2004). Customer Satisfaction and Shareholder Value. *Journal of Marketing*, *68*(4), 172–185. doi:10.1509/jmkg.68.4.172.42723

Barin Cruz, L., & Avila Pedrozo, E. (2009). Corporate social responsibility and green management. *Management Decision*, *47*(7), 1174–1199. doi:10.1108/00251740910978368

Barnett, M. (2007). Stakeholder influence capacity and the variability of financial returns to corporate social responsibility. *Academy of Management Review*, *32*(3), 794–816. doi:10.5465/amr.2007.25275520

Bhattacharya, C., & Korschun, D. (2008). Stakeholder Marketing: Beyond the Four Ps and the Customer. *Journal of Public Policy & Marketing*, *27*(1), 113–116. doi:10.1509/jppm.27.1.113

Bhattacharya, C., Korschun, D., & Sen, S. (2008). Using corporate social responsibilty to win for war of talent. *MIT Sloan Management Review, 49*(2), 37-44. Available at: https://sloanreview.mit.edu/article/using-corporate-social-responsibility-towin-the-war-for-talent/

Carroll, A. (1979). A Three-Dimensional Conceptual Model of Corporate Performance. *Academy of Management Review*, *4*(4), 497–505. doi:10.5465/amr.1979.4498296

Carroll, A. (1991). The pyramid of corporate social responsibility: Toward the moral management of organizational stakeholders. *Business Horizons*, *34*(4), 39–48.

Chapple, W., & Moon, J. (2005). Corporate Social Responsibility (CSR) in Asia: A Seven-Country Study of CSR Web Site Reporting. *Business & Society*, *44*(4), 415–441. doi:10.1177/0007650305281658

Hallbăck, V. (2011). *Drivers and Barriers for Corporate Social Responsibility in Multinational Corporations A case study of Wărtsilă*. Masters. Water and Environmental Studies Department of Thematic Studies Linkăping University.

Handy, C. (2002). What's a business for? *Harvard Business Review*, 54. Available at: http://www.ecrc.org.eg/Uploads/documents/Articles_A%20guide%20to%20corporate%20social%20responsibility.pdf

Kostova, T., & Zaheer, S. (1999). Organizational Legitimacy under Conditions of Complexity: The Case of the Multinational Enterprise. *Academy of Management Review*, *24*(1), 64.

Krishna Erramilli, M., Agarwal, S., & Dev, C. (2002). Choice Between Non-Equity Entry Modes: An Organizational Capability Perspective. *Journal of International Business Studies*, *33*(2), 223–242.

Lafferty, B., & Goldsmith, R. (2005). Cause"brand alliances: Does the cause help the brand or does the brand help the cause? *Journal of Business Research*, *58*(4), 423–429.

Laudal, T. (2011). Drivers and barriers of CSR and the size and internationalization of firms. *Social Responsibility Journal*, *7*(2), 234–256.

Michelini, L., & Fiorentino, D. (2012). New business models for creating shared value. *Social Responsibility Journal*, *8*(4), 561–577.

Miluwi, O. D. (2013). Corporate social responsibility: Global idea and national importance in the 21st century. *International Journal of Advanced Research in Management and Social Sciences*, *2*(3), 101. Available at: http:// www.garph.co.uk

Mirvis, P., & Googins, B. (2006). Stages of Corporate Citizenship. *California Management Review*, *48*(2), 104–126.

Muller, A., & Kolk, A. (2008). CSR Performance in Emerging Markets Evidence from Mexico. *Journal of Business Ethics*, *85*(S2), 325–337.

Pohl, M., & Tolhurst, N. (2010). *Responsible Business*. John Wiley & Sons.

Porter, M., & Kramer, M. (2006). the link between competitive advantage and corporate social responsibility. *Harvard Business Review*, *84*(12), 78–92.

Quest Sustainability Framework, C. S. R. (2004). *A Historic perspective of the CSR movement*. Available at: http://www.csrquest.net/uploadfiles/1D.pdf

Rahbek Pedersen, E., & Neergaard, P. (2009). What matters to managers? *Management Decision*, *47*(8), 1261–1280.

Reficco, E., & Marquez, P. (2009). Inclusive Networks for Building BOP Markets. *Business & Society*, *51*(3), 512–556.

Roloff, J. (2007). Learning from Multi-Stakeholder Networks: Issue-Focussed Stakeholder Management. *Journal of Business Ethics*, *82*(1), 233–250.

Rupp, D., Ganapathi, J., Aguilera, R., & Williams, C. (2006). Employee reactions to corporate social responsibility: An organizational justice framework. *Journal of Organizational Behavior*, *27*(4), 537–543.

Schwartz, M., & Carroll, A. (2003). Corporate Social Responsibility. *Business Ethics Quarterly*, *13*(4), 503–530.

Sen, S. (2006). The Role of Corporate Social Responsibility in Strengthening Multiple Stakeholder Relationships: A Field Experiment. *Journal of the Academy of Marketing Science*, *34*(2), 158–166.

Strike, V., Gao, J., & Bansal, P. (2006). Being good while being bad: Social responsibility and the international diversification of US firms. *Journal of International Business Studies*, *37*(6), 850–862.

Udayasankar, K. (2007). Corporate Social Responsibility and Firm Size. *Journal of Business Ethics*, *83*(2), 167–175.

Visser, W. (2006). Revisiting Carroll's CSR Pyramid: An African Perspective. In E. R. Pedersen & M. Huniche (Eds.), *Corporate Citizenship in Developing Countries* (pp. 29–56). Copenhagen Business School Press.

Windsor, D. (2001). The future of corporate social responsibility. *The International Journal of Organizational Analysis*, *9*(3), 225–256.

Yunbu, Z., & Yuqi, Z. (2012). *A Comparative Case Study on Corporate Social Responsibility (CSR) between SMEs and MNCs. Masters*. Halmstad University.

Chapter 2
Corporate Social Responsibility and Poverty Alleviation

ABSTRACT

Poverty is one of the significant issues of the world. There are several causes of poverty. Numerous countries of the world adopt sustainable policies for its reduction. There are also direct and indirect responsibilities of the corporate sector to play a vital role in its reduction. The aim of writing this chapter is to explain the significant causes of poverty around the world. Furthermore, this chapter also explains how the private and, more specifically, the corporate sector can influence overall poverty reduction.

INTRODUCTION

Indeed, defining poverty is not an easy concept; wide ranges of definitions exist in the literature based on different disciplinary approaches and ideologies. As (Grusky and Kanbur, 2006) express in their work, after post-world war II defined poverty in monetary terms, moreover express in terms of using the level of income or consumption to measure poverty, and (Lipton and Ravallion, 1993), express poverty based on head counts, they defined the poor by the headcounts of those who fall below given the level of income and consumptions or poverty lines.

People can be counted among the poor people or in poverty when deprived of income and other essential resources to spend their daily lives such as food, shelter, and other material things, enabling them to play an active role in society

DOI: 10.4018/978-1-7998-3988-0.ch002

Townsend (2006). Similarly, the world bank defines poverty as the inability to attain a minimal standard of living in an average society. Furthermore, poverty includes hunger, lack of shelter, illness, and then inability to visit a doctor, such as lack of medical facilities, lack of schooling, unemployment, and lack of basic human necessities such as clean water extra.1 Furthermore, World Bank also defines poverty as "A person is supposed to be poor if his or her consumption or income level falls below some minimum level necessary to meet basic needs ("poverty line").2

POVERTY AS THE FIRST TARGETED GOAL IN MDG AND SDG

The Millennium Development Goals are the world's most significant commitment to humanity, which led the human race towards better life and development. It is a bundle of development goals and targets set by independent states to reduce poverty and make availability of basic human needs for everyone, thus reducing the gap between developing and underdeveloped societies. Initially, the theme of MDG was only associated with "global strategy"; thus, it turns into "global plus national," individual states and countries start making their policies under the light and guidance of these global strategies. The current theme of MDG and targets drive through series of outcomes of meetings and conferences held at various international forums and platforms started from the early period of 1990. Table 1 indicates the venue and themes of all these conferences and meetings, which turn these strategies into millennium development goals.

The first-millennium development goal was set to reduce extreme poverty and hunger, then forwardly education for all, gender equality and women empowerment, reduction in child mortality, maternal health improvement, fight against HIV/AIDS and other diseases, and environmental sustainability, and increases global partnership for development. As (McArthur 2014) stated, MDGs were a product of iterated distillation, extracted from a wide array of global processes, with many actors involved over the several years, which is probably true moreover MDG become the world's central reference point for development cooperation and guidance (see figure 1).

Table 1. Foot Prints of Conference

Date	Location	Theme of conference
5 to 9- March -1990	Jomtien Beach, Thailand	The world summit Education for all.
30-September- 1990	New york, USA	The world Summit for Children development.
3-14-June-1992	Rio De Janeiro, Brazil	The United Nations Conference on Environmental Development.
3-4-September-1994	Cairo, Egypt	The International Conference on Population and Development.
14-March-1995	Copenhagen, Denmark	The United Nations, World Summit for Social Development.
4-15-September-1995	Beijing, China	The world summit for woman's rights.

Source: Author Own

Figure 1. Millennium Development Goals

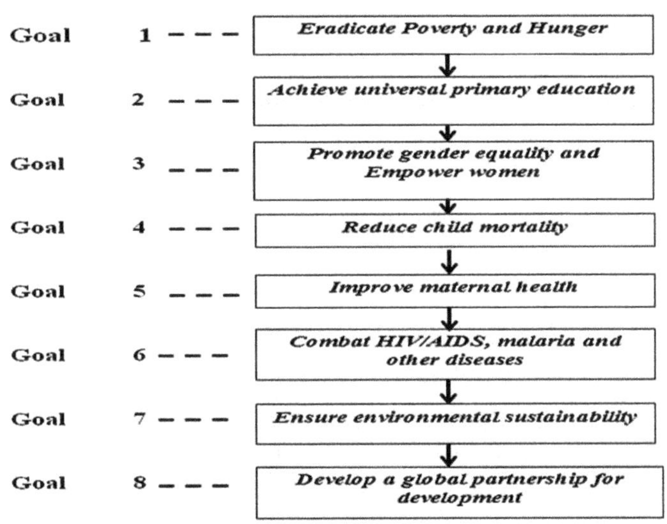

Apparently, after poverty, which the first goal, the next six goals focus on the significant underlying causes of poverty, lack of access to education, health care, employment opportunities for all, gender inequality, poor living conditions, and environmental threats. The last goal indicates the development of global partnerships, such as how developed and industrialized countries work together with low-income and emerging countries to enhance the standard of living of developing countries.

POVERTY AS A GLOBAL ISSUE

Every development strategy aims to eliminate poverty and injustice and to encourage sustainable development. Development policy also makes it easier to find solutions to other global problems, including hunger, which is the primary cause of poverty, especially in developing countries. Education and health indicators are also higher developed and more prosperous countries. Less than one child in 100 in rich countries does not achieve the fifth birthday. However, on the other hand, the ratio is 5 to 7 children from 100 unable to reach the fifth birthday. The goal of all policies should be to improve developing countries' resources to be less dependent on development assistance or foreign Aid. One of the significant roles, which can play in achieving stable life for everyone, is sustainable development, which is based on economic development, social progress, and environmental sustainability. **"It was the best of times; it was the worst of times, it was the age of wisdom, it was the age of foolishness, it was the epoch of belief, it was the epoch of incredulity …"3.** This particular phrase is enough to describe the high level of inequalities in this world nowadays. On the one hand, the rich people in the world enjoying all comfort and luxuries of the world, and on the other hand, there are millions of people who are spending their lives in extreme poverty, and most of them not able to afford one time of meal which is enough for the body nutrition. In 2017 821 million people were undernourished, and it is also expected that, by the end of 2050, 2 billion people will be undernourished.4

Similarly, one between two international borders, one country is enjoying peaceful sleep, and similarly, on the other side, there are 24/7 military escalations due to war. Furthermore, one of the International One country's sides has freedom of speech and democracy and on the other hand one country under the control of dictator and without any freedom of speech by the general population.5

The majority of the studies mention that poverty, social inequalities, internal and external economic factors, and financial instabilities in combined form induce political stability (Draman, 2003). More specifically, due to the war against terror & internal and external conflicts in the middle east and upper African region, millions of people migrate from their homeland and living in refugee camps without any employment and necessary facilities required for living daily. All these factors in combined form induce and increase poverty as well.

Table 2. List of Global Issues

Thematic Area	Issue
Global Economy	International Trade / Financial Stability / Poverty/ International Migration/ Inequalities / Food Security /Intellectual Property Rights / Debts Relief
Human Development	Education / Medical Issues / Refugees
Environments	Climate Change / Fresh water access and Sanitation / deforestation / Sustainable Energy / Loss of biodiversity
Peace and Security	Military escalations / Wars / Drugs / Money laundering / Genocide / Terrorism
Global Governance	Reforms of United Nations System / International Orders / Human Rights / Corruption / Conflict preventions / Global Security

Source: Introduction to Global Issues by VINAY BHARGAVA

Table no 2 explains the majority of the global issue in a collective form. Among the global issue, economic prosperity is on the top of the list. All the issues which are curial for economic prosperity are technically interconnected with each other. International trade can be increased due to high production. Production is carried out by using the factor of production, land, labor, and capital. In the current situation nowadays, one question is always arises, sustainable use of land. As unsustainable use of land resources along with unsustainable production methods already created massive environmental issues. Deforestation not only harms the local inhabitants due to this, but all the natural mechanisms of nearby areas also suffer a lot. Unwell come rains and storms are the primary cause of deforestation. By 2050 due to climate change, approximately 11 million more people will suffer from poverty.*, therefore research predicts that it is tough to meet SDG 1 entirely by the end of 2030.

One of the harmful effects of corruption can be observed in developing countries. Poverty and social inequality usually arise due to mismanagement of public funds and corruption. Similarly, corruption induces furthermore organized crimes such as money laundering and tax evasion. Both money laundering and tax evasion reduces governmental revenues and massively affect the government investment process. In the case of developing countries, it increases poverty as well Janjua and Rehman (2019).

In terms of health, at the moment, one of the most significant emerging issues faced by the world in the current pandemic crises (Covid-19). Approximately 6,731,793 people infected with it, 393,721 lost their lives, and 3,271,515 recovered from it.† Death numbers are expected to increase shortly due to a lack of relevant medicine of that particular covid-19. Due to that pandemic crisis, most countries of the world were under a lockdown situation. Schools, universities, offices, and manufacturing units were utterly close. Similarly, on the other hand, for a while globally, flight communications were also suspended. That particular lockdown ultimately impacts all the economic and social activities. Due to the recent freeze in overall economic activities globally, it is expected to have a significant recession and massive poverty wave. As Professor Adil Najam (Boston University) indicated in his interview in December 2019; that even in the era of information and the industrial revolution, the world is not ready for any diseases with belong to a specific location and then suddenly spread all across the globe within few days. If that happened, it would impact every individual of the world, thus due to the factor of globalization.

Similarly, he also said that particular crises suppose to be acute crises for all the world leaders and other political powers, as in the current era, there no single order of the world is exciting; thus, it multi-polar world that we are experiencing now. In the past few months, the world is under a lockdown situation, massive economic recessions are expected, people are losing their job, and poverty across the globe increases.

One of the significant impacts which the world will experience is not doubted poverty. Besides, pandemic crises of poverty never ended in the world. There were always rich people and poor ones in every corner of the world in all eras. Similarly, even in the fourth industrial revolution and in globalization, the income inequalities worldwide are increases, which means the gap between poor and wealthy people is increasing with massive accelerating speed. Moreover, inequality in most countries is growing, even in cases where all incomes have risen steadily. However, the overall class distribution in terms of rich and poor are still a big issue.‡ It is also true that the overall poverty around the world decreases, but on the other hand, it also matters how scientists and economists of the world define poverty, what exactly poverty is for them. Figure 2 indicate the web of poverty.

Figure 2. Web of poverty

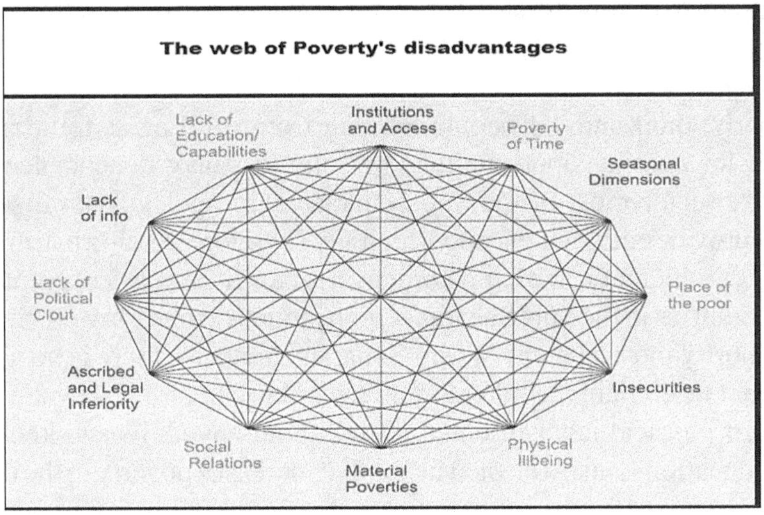

Besides overall poverty, one of the emerging issues of the world is hunger. Even the world is become global village due to rapid globalization, but approximately 821 million people still living in hunger, and similarly, 1 in 9 individuals in this world still go to bed with an empty stomach each night.6 However, Najam (2019) indicates that the world's current period will always remember in history as we have food that is available to feed everyone in this but still in this world some of the people every night sleep Hungry. Due to recent pandemic crises, it is expected to have more hunger in the world. It is true to say that poverty and hunger have a direct relationship with each other. More the poverty, more will be hunger. One of the critical factors, which increases poverty and hunger worldwide, is global climate change. As we have discussed early, among 17 SDG, four goals are related to global climate change. One question arises, is it possible that climate change can cause poverty and hunger? Indeed, it is.

As we have already discussed earlier, poverty is a significant issue in the global world nowadays. Majority of the poor people living in Sub-Saharan Africa and South Asia countries. Most of these countries are dependent on their natural resources; furthermore, they are fragile and conflict-affected states. Similarly, according to an estimate, 1.7 billion people live in severe poverty without access to social services and security. Among the challenges to complete the target of sustainable development goals, poverty reduction is one the major in developing countries. In developing countries, the majority of poor people living in rural areas and mostly depend on agriculture. Due to recent adverse climate change, there is a decline in rainfall in most of the Sub-Saharan region, which directly affects agricultural production and increases poverty.

Similarly, thousands of people migrate from rural areas to urban areas to search for earning opportunities, but due to heavy dependence on the agriculture sector most of the Sub-Saharan region not industrialized, thus unable to provide employment opportunities. Therefore, rural-urban migration becomes a problematic and extra burden on urban cities. Lack of employment in most countries in the Sub-Saharan region induces crimes as well. Similarly, in the majority of rural areas of Sub-Saharan countries, there is no access to education. Once young people migrate toward urban cities, they are usually looking for physical labor-oriented jobs without any skills and knowledge. Lack of education is also a critical factor that increases poverty in the majority of developing countries.

Non-seasonal rains, unexpected floods, and hurricanes are few examples of rapid climate change in the world. Although with the help of an algorithm and big data science, the meteorologist of the world can forecast regarding rain, but on the other hand sometimes it is hard to predict overall intensities of rain as well. The situation is getting worse when a massive storm damages the field and crops. Thus harvesting vegetables is not a single phenomenon; it depends on several months. Although this is the period of the industrial revolution, Overall production in the world showing us an upward trend but on the other hand industrial pollution in terms of carbon dioxide emission and water pollution is also emerging issues of the world. Thus water and air pollution are the primary cause of rapid climate change.

It is the era of globalization, which is the outcome of the fastest-growing emerging technology, but on the other hand, there is still always a question of why this world still cannot catch a direction? Furthermore, the answer that comes to everyone's mind is that there is something wrong, somewhere, and what is wrong, that is a challenging question. One more critical aspect, which arises among the world researchers, is that emerging technologies bring revolution in this world, but similarly, on the other hand, more problems are lined in front of us. In terms of the world's problem, few of the countries, even in technology, can provide jobs to young people. Nearly 500 million new jobs will need to be created by 2020 to provide opportunities to unemployed people.

Similarly, with the help of renewable energy technology, we overcome global warming, but still, there is a climate change issue. The Earth's average land temperature has warmed nearly one °C in the past 50 years due to human activity, global greenhouse gas emissions have grown by nearly 80% since 1970, and atmospheric concentrations of the major greenhouse gases are at their highest level in 800,000 years. Similarly, there have been significant gaps in the financial system and other flaws in the global financial crisis that may result from such an integrated global economy. Some years after the recession, weak growth, unorthodox monetary policies in major economies, and restricted public spending are still struggling in the global economy. We must find forms of resilience and market resistance in the financial system. The recession has led to a significant decline in public confidence and faith in financial institutions. The internet is changing the way we live, work, produce and consume. With such extensive research, digital technologies cannot help but disrupt many existing business and government models. We are entering the age of the Fourth Industrial Revolution, a technological transformation driven by a ubiquitous and mobile internet. The challenge is to manage this seismic change to promote the long-term health and stability of the internet. Within the next decade, it is expected that more than a trillion sensors will be connected to the internet. By 2025, 10% of people are expected to be wearing clothes connected to the internet, and the first implantable mobile phone is expected to be sold. If almost everything is connected, it will transform how we do business and manage resources more efficiently and sustainably.

Nevertheless, how will this affect our privacy, data security, and our relationships? Today, 43% of the world's population is connected to the internet, mostly in developed countries. How will we achieve the United Nations' goal of connecting all the world's inhabitants to affordable internet by 2020? Over the past few decades, the world has seen significant advancements in health, and primarily, as a result, people are generally living longer, healthier lives. However, severe global health challenges remain, ranging from dealing with pandemics to the rise of non-communicable diseases (NCDs) to the prohibitive costs of care, particularly in developing countries. The number of people on the planet is set to rise to 9.7 billion in 2050, with 2 billion aged over 60. The global health system will need to adjust to this massive population growth, which will be concentrated in the poorest countries, and increasing numbers of elderly. It means shifting the current focus on treating sick people to prevent illness and preserve populations' health. By 2050, the world must feed 9 billion people. Among the global issue, economic prosperity is on the top of the list. All the issues which are curial for economic prosperity technically all are interconnected with each other. International trade can be increased due to high production. Production is carried out by using the factor of production, land, labor, and capital. In the current situation nowadays, one question is always arises, sustainable use of land. As unsustainable use of land resources along with unsustainable production methods already created massive environmental issues. Deforestation harms the local inhabitants, due to this, all the natural mechanisms of nearby areas suffer a lot. Unwell come rains and storms are the primary cause of deforestation. It is also estimated that, by 2050, approximately 11 million more people will suffer from poverty due to climate change.7, therefore research predicts that it is tough to meet SDG 1 entirely by the end of 2030.

One of the harmful effects of corruption can be observed in developing countries. Poverty and social inequality usually arise due to mismanagement of public funds and corruption. Similarly, corruption induces furthermore organized crimes such as money laundering and tax evasion. Both money laundering and tax evasion reduces governmental revenues and massively affect the government investment process.

POVERTY IN DEVELOPING COUNTRIES

As we have already discussed earlier, poverty is a significant issue in the global world nowadays. Most of these countries are dependent on their natural resources. Furthermore, they are fragile and conflict-affected states. Similarly, according to an estimate, 1.7 billion people worldwide live in severe poverty without access to social services and security. Among the challenges to complete the target of sustainable development goals, poverty reduction is one the major in developing countries. In developing countries, the majority of poor people living in rural areas and mainly depend on agriculture. Due to recent adverse climate change, there is a decline in rainfall in most of the Sub-Saharan region, which directly affects agriculture production and increases poverty on hand.

Similarly, thousands of people migrate from rural areas to urban areas to search for earning opportunities, but due to heavy dependence on the agriculture sector, most of the Sub-Saharan region not industrialized, thus unable to provide employment opportunities. Therefore, rural-urban migration becomes a problematic and extra burden on urban cities. Lack of employment in most countries in the Sub-Saharan region induces crimes as well. Similarly, in the majority of rural areas of Sub-Saharan countries, there is no access to education. Once young people migrate toward urban cities, they are usually looking for physical labor-oriented jobs without any skills and knowledge.

Lack of education is also a critical factor that increases poverty in the majority of developing countries.

Table 3. Multidimensional Poverty in Different Region of World

Regions	Population in severe multidimensional poverty (Percentage)
Arab States	6.9
East Asia and the Pacific	1.0
Europe and Central Asia	0.1
Latin America and the Caribbean	2.0
South Asia	11.3
Sub-Saharan Africa	35.1

Source: United Nations Development Program

Furthermore, table 3 indicates that 35.1% of the Sub-Sahara African population is living in extreme poverty, and Europe and Central Asia consist of the minor percent of Multidimensional poor people in their region, which is 0.1% of the population.

POVERTY AND CORPORATE SOCIAL RESPONSIBILITY

CSR is a universal phenomenon, and in the contemporary world, all multinational corporations adopt it, regardless of size, sector, and country of origin (Pimpa, 2011). On the other hand, it is also the true majority of existing literature reveals that CSR is the responsibility of sizeable Multinational Corporation (Perrini, F; Russo, A; Tencati, A; 2007), which is not valid as working ethically without harming the society is the responsibility of all the corporations regardless of their size. Besides every individual, whether they are a part big organization or even a smaller organization, they should not involve in any action which harms the environment moreover cause the global environment. Similarly, it is also true the big organization spread more business around the world. Therefore, their social world is not only based on their origin; thus, it is spread worldwide as (Maignan, Isabella, O.C, Ferrell, 2001) in their work mention that usually CSR is imposed by a stakeholder in such a way that business meets its economic, ethical, legal, and discretionary responsibilities. Therefore CSR in a more precise way can be a mixture of strategic voluntary, and legal moves. The role of efficient and effective leadership at the local and international level cannot ignore, to address all the key issues collectively. The Multinational Corporation leader can play an essential role in the cooperation of local community leaders in identifying problems related to poverty and then providing their support and technical assistance in the poverty eradication process (Ragodoo, 2009).

Similarly, on the other hand, it is also the responsibility of a local leader to guide the local community regarding the hazard of climate change. In case of any unsustainable method adopted by the local community, local leaders must step out and adequately guide them along with experts in particular areas. This phenomenon is also addressed by Sustainable development goals, which are **"Strengthen the mean of implementations and revitalize the Global Partnership for Sustainable Development."**

As we have discussed earlier, poverty is a global issue, although poverty can be observed in developed nations and underdeveloped nations. The demand for greater involvement of businesses, especially the corporate sector, in sustainable development objectives by United Nations development agencies and other governmental agencies is increasing very rapidly; however, besides sustainable development goals related to the environment, primary focus recently given to goals that could to use for eradicating poverty. Nevertheless, traditionally, corporate social responsibility (CSR) programs have not historically covered the social Problems related to poverty (Medina-Muñoz, 2020). These massive problems are related to health, education, food and nutrition, and shelter.

Historically, social concerns such as poverty and underdevelopment are not the concern of entrepreneurs, especially for the business community. Companies have only one social obligation, which is traditionally towards its investor and shareholder; thus, companies and the business community need to invest the capital of shareholders in such activities, increasing the profit and maximizing the income. There is nothing more than an actual adoption of a socially responsible doctrine that will kill the private business system; business is needed to gain income and contribute to the bottom line, and that is what business can and must do (Friedman2020).

In general, a business's social responsibility revolves around the economic, legal, ethical, and discretionary expectations that society has of organizations at a given point in time. Furthermore, as Carroll defined, CSR's four-dimensional definition involves a business's conduct so that it is economically profitable, law-abiding, ethically oriented, and socially supportive. The discretionary dimension involves voluntarism and philanthropy. Furthermore, as (Ismail 2011) it is not limited to shareholders alone but applies to various stakeholders; the company has a broader obligation. Therefore, it is proper to argue that these stakeholders are every individual of society in border terms. The case backs that the government alone can certainly not claim to have a sole obligation to better their people's lives as it exceeds their capabilities, thus hard to manage everyone.

On the other hand, it is a more complicated situation in populated countries, where the population's burden depends too much on the government. If the government is unable to meet its citizens' growing demand, then this is where the companies should assist the government. Moreover, in developing countries, handwork with the government is usually conducted by MNC (Multinational Corporations) as local companies are not strong enough. Furthermore, these companies also do not have the technology, which can be useful for social work.

In some cases, MNC usually engage their self's more than their exiting capabilities and capacities. As endorse that phenomenon in his work (McWilliams et al.,2006) In broader terms, CSR is a situation in which the company goes beyond enforcement and participates in its acts that seem to encourage some social good, beyond the company's interests and what is needed by law thus overall compliance. In terms of social work, (Maç & Çalış,2011) in their analysis enlist social work which covers under the head of CSR. Thus the companies usually adopt for their social work. This social worker is related to Climate, education, cultural art, funding, and donation. Out-of-the-box activities may include creating environmentally sustainable goods, environmental training, establishing cooperation with universities and technical secondary schools in the automotive sector, the development of training programs, the contribution of educational institutions to the technical infrastructure, and the sponsorship of cultural and art activities. A study conducted by (Inyang et al., 2011) concluded that business organizations have already enlisted their social steps that indicate their commitment to CSR. However, most have only taken up some philanthropic operation for their stakeholders. Usually, their stakeholder is direct or indirect investors. It has also been observed that companies usually engage themselves in social work to fulfill their legal obligations.

MULTIDIMENSIONAL POVERTY INDEX

The determination of a poverty line cannot be based on an arbitrary selection of a low-income level. Only scientific criteria independent of income can justify where the poverty line should be drawn. The multiplicity and severity of different types of deprivation can constitute those criteria. Therefore, the key is to define a threshold of income below which people are found to be thus deprived. The measure of multiple deprivations must be decided based on evidence about every sphere of the range of social and individual activities people perform to fulfill individual and family needs and social obligations. The Multidimensional Poverty Index (MPI) has been developed by Alkire and Santos (2010) for the 2010 Human Development Report. It is an index of acute multidimensional poverty and is based on the Alkire and Foster (2011a) dual cut-off method for poverty identification.1 The MPI (M) itself then can be thought of as the product of the MPI headcount H (measuring the share of the population that is multidimensional poor), and the weighted deprivation share of multidimensional poor households A (measuring the weighted percentage of indicators, in which the multidimensional poor are on average deprived). Alkire and Santos (2010) identify three dimensions to be included in the MPI: health, education, and living standards see figure 3.

Figure 3. MDPI
(Alkire and Santos 2010)

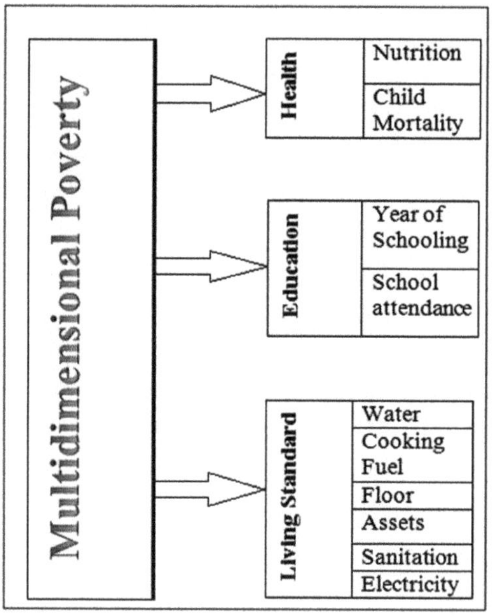

The third component of MDPI, the multidimensional poverty index is consists of the standard of living. As an indicator for impoverished people, six measures consider the contribution of deprivation of living conditions to overall multidimensional poverty. It consists of household usage of cooking fuel, which indicates whether the families or individuals have access to sustainable fuel or use cook of wood or charcoal or sung. After cooking fuel, it consists of access to electricity. As in 2018 approximately, 90% of the world population have access to electricity; there is still 10% of the world population living without electricity.

Figure 4. The percentages of multidimensional poor people

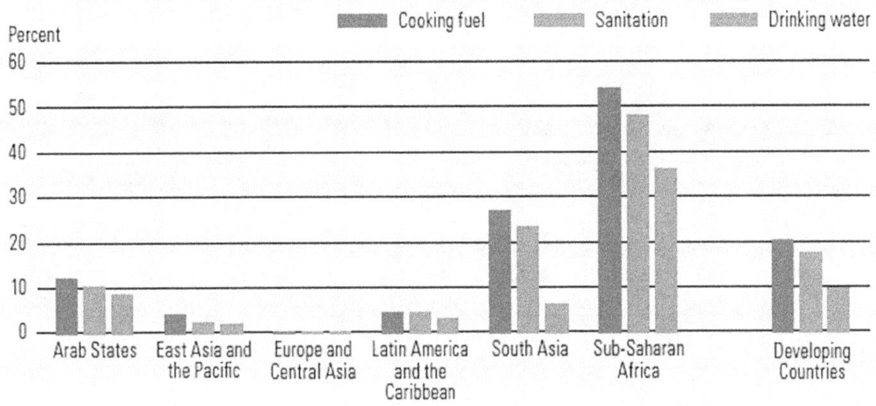

Table 4. Access to electricity in 2018 top 10 countries without access

Countries	Access to electricity in 2018
Burundi	11.02425
Chad	11.75936
Burkina Faso	14.4
Niger	17.6
Malawi	18.02
Congo, Dem. Rep.	18.97766
Madagascar	25.90781
Liberia	25.91827
Sierra Leone	26.1
South Sudan	28.20186

Source: World Bank (2020)

The majority of these countries, which do not have access to electricity, are located in sub-Sahara regions see figure 2.4. In Burundi, approximately 88% of their population is living without access to electricity in 2018 see Table 4. South Sudan is at 10th number in which approximately 73% of their population is living without access to electricity see table 5.

Figure 5. Access to electricity
(WorldBank, 2020)

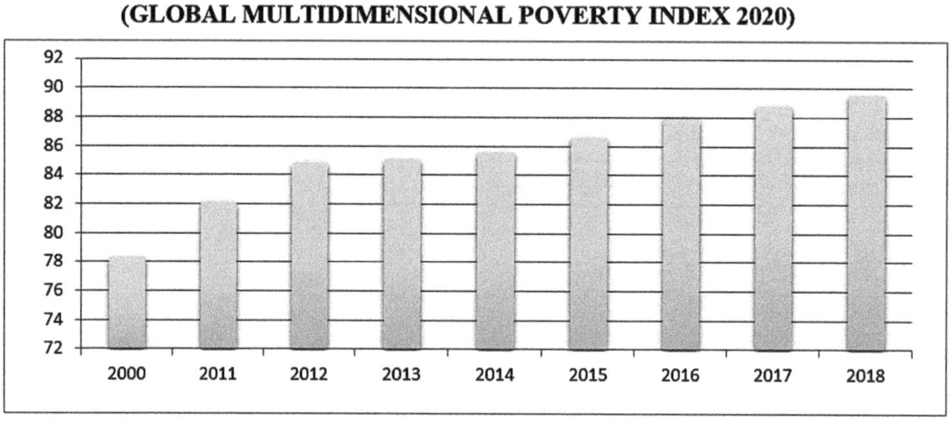

After access to electricity, the standard of living component consists of access to safe drinking water and sanitation. According to (UNICEF-WHO 2019), globally, 1 in 3 individuals do not have access to healthy drinking water. According to a recent UNICEF report and the World Health Organization, billions of people worldwide continue to suffer from inadequate access to water, sanitation, and hygiene. Around 2.2 billion people worldwide do not have drinking water services safely operated; 4.2 billion people do not have sanitation services safely managed, and 3 billion lack basic hand washing facilities. Furthermore, In 2017, 3 billion individuals lack basic hand washing facilities at home with soap and water. It also reveals no basic hand washing facilities for nearly three-quarters of the Least Developed Countries' population. Every year, 297,000 children less than five years of age die from diarrhea associated with insufficient WASH. Poor sanitation and polluted water are also associated with the spread of cholera, hepatitis A, typhoid, and dysentery. Since 2000, 2.1 billion people have gained access to basic sanitation facilities, but the waste generated is not handled safely in many parts of the world. It also shows that 2 billion people, of whom 7 out of 10 live in rural areas and one third live in the Least Developed Countries, still lack basic sanitation.

CONCLUSION

In the current situation there, in several countries, due to external and internal conflicts majority of young people aged 15 to 35 are on the streets and protesting for their rights. Their right includes stable employment, issues of climate change, freedom of speech and independence. For fighting against poverty, private companies should work along with public companies, as this mechanism will create more jobs and bring stability to society.

REFERENCES

Draman, R. (2003). Poverty and Conflicts in Africa: Explaining a complex Relationship. In *Experts Group Meeting on Africa-Canada Parliamentary Strengthening Program* (pp. 1-18). Academic Press.

Friedman, M. (2020). *Capitalism and freedom*. University of Chicago press. (Original work published 1962)

Grusky, D., & Kanbur, R. (2006). *Introduction: The conseptual foundations of poverty and inequality measurmnet. In Poverty and Inequality*. Stanford University Press. doi:10.7228/manchester/9780719065781.003.0001

Inyang, B. J., Awa, H. O., & Enuoh, R. O. (2011). CSR-HRM nexus: Defining the role engagement of the human resources professionals. *International Journal of Business and Social Science*, *2*(5), 118–126.

Ismail, T. N. T. (2011). Corporate social responsibility: The influence of the silver book. *International Journal of Business and Management Studies*, *3*(2), 371–383.

Janjua, L. R., & Khan, S. A. R. (2019). *Global Perspectives on Green Business Administration and Sustainable Supply Chain Management*. IGI Global.

Maç, S. D., & Çalış, Ş. (2011). Labour practices in the content of corporate social responsibility: An evaluation on automotive manufacturer companies' websites. *International Journal of Business and Management Studies*, *3*(2), 317–331.

Maignan, I., & Ferrell, O. C. (2001). Corporate Citizenship as a Marketing Instrument: Concept, Evidence and Research Direction. *European Journal of Marketing*, *35*(3/4), 404–424. doi:10.1108/03090560110382110

Matunhu, J. D. (2011). *Poverty and corporate social responsibility in Africa: A critical assessment*. Academic Press.

McArthur, J. W. (2014). The origin of the Millennium Development Goals. *SAIS Review (Paul H. Nitze School of Advanced International Studies)*, *34*(2).

McWilliamsA.SiegelD. S.WrightP. M. (2006). Corporate social responsibility: International perspectives. Available at SSRN 900834.

Medina-Muñoz, R. D., & Medina-Muñoz, D. R. (2020). Corporate social responsibility for poverty alleviation: An integrated research framework. *Business Ethics (Oxford, England)*, *29*(1), 3–19. doi:10.1111/beer.12248

Perrini, F., Russo, A., & Tencati, A. (2007). CSR Strategies of SMEs and Large Firms, Evidence from italy. *Journal of Business Ethics*, *74*(3), 285–300. doi:10.100710551-006-9235-x

Pimpa, N. (2011). Multinational Corporations: Corporate Social Responsibility and Poverty Alleviation in Thailand. In *The first International conference on interdisciplinary Research and Development* (pp. 1-8). Academic Press.

Ragodoo, N. (2009). The contribution of the hotel sector to the local community: The case of Mauritius. *International Journal of Environmental, Cultural, Economic and Social Sustainability*, *5*(3), 25–37. doi:10.18848/1832-2077/CGP/v05i05/54680

Townsend, P. (2006). *What is poverty? An historical perspective (Poverty in focus, UNDP)*. International Poverty Center, London School of Economics.

ENDNOTES

* World Bank Global Monitoring Report 2015

† https://epidemic-stats.com/coronavirus/

‡ Schwab (2016), The Fourth industrial revolution, World Economic Forum

1 www.worldbank.org

2 https://www.worldbank.org/en/topic/poverty

3 Charles Dickens' novel, *A Tale of Two Cities, Para.1, Line, 1*

4 https://www.un.org/sustainabledevelopment/hunger/

5 Democratic People Republic of Korea (North) and Republic of Korea (South).

6 https://www.foodaidfoundation.org/world-hunger-statistics.html

7 World Bank Global Monitoring Report 2015

Chapter 3
Islam and Corporate Social Responsibility

ABSTRACT

Several studies have been conducted to explore corporate social responsibility and its essence for the current world. The majority of the books and existing literature have presented the Western point of view of CSR; however, this chapter aims to explore corporate social responsibility from the viewpoint of Islam. The discussion reveals that Islamic corporate social responsibility provides a systemic framework of CSR practice, which is beneficial for everyone in the society. The core sustainability can be achieved as this in the form of social, economic, and environmental sustainability.

INTRODUCTION

The history of religion is ancient; as long as the human race exists in this universe, religion is a universal social phenomenon, a severe concern by every living man or woman, based on beliefs and practice. Even from the past till now, religions count as the most substantial social control source on groups of people bound together by similar faith. Similarly, (Nath 2015) summaries in his work the importance of religion in society by stating, people get mental peace by the following religion, furthermore religion work as an instrument that converts animal qualities to human qualities, and similarly, religious education promoting social welfare thus in this way poor people can become an essential pillar of society. In his work, he further indicates that religious

DOI: 10.4018/978-1-7998-3988-0.ch003

institutions and guidance are essential factors that help control individual behaviors in society. In terms of economics, the majority of world religions encourage balance in society. Moreover, religion works as an instrument and an essential factor influencing the political system of any country. One of the essential projections indicated by "The Future of World Religions: Population Growth Projections, 2010-2050", Muslims thus particularly Islam, is the only major religious group projected to increase or expended father than the world population as a whole.1 The word religion is derived from a Latin word (Religare), which means to bind together, indicated by Ronald L. Johnstone in his book.2 According to the estimation of PEW Research Centre, Washington USA, there are approximately more than 4300 religions in this world, among all of them most Christianity is on the top with a follower of 2.3 billion and then Islam with a follower of 1.8 billion.

However, on the other hand, Milton Friedman (1970) Suggested that corporations are sole organizations only for profit-making; thus, their primary concern is only profit-making. Similarly, another explanation why CSR does not support social welfare is that since they are in 'pursuit of benefit,' they have no social potential. Benefits refer to the monetary benefits (Davis, 1973).

At the macro level, Taking advantage of the economic and regulatory asymmetries present in the global market is the emergence of global competition and the economic expansion between developing countries and developed countries; however, more especially Islam does not allow in terms of religion any exploitation. Similarly, in the view of Islam, CSR includes all individuals and organizations in the world. To be directed in forming a moral self that differentiates between right and wrong, and never lose sight of God and humanity's obligations Elasrag,(2015). As in the context of Islam, the welfare of the community is also essential. Islam also stresses the community's wellbeing over individual rights Shamim & Karim (2010).

For understanding the ethical origins of CSR, it is clear why the religion of Islam, but with this idea, every other religion in the world has an extremely high connection. Religion is an integral part of every ethics discussion, and so on, of the corporate ethics at the core of CSR. The explanation for this is that many religions have personal conduct value structures that guide followers in deciding between right and wrong. However, the primary roots of CSR can found in every religion, such as triple gems of Jainism, Judaism's halacha, in Islam Sharia, in catholic the canon law, in Buddhism the eightfold path, and in Zoroastrianism, it is mention as good thoughts along with good words and deeds Brammer et al. (2007).

Corporate social responsibility includes all individuals and organizations in the world view of Islam. To be directed in forming a moral self that differentiates between right and wrong, and never loses sight of God and humanity's obligations. Islam has not lost its widespread impact on societies in which it is practiced and is a 'full way of life' for adherents with unique economic life implications. The role that responsible business should play in the growth of a culture, society, and economy is based on social justice and equality rather than efficiency or profit generation Elasrag (2015). In a more specific way, Islamic corporate social responsibility is based on Islamic human wellbeing and the good life in the Islamic sense of social responsibility, which emphasizes brotherhood and socio-economic justice and demands a balanced fulfilment of human material and spiritual needs. Vicegerencia is where a person is accountable to society and also to himself. On this planet, all possessions belong to Allah.

Furthermore, its primary roots are also based on one phenomenon: wealth is a grant from Allah. Allah entrusts every human being to share and use it wisely and obey Allah's guidance and preserve justice on the planet Harun et al. (2015) The practice of positive Islamic teaching deeds, such as helping poor people by giving sadaqah, which is volunteer practice. Then obligatory practice for helping needy Zakat consider those practices that spread brotherhood within the society and reduce their greed. Furthermore, among Islam's teaching, every individual's responsibility is to protect Allah's property. Similarly, in terms of business practice, when a company introduces Islamic corporate social responsibility initiatives that involve the social, environmental, employee, and customer-related programs that draw on the sense of the voluntary contribution of the organization, it should invite and encourage workers to adopt the same voluntary attitude and actions towards their fellow employees.

The corporate community must be conscious of its obligation, more especially its responsibilities towards society. CSR does not mean just engaging in charitable events or activities. However, it includes taking responsibility for the advancement of society by envisaging potential socio-economic justice plans and being mindful of their responsibility for society's wellbeing. The business community is highly qualified to create a strategy for social change and align its development priorities with the country and participate in joint projects with other organizations.

It is true to say that the moral dimension of Islam's corporate social responsibility is based on the interaction of all the ingredients of economics such as individual, society, and market. In terms of individual, there is always a heavy responsibility on individual shoulders. As in the Islamic economic system, over profits, income-earning through interest, and monopoly are strictly prohibited, whereas if any individual is performing work, dishonesty in his work is not allowed. By Sharia goals, the Islamic market is the facilitator of settlement between various parties' diverse interests and goals. Thus it is true that business organizations that exist in the market with their economic interests and objectives, the settlement of those interests should comply with Sharia rulings, which will lead to the achievement of the higher Sharia objectives.

Islamic beliefs are based on the Quran and then further explained by Prophet Mohammed (PBU H) through his teaching. These beliefs include believing in One Unique and Single God (Allah), Believing in The Angels, Believing in The Revealed books, [Torah (Given to Moses), Zaboor (Given to David), Injeel (Given to Jesus) and Quran (Given to Mohammed (P.b. U.H.)), The Final Revelation of Allah.], Believing in the prophets of Allah, including Moses, Abraham, Jesus and last prophets Mohammed (P. B. U. H), and in the last believing in the hereafter, the day of judgment, the afterlife, heaven, and hell.

Furthermore, a fiver pillar indicated by the Quran and practiced by Mohammed (PBUH) are practical aspects of Islam. All these pillars make Muslims conscious of Allah and bring harmony and peace in their lives. Similarly, these fundamental pillars fulfill their spiritual need as well. Moreover, this world is not an illusion to the Muslims; thus, it is the place to work according to Mohammed's practice guidelines (PBU H) and enjoy as well. All the Muslims around the world's lives righteous life based on Allah's principles and words indicated by The Quran, with a hope enter in Paradise in the hereafter. Given in the figure 1, describe five pillars of Islam.

Shahada is the first and fundamental pillar of Islam. Being Muslim, everyone must believe in Shahada, which states that "***There is no God but Allah, and Muhammad is his messenger***." It is the fundamental expression of Islam believes, and it further underscores the monotheistic nature of Islam. This expression also indicates that all the power in the universe only belongs to Allah; thus, Allah is the creator of this entire universe.

After, ***Shahada*** the second most important pillar of Islam is ***Salat*** or ***Namaz.*** It is obligatory for every Muslim to must pray five times a day. For the last 1400 years, millions of Muslims worldwide offer Salat five times a day. Salat or Namaz is no a phrase to be spoken. Thus it involves uniting the mind, soul, and body in worship. A whole series of set movements should be performed to perform Salat, illustrated by our Prophet Mohammed (PBUH). In the Holy Quran, Allah commands all Muslims to offer ***Salat*** or ***Namaz*** 700 times. Furthermore, Namaz or Salat is also teaching us to clean souls and physical bodies; thus, before performing Salat or Namaz, every Muslim must perform ***Wudhu*** *(a ritual washing).* Similarly, Salat or Namaz also

Figure 1. Five Pillars of Islam

indicate equality and brotherhood among all Muslims; while offering Namaz or Salam in the mosque, all the Muslims line up shoulder by shoulder to each other despite any race, color, or any other materialistic factor (rich or poor).

Zakat is the third pillar of Islam. It is obligatory for every Muslim to must pay ***Zakat*** (money or other monetary units as a charity) according to the prescribed amount by ***shariah*** every year to make their wealth clean.

It is true to say that the value or essence of social responsibility has been recognized throughout history, and in Islam, in more structure, it was introduced as Zakat in the 7th century. Therefore, many organizations worldwide are now recognizing that corporate social responsibility positively influences society and staff members and its all stakeholder(Elasrag,2015).

In recent years, the relationship between Business ethicists and management theorists has dedicated much time to think about the relationship between

Table 1. Ethical standard of CSR

Model	Dimension
Relativism	Ethical choices or decisions are taken based on self-interest and Needs, excluding any outside input or input.
Utilitarianism	In general, Utilitarianism is considered outcome-oriented thus, in this dimension, Ethical decisions are made based on measuring costs and benefits. Furthermore, under this dimension, the outcome or the derived benefits, if good for most of the group, are considered ethical.
Universalism	Ethical decisions emphasize the aim of the decision or action. Everyone should make similar decisions under similar conditions; thus, the duty should be done by all.
Rights	Ethical decisions emphasize freedom as a core belief and stress individual rights along with freedom of choice.
Distributive Justice	Ethical decisions revolve around a single value of justice and equity. There should also be, fair distribution of resources and benefits along with fairness and equality.
Eternal Law	Ethical judgments are made based on the eternal law, which is revealed in scripture.

Source: Elasrag (2015)

business and society. Six critical ethical standards Models represent ethical thought and add to corporate social responsibility (Mohammed, 2007). These models are summarised in Table 1.

Furthermore, "God commands you [people] to return things entrusted to you to their rightful owners, and, if you judge between people, to do so with justice." Quran [4:58]. It is also obligator for every Muslim to must **Fast/ Saum** every year in the holy month of Ramadan. **Fasting / Saum** is the fourth essential pillar of Islam. Fasting or Saum starts from dawn and finishes at sunset. During this entire period, Muslims abstaining their self from any food, drink, or sexual relations. It teaches Muslim self-control; furthermore, it is a highly spiritual activity constantly reminding the believer (Muslims) to be conscious of Allah.

Similarly, **Saum / Fasting** also teaches Muslims to control their tongue to be respectful and be forgiving. The majority of Muslims in the Holy month of Ramadan donate vast amounts of money as charity to the needy and poor people. On the other hand, there are exceptions made for sick, more aged, and pregnant women. All are expected to refrain from **fasting /Saum** during the day.

PHILANTHROPY IN ISLAM

Islam is the religion of peace, love, and respect; Furthermore, Islam teaches us the lesson of humanity. The teaching of The Quran and life of Mohammed (P.B.U.H) explain us to behave like a human in every dimension of life. It explains to all the Muslim of the world the listen of tolerance and respect with the non-followers of Islam. Mohammed's (PBUH) teaching guides us to all the Muslim to express love, peace, and respect even during the time of wars. Allah's order in the Quran and Hadith teach us that every Muslim must take care of state and private properties, even not harm the environment. Not even during peacetime, Mohammed (P.B.U.H.) ordered all the Muslims worldwide to pay the "Haq" called moral obligations to whom any individual directly or indirectly interact.

It is true to say that the moral dimension of Islam's corporate social responsibility is based on the interaction of all the ingredients of economics such as individual, society, and market. In terms of individual, there is always a heavy responsibility on individual shoulders. As in the Islamic economic system, over profits, income-earning through interest, and monopoly are strictly prohibited, whereas if any individual is performing work, dishonesty in his work is not allowed. Under Sharia goals, the Islamic market is the facilitator of settlement between various parties' diverse interests and goals. Thus it is true that business organization which exists in the market with their economic interests and objectives, the settlement of those interests should comply with *Sharia* rulings which will lead definitely to the achievement of the higher *Sharia* objectives.

However, in terms of philanthropy in Islam, its exit into two kinds Zakat and Saqda. In Zakat, all Muslim individuals and organizations must pay 2.5% of their profits or earn once every year to the poor people or charitable organizations as prescribed in the Holy Quran.

In terms of Zakat, the number of individuals or organizations they need to pay is calculated according to the Nisab. This minimum threshold for Zakat is known as Nisab in Arabic. Nisab is known as the minimum percentage, which is applied to certain commodities as prescribed in Sharia. Furthermore, Zakat is one of the five pillars of Islam. As in the book Hadith, then Malik's Muwatta regarding volunteer charity, the words ate quoted from Yahya ibn Said from Abu'l-Hubab Said ibn Yasar (PBUH) said, "Whoever gives sadaqah from good earning - and Allah only accepts the good. It is as if he placed it in the palm of the Merciful to raise it, as one of you raises his foal or young camel until it is like the mountain " Thus it is true to say that, besides obligatory charity which is Zakat, the people who give sadaqah from their hard-earned money always consider as loveable people among the Allah and for sure they will get a high reward in the day of justice as well.

The typical organization formed for earning purposes thus for profit-making are usually trustees in the Islamic perspective, and they are accountable to the fund's owner. Thus people who are owners are referred to the shareholder. That entire particular concept is defined as Amanah in Islamic literature. Furthermore, the Islamic perspective also ensures the fair and reasonable use of the funds along will fair distribution. Fair refers to the optimal use of funds without any dishonesty and corruption. Fair distribution means the funds' earning profits will be equally distributed among the entire shareholder, thus the people who provided funds for the business. Unfair utilization and corruption refer to the Kheayanah in Islam. Islam strictly prohibited the Kheayanah.

In terms of management and operational activities of business organizations, Islam provides guidelines also. Islamic perspective emphasizes discussions and consensus between the investor and the business's organizers; thus, management as discussion provides chances to the more knowledgeable persons or manager to present their perspective among the investors and stockholders. That particular phenomenon is known as Shura. All these concepts of Amanah, Kahyanah, and Shura are referred to as business ethics.

Management should be closely observed; thus, all the business activities should be recorded relatively; in terms of benefit and loss resulting from company activities. The recording should be transparent and accessible to every shareholder.

As The Prophet Mohammed (PBUH) said that, "Those who cheat is not of us," which means Islam principles strictly prohibited any cheating thus dishonesty. Therefore, it is the responsibility of all people directly or indirectly associated with the business organization to honestly and fairly perform all their duties.

"O you who believe! When you deal with each other in transactions involving future obligations in a fixed period, reduce them to writing. Let him who incurs the liability dictate, but let him fear his Lord God, and not diminish aught of what he owes" (2:282)

Allah's above words teach us that whenever two or more people are involved in any business relationship, thus the business activities are supposed to happen in the future it is advisable that the contract between all the involved parties should be written in black and white form. As writing in black and while form always helpful to discourages disputes of involved parties.

In order to achieve socio-economic justice and equality, the main goal of the shariah system or shariah law is to ensure a community that is free from all signs of in-justice and inequality As the major components or attributes of shariah law are a verdict of Allah, which is mention in the Holy Quran and further it is narrated by the Prophet Mohammed (PBUH).

In terms of business, the Islamic business organization's concept usually adopts corporate social responsibility derived from the Tawheed, which identifies the relationship between Allah, human as an individual, and the environment as nature Muhamad et al. (2008). Furthermore, these three attributes combined are generally known as a framework for Islamic business practice, representing corporate social responsibility. One of the primary factors that made that framework purely Islamic is the Shariah principle and Ribbah (Interest) free business practice. The major laws, economic practices, and development are narrated with Shariah Law's viewpoint in the presence of social justice (Adaal). In figure 2 represents three attributes of the framework of Islamic business practice.

Similarly, a few critical components of Islamic business practice, strictly prohibited, are price manipulation, especially in drought or pandemic crises, interference of free-market fraud, and bribery. However, it is proper to argue that all things create social injustice and economic inequalities. More

Figure 2. Framework of Islamic business practice
(Khatun & Alautiyat 2012)

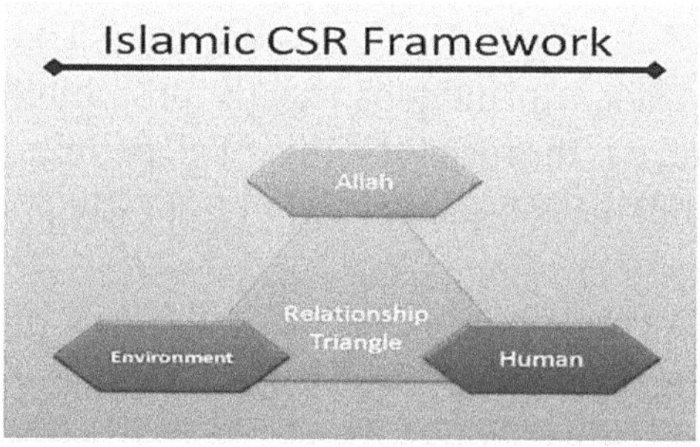

concretely, the legal practice is considered Halal, and these are narrated in the Quran, sunnah, and Hadith. On the other hand, all the prohibited practices are considered Haram, such as Ribbah, fraud injustice. The Islamic business code of ethics illustrates five essential attributes of humans in which individuals interact and carry on their business practices. These five attributes also indicate individual's and parties' rights and their duties. These are justice and equality, fairness, benevolence, sincerity, and trust Muhammad et al. (2008).

None of the society or even any individual family cannot survive with justice and its practice. "Allah commands justice, the doing of good and liberality to kith and kin. He forbids all shameful deeds and injustice and rebellion; he instructs you, that ye may receive administration." (16:90). In terms of justice in business practice, it indicates the employer's behavior or management towards its employees. Thus exploitation of anyone's weakness is strictly prohibited in Islamic business practice.

Furthermore, after justice, the basic principle of Islamic business practice is truthfulness in every aspect of business activities as Allah speaks the truth and orders all the Muslims of the world to be straightforward in their every business dealing. Furthermore, Prophet Mohammed (PBUH) was accepted by all the community due to his truthfulness. He was called due Saqid and Ameen due to actual deeds and his business practices. Therefore, Prophet Mohammed (PBUH) orders all Muslims to follow truthfulness in every aspect of business activities as in sales, purchase, trade, and business contracts. Apart from justice, which is an essential component of society, the minimum level of fairness that everyone must obey is to protect or secure others' rights. In terms of the Islamic organization perspective, the relationship between the higher management or executives and workers should be based on benevolence(Ehsan) without any expectations. These practices are nowadays easily traceable in the sense of social benefits which are provided by the majority of the companies such as medical and education facility for the children's

In word and deed, honesty is commonly understood to be fact. Therefore, Islam attaches great significance in every walk of life to the honesty of intentions and acts. The performance of duties demands that all people in organizations operate with integrity and loyalty. Islamic organizations' CSR policies and practices usually cover four major CSR dimensions. These dimensions include Culture, Workplace, Climate, and Marketplace in which all CSR policies revolve, and therefore, CSR policies should be made to fulfill all Muslims' social objectives (thus, ummah).

It is true to say that all these four dimensions, which are primary roots of CSR policies and practices in Islam, should be prioritized according to two further attributes such as obligatory (wajib) and recommended (mandub). This framework indicates that those with the critical category's faith factor are the CSR operations that obtain the highest priority in the Islamic framework. CSR

Figure 3. Obligatory and Recommended CSR practices framework
(Darus et al. 2013)

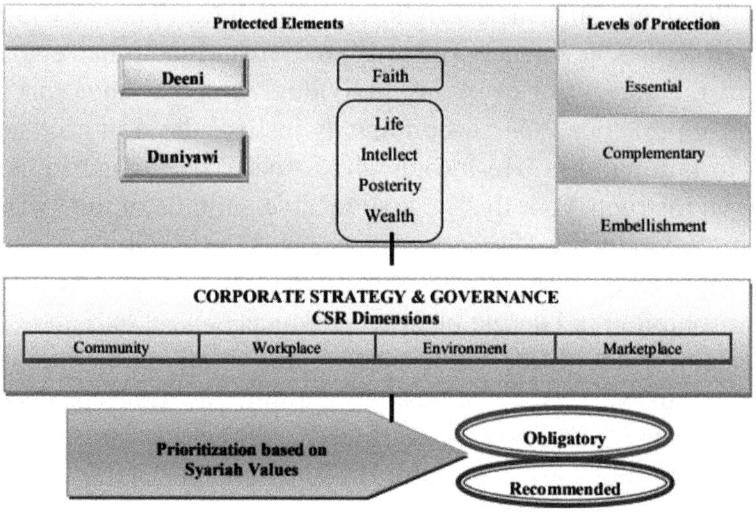

activities that come under the Critical category should be given more weight than Complementary and Embellishment activities in terms of quantification and valuation, while CSR activities that receive the lowest priority are those with the Embellishment category's wealth part. Islamic organizations do not conduct reprehensible and prohibited practices because they contradict the establishment of Islamic organizations. Given in figure 3, indicate that particular framework.

In line with the nature of Islamic values and the implementation of Sharia, some authors argue that CSR would necessarily be practiced by a company that claims to operate its functions according to the principles of shariah. Islam makes no distinction when it comes to ethics regarding whether it is for personal or commercial use. In other facets of daily life, business ethics cannot be distinguished from individual daily life Arsad et al. (2015). Islamic philanthropic responsibility Islam encourages its supporters to do business without damaging others or the world for profit. It is anticipated that individuals will ensure justice for owners and security for humanity.

For nearly 14 centuries, the notion of social obligation and justice has been an integral part of Islamic society. Although Islamic philosophy is rich in precepts pertinent to CSR based on the shariah (the Islamic legal and social system) derived from the Holy Qur'an and Hadith, these precepts have not yet been systematically synthesized to present a systemic model with an explicit notion of CSR in Islam.

CONCLUSION

After reviewing different Islamic Corporate Social papers and journals Responsibility, the researcher considered that most organizations do not know that it would have a positive effect on their actions by introducing the ICSR program for workers, not only as an employee but as a responsible human being and a good servant in the eyes of Allah. Therefore, the organization must continue to adopt ICSR programs and invest its benefits in the entire society's sustainable development. Our discussion reveals that to maintain harmony, justice, peace, and equality in society, it is necessary for the organization and corporate sector to adopt policies highly recommended in Islamic thoughts. These policies and practices provide equal rights for everyone. It also discourages the exploitation of the weak with the society and enhances helping the needy and poor people within the society through Zakat and Sadaqah.

REFERENCES

Ali, A. Y. (1987). *The Holy Quran (Koran).* Madinah: King Fahd Printing Complex.

Arsad, S., Ahmad, R., Fisol, W. N. M., Said, R., & Haji-Othman, Y. (2015). Maqasid shariah in the corporate social responsibility of Shari'ah-compliant companies. *Research Journal of Finance and Accounting*, *6*(6), 239–247.

Brammer, S., Williams, G., & Zinkin, J. (2007). Religion and attitudes to corporate social responsibility in a large cross-country sample. *Journal of Business Ethics*, *71*(3), 229–243. doi:10.100710551-006-9136-z

Darus, F., Yusoff, H., Abang Naim, D. M., Mohamed Zain, M., Amran, A., Fauzi, H., & Purwanto, Y. (2013). Islamic Corporate Social Responsibility (i-CSR) Framework from the Perspective of Maqasid al-Syariah and Maslahah. *Issues in Social & Environmental Accounting, 7*(2).

Davis, K. (1973). The case for and against business assumption of social responsibilities. *Academy of Management Journal, 16*(2), 312–322.

ElasragH. (2015). Corporate social responsibility: An Islamic perspective. Available at SSRN 2603832.

ElasragH. (2015). Corporate social responsibility: An Islamic perspective. *Available at* SSRN 2603832.

Friedman, M. (1970). The social responsibility of business is to increase its profits. *Foundations of Business Thought*, 221.

Harun, I. F. B., Isa, A. B., & Najuna, F. (2015). *The Implementation of Islamic Corporate Social Responsibility Programs and Its Impact on Employees Behavior: A Case in Petronas Cari Gali Sdn*. Bhd Kota Kinabalu.

Khatun, K. M., & Alautiyat, H. (2012). Corporate social responsibility: An Islamic perspective. *Int. I. Bus. Technopreneurship*, *2*(3), 415–423.

Mohammed, J. A. (2007). *Corporate social responsibility in Islam* (Doctoral dissertation). Auckland University of Technology.

Muhamad, R., Sukor, M. E. A., & Muwazir, M. R. (2008). Corporate social responsibility: An Islamic perspective. *Asian Journal of Accounting Perspectives*, *1*(1), 43–56.

Muhammad, M. Z., Ilias, A., Ghazali, M. F., Abdullah, R. C., & Amin, H. (2008). An analysis of Islamic ethics in small and medium enterprises (SMEs). *UNITAR e-Journal, 4*(1), 46-58.

Shamim, M., & Karim, N. (2010). Corporate social responsibility: Contemporary thought and Islamic perspectives. *Thoughts on Economics*, *21*(1), 45–66.

ENDNOTES

1 *Pew Research Centre, April 2, 2015, "The Future of World Religions: Population Growth Projections, 2010-2050."*

2 *Religion in Society, A Sociology of Religion (2015).*

Chapter 4
Corporate Social Responsibility and the Fourth Industrial Revolution

ABSTRACT

The aim of writing this chapter is to describe the nexus between emerging technology in terms of fourth industrial revolution and corporate social responsibility in the presence of driven challenges and opportunities. This chapter also explains the current implications of the fourth industrial revolution to understand the current challenges, to address and find out opportunities. Similarly, this chapter also analyses that role of information technology overall as a factor of globalization. Furthermore, in term of the emerging issues, which are significant challenges of the world, such sustainable development consists of economic, social, and environmental factors. The discussion reveals that, to achieve sustainable development in the presence of fourth industrial revolution, it is the responsibility of the corporate sector to use all technologies in a socially and economically friendly manner; therefore, the maximum advantages could be derived from its use.

INTRODUCTION

In the last five years, massive inventions of the fourth industrial revolution reshaped the government and business. Similarly, the technological advancement so-called fourth industrial revolution ultimately changed our

DOI: 10.4018/978-1-7998-3988-0.ch004

lifestyle dramatically. However, it is correct to argue that referring to the fourth industrial revolution. Eventually, people will not have control over either technology or the disruption that comes from it. Moreover, it can predict that the fourth industrial revolution will create numerous opportunities such as it will help reduce barriers between inventors and markets, which eventually decrease the monopolies. There will be a more active role of artificial intelligence in every domain, fusion effect of technology; thus, different techniques replace old technologies such as blockchain technology and advanced use of the Internet such as the Internet of things.

The critical invention which will ultimately reduce the barrier between inventors and the market due to the fourth industrial revolution is the invention of 3D printing for prototyping. With the help of 3D printing, new invention ideas quickly converted into new products with a minimal step-up cost. Entrepreneurs can promptly enter the market without traditional constraints of time. Therefore the typical barrier of time ultimately removed from the market equation (Xu et al 2018). Furthermore, the 3D products appeared to be lighter in weight and reliable with less wastage. Similarly, 3D products can be produced as per every individual need; therefore, it will be ideal for mass customization techniques. It is also expected that different people start preparing products at their homes with the help of 3D technology with their precise specification rather than buy from outside—that how it will ultimately remove the monopolies of big manufacturing corporate from the market.

The other technological invention, which is considered the critical invention of the fourth industrial revolution, is artificial intelligence, which can quickly solve complex problems with the help of algorithms. The main drawbacks that the world could experience due to the adoption of artificial intelligence are the upward trend of unemployment as millions of people might lose their jobs. However, due to the fact, there is a considerable responsibility of the government to adopt the artificial intelligence, as the government needs to support both the corporate and individual sectors to ensure that both stakeholders benefit from the artificial intelligence-powered digital economy. Indirectly it means that the government is preparing the labor force for rapid change in job markets and enabling people to adopt this technology and increase productivity, thus, which is the key driver of economic growth (Chui, 2017). Therefore, it is also expected that due to the unemployment crime rate will increase, hacking and cybercrime will be more common, and it will also increase social inequalities. Similarly, accountability will be more complicated due to the extensive use of artificial intelligence (Schwab,2016).Furthermore, the other important technology of the fourth industrial revolution is Internet of things (IoT), which offer advance connectivity of devices, system, domains, and services. The key benefits that can drive from IoT are improved quality of life, saving in time, and logistical efficiency. Similarly, it will also help in creating new business. Eventually, it will transfer life toward the smart effect, based on knowledge and connectivity. It is also expected that shortly, most of the traditional products will be replaced by digital products, due to (IoT). Along with AI, IoT and 3D printer, robotics, and big data analysis are also count as a critical invention of the fourth industrial revolution.

However, it is also true to argue that the fourth industrial revolution might not able to provide benefits to everyone. Although until now, the outcome of the third industrial revolution not yet reached entirely on the people of the third world or developing countries. Many people from developing and least developing countries still do not have access to electricity, access to fresh and safe drinking water, the Internet, and other machinery. Many aspects of the fourth industrial revolution are highly advanced, and that particular technology is still not adopted by the society and culture of third world countries.

One of the adverse effects of the fourth industrial revolution that might appear in the future can be high inequalities. The world might divide more into classes and social clusters. On the other hand, in advanced technologies, they have their exiting challenges. These challenges are arises due to geopolitical instability and security. In terms of safety, it is not only related to security at the national or international level. In any corporation, once employees connect their device with their company network, the security challenges start arising for the organization. These challenges can prevent the theft of company data and hacking of the system and network, ultimately making more complications.

One of the critical challenges that advanced technologies are facing nowadays is a massive inflow of migrants, and after that, they provide them all the basic needs of life, such as jobs and shelter. Another big crisis which is appeared recently in advanced technologies is due to security. A competitive advantage of which always possess by developing countries due to their low labor and raw material cost might be replaced with the factor of re-shoring due to new technologies of the advancement of the fourth industrial revolution as the existence of a 3D printer, and then the Internet of things.

In terms of business, four main effects might arise. Initially, customer expectations are shifting; thus, they are demanding more satisfaction, which induces more technological changes. Secondly, overall products are being enhanced by data, more data is collected from the customer, and their behavior patterns also noticed at the micro-level. A third effect is that new partnerships are being formed worldwide despite the geographical distance and regional stakes. And in the last, the significant impact is the transformation of the traditional model into a digital model. One of the critical mechanisms that researchers still not entirely describe as the output effect of the fourth industrial revolution is the operation and limit of activities conducted by public institutions and organizations. In particular, the main aim of the corporate sector is to maximize their profits; therefore, they usually compel government at the regional and national levels. Private companies are still willing to partner with other firms, even against the government's will. Similarly, due to the fourth industrial revolution, the power shifts from states to the non-states actors. The foster new technologies and social interactions allow virtually everyone to impact in a way that was unimaginable a few years ago.

The fourth industrial revolution could have a variety of implications for society and the economy (Prisecaru, 2016). Initially, a large part of the world's population will possibly use the channels of social media to communicate, learn, and modify information. Secondly, various innovative manufacturers and competing industries will have easy access and improve the quality and prices of the goods and services on their digital platforms for marketing, sales, and distribution. The transition due to the fourth industrial revolution has main effects on the business environment: its influence on customer preferences, product quality, the creation of collective innovation, and organizational changes.

KEY ATTRIBUTES OF GLOBALIZATION DUE TO THE FOURTH INDUSTRIAL REVOLUTION AND RESPONSIBILITY OF CORPORATE SECTOR

Life sciences and emerging technology developments and the like have opened up vast new possibilities for development and trade. Innovations like the Internet have made it possible to access information and tools around the world. Besides opening up vast possibilities, the use of modern technologies poses particular risks when combined with the quest for profit and this "worldwide" reach. The threats can be interpreted in that sense as the chance of harm caused by technological and economic changes. For instance, hazards associated with industrial production can spread quickly beyond the immediate context in which they are produced. Threats are globalizing, in other words. Capitalism is fundamentally disruptive and continuously changing, taking on very different forms around the world. While it creates wealth for a significant number of individuals, many more have undergone market growth, the expansion of economic activity and the degree to which societies worldwide are and continue to enjoy increased prosperity, for example, through schooling, agricultural reform and the legal framework for acts. Public policy has deepened. In the same way, the public intervention that can fundamentally alter the result of local and global economic ties is argued (Baş,2009).

a) More Enormous in Nature

The essence of globalizing itself has changed, the way globalization influencing our economic and social life, it seems to be modern and new. The new the globalization operation with a more exceptional degree of resolution at the national level of economic in every stage sector by sector. In terms of novelistic approach, it can also be argued that, in the presence of the more technological advancement, will this new globalization able to solve problems of the people from developing countries? Will it able to reshape their standard of living? Furthermore, what will be the implication of emerging technology in the new globalization era? These entire questions are the hot debate among the world researchers and scientist.

Similarly, there are many aspects of the natural order exit. These aspects are human, human activities, organization and material resources of the earth (Devezas, 2012). It can be argued that will it be possible that organization get benefited from new globalization without harming humans and material resources of the world? Furthermore, it is also true that the overall world system achieves economic growth and development very rapidly, but on the other hand, we harm this entire world. Global warming due to the high emission of high greenhouse gases is the outcome of rapid industrialization. Despite that fact, developed nations rapidly get rid of those industries which harm their internal environment. In the long run, it had been observed that in long-run dynamic while achieving economic growth, the level of environment pollution fall thus Environment Kuznets curve found right for developed countries.

However, on the other hand, due to fact of globalization, some of the developed countries moved their production in developing countries which environmental laws and overall governance are not too strict, therefore, P.H.H. (pollution heaven hypothesis found valid for those countries).

Figure 1. Old vs New Globalization
(Richard Baldwin, 2016)

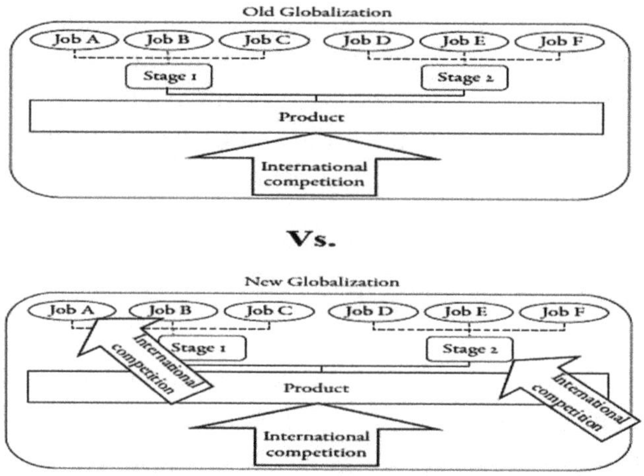

Similarly, in terms of globalization, corporate or countries usually go for internationalization of their products and services. International Corporation increases the demand for goods and services, thus, which create more jobs at every stage and every cluster of the economy. Thus eventually increase the production level of the country. Nevertheless, on the other hand, the more degree of internationalization thus international cooperation will increase international competitions, international competition hit or effect particular job, but in with a more excellent degree of resolution, it will hit stage 2 thus all the jobs (D.E.F.) as mention in figure 1.

b) Faster and More Individualized

In a particular market, the expansion of production and exports continued to raise the fortunes of productive factors most intensively employed by increasing industries. Therefore, in most G7 nations in developed countries, the fortunes of new labour-intensive industries have increased, so that untrained labour considers the first-round effects of globalization highly harmful. Enhanced transparency, therefore, has spurred the fortunes of skill-intensive industries, which has benefited professional workers by furthering globalization. The New Globalization has shifted competitiveness from industry-specific competition to stage-by-stage competition through the fragmentation of production processes. Since the effect was more selective, the impact of globalization was personalized. In other words, if the offshore raising boosts the productivity of the stage at which the workers are present; globalization may benefit a different kind of worker in a market. However, if they did not operate on an offshore point, the same work with the same ability in the same business might be affected.

Similarly, most the time, the effect of new globalization is speedy, and sudden, within very less period, a massive number of workers lose their stable jobs. Thus, recent example can be seen in terms of financial institutions which recently shut down their operation in their country of origin and moved to Eastern European countries although these companies belong to service sector but on the other side, even with time they were more digitalized and more advance in their home countries. Nevertheless, due to international competition, they industrialized more, and they moved out of from their country of origin (For example I.B.M. operations in Slovakia, JP Morgan Operations in Poland, Standard chartered operations in Poland and India).

c) Less Predictable and Controllable

Old globalization has primarily been driven by cuts in shipping or cost of transportation goods prices. Nevertheless, lower trade cost of goods, with time tends to affect traded well in a similar way. As the global competition went from sector to stage, history was less reliable as a guide for the future. Therefore in nature, it can argue that unpredictability is one of the significant attributes of new globalization. Thus, what can happen next? How will technology affect the internationalization process?

Furthermore, in recent time, it arises multiple concern due to its intense dynamic nature, therefore, the prediction in which way new globalization will grow is hard as well, it spread in the world is seems like uncontrollable as well. However, due to the fact of new globalization and emerging technologies bring revolution in this world. Thus the G.D.P. of the world grow father then population but are we capable of sustaining that much growth so that our world system stays in balance form. That particular dimension of new globalization needs to handle with care. The main challenge is to decide what stages or levels of modern globalization are to be pursued. The "glue" responsible for the micro clustering in the first place is difficult since economists cannot understand in any detail. It is not sufficient to know the direct cost of telecoms, because it deals with the essence of the stages and their interconnections with other stages and levels in complex and poorly understood ways (Baldwin,2016). Thus, the governments were in charge of the gates of the old imperialism, to put it differently. No one in particular, however, controls the sluice gates of the New Globalization.

CORPORATE SOCIAL RESPONSIBILITY AND FOURTH INDUSTRIAL REVOLUTION

Economics Needs a Scientific Revolution (Bouchaud, 2008). Typical, the depth of the word scientific revolution is not easy to understand in the current dynamics of the world. The possible argument which increases its complexity of understanding scientific revolution is day-by-day inventions and innovations. Since at the macro level, the world's problem is homogenous, such as global warming, but at the micro-level in terms of individual state or stakeholder, the difficulties are heterogeneous, thus representing a distinct individual or stakeholder. For example, in terms of environment, carbon dioxide emission will harm every individual irrelevant to its origin, country, or developed country. However, similarly, on the other hand, lack of education, access to freshwater, and electricity and spreading of HIV are issues of developing countries as some of the countries of the sub-Saharan region. As John Naisbitt: "The most reliable way to forecast the future is to try to understand the present." However, in the current time, the understanding present seems to become more complicated, as it is stated, Social-economic systems are complicated, and free markets are wild. No framework can describe wild markets in classical economics (Devezas, 2012)

In general, the difficulty of understanding the current time is depending on many factors. One of the most critical factors which can be is technology. Similarly, a definition of technology is challenging to develop, people know it, and they can distinguish between what is made of human beings and what is naturally occurring (Brey, 2009). Nevertheless, on the other hand, Technological knowledge makes it possible to distinguish between the natural (not a technology) and the created by people (a technology) (Carroll, 2017).

Traditionally, it is also argued that technology consists of two attributes, a physical dimension that includes goods, devices, equipment, drawings, techniques and processes, and Knowledge part comprising management, marketing, production, quality control, efficiency, skilled labor, and functional areas(Kumar et al. 1999).

Technology has become a key component of the business world or sector. Thus the technology is designed as corporate information on the production process and product design characteristics and performance (Reddy& Zhao, 1990). However, in terms of corporate information, it was always questioned whether technology is possible or not? More notably, how technology possibly interpreted in the typical process of company expansion. When it can to the expansion process, usually it arises two possible situations, local development or cross-border expansion. Concerns have arisen; Technology and technology transfer typically encompass many different concepts and perspectives depending on the objectives, research background, researchers, developers, users, research fields and disciplines of the organization, and the underlying perspectives (Wahab et al 2012). Technology is derived from the word Techne, which referred to as Art or skill (Skrbina, 2014). The current use of such terms suggests that a degree of expertise or creative abilities should be included with what they describe. Similarly, technology referred to the Art or skill handling any specific task. These particular tasks count as complicated in their specific timeline. Thus it technology referred to solve these entire complicated tasks in the given time. In the more border way, in the presence of factor of globalization, it is argued that these specific skills and Art is transferable itself, as technology makes it possible to transfer. In the modern world, doing things by Art and the latest skill is the requirement of time. Without implementing the last skills and artistic approach in current work, development, and innovation cannot achieve; thus, it is the requirement of the current world.

Furthermore, development and innovation are directly affecting the level of production in the current period. Higher the use of innovation higher will be the output. Therefore it is true; technology in terms of skill is a critical component of the industrialized and automated world. Furthermore, the artistic approach is the managerial techniques which accelerate industrialization. Thus, technology is strongly related to GDP (with a Pearson correlation coefficient of 0.88) the proportion of the population of a nation using the Internet also indicates the strength of globalization's technology side.

In comparison, the human population and economical production of the planet have also risen more rapidly than exponentially (i.e., in a super-Malthusian manner) (Devezas, 2012). A challenging debates aeries, how it became possible? Which factor affects the fast acceleration of growth? In simple words, the answer can be explained with a single word, which is Technological advancement. In a more sophisticated way, it can be expressed with a word, emerging technologies. For academic research, emerging technologies seem to be a subject of discussion and a core topic for policy discussions and initiatives. In simple words, Emerging technologies are those technologies that impact on the economy and reshape the overall society (Ávila-Robinson & Miyazaki,2014). It is also expressed in term of generic, along with a beneficial tool which solves the uncertain situation of any period with an emergence process (Boon & Moors, 2008). Emerging technology can be explained with a simple example, the relationship between technological progress and any upcoming era. Let us say if we call our memory, every next consecutive next brings for us some new tools and innovations. At the moment we are standing in 2020, and if we recall our memories in 2010, the available technology which we have now, we are unable to imagine those in 2010, and same like if we go more ten years, in the year of 2000 the technologies which we had in 2010 was not available in 2000. Nevertheless, still one critical question, we are advance in terms of technology in 2010 as compared to 2000, and in 2020 we are advance more than 2010 m but why still this economic system in the shape of the world, facing emerging issues of society, in terms of governance, health, and stability.

As the "New Oxford American Dictionary," the express word 'emerge' or 'emergent' means coming into being or becoming valuable and prominent. Similarly, it can be express in terms of issues and then the solution. As in current world dynamic, the world is moving extremely fast as we have discussed that earlier, but similarly, on the other hand, the fast acceleration of the world solving issues but side by side news issues are emerging in the world and solving these emerging issue we need to relies on emerging technology. These emerging technologies bring a revolution in the world, but similarly, on the other hand, the technological revolution possibly transforms the world economic order in a more sophisticated way. Thus these technologies change the form old business model and integrated into the new system as emerging technologies. There it can be argued that new different emerging technologies will have a different impact on the nature of the global economic and social problems (Nowak & Kluź, 2020).

Due to the fact, big data science is the critical component of the fourth industrial revolution; therefore in future decisions are not hypothesis-driven but instead focused on broad data that are deciphered by model recognition – and not by humans. Shop floor technology translates ways in which operators create their software and solutions to make their tasks simpler and automatic. The fourth Industrial Revolution case can be installed at a minimal cost, enabling plants to operate in several areas simultaneously. Therefore, it is also predicted that many small units would finish due to the fourth industrial revolution. The Fourth Industrial Revolution's critical drivers in manufacturing are three technological megatrends: connectivity, intelligence, and flexible automation. Connectivity can quickly achieve by the world nowadays, as a massive number of people in the world, due to mobile and smartphone all the time, connect. Intelligence Is due to big data science and artificial intelligence involvement in our everyday operations of the life cycle.

Similarly, flexible automation indicates the use of robotics in production and industrial units. Companies increase their competitive advantage by offering operating excellence. They aim to optimize their production system and increase the productivity and quality performance of their operations. They usually begin to innovate at one or more manufacturing locations and then roll out. Furthermore, the use of crucial innovation of the fourth industrial revolution in supply chains is a new way of working together for humans and machines. Digitization of production and storage processes contributes to both efficiency and sustainability. Human experience remains essential for analysis and guidance but can be combined with artificial intelligence used in computer and process data for deep insights and the resolution of complex problems. The real value of digital transformation is brought to life by this coexistence of people and technology (Klaus,2017).

However, the fourth industrial revolution is not just about intelligent and interconnected devices and systems. The scope is even more significant. At the same time, waves of further development are emerging in fields ranging from gene sequence to nanotechnology, recycling, and quantum computing. The fourth industrial revolution varies fundamentally from previous revolutions due to the convergence of these technologies and their interaction through physical, digital, and biological fields. In the current situation, the fourth industrial revolution requires strong leadership, which helps create awareness of ongoing changes in all sectors and explain to the world that we do not have to worry about our cultural, social, and political structures. Consequently, at the national and global levels, the institutional structure for regulating the diffusion of innovation and preventing disruption is insufficient. Few among these technologies are discussed in the below section.

a) Artificial Intelligence and Machine Learning

It is defined as the area of study in the field of computer science which able to machines engaging in the problem-solving process as like a human through a detailed mechanism of learning, reasoning and self-correction. Thus this technology is the extension of human intelligence with the emerging use of computers. In the past physical power were exerted through the use of mechanical tools. So in simple words, AI can be explained the emerging technology, as a system which thinks like humans, act like humans, furthermore think and act rationally. Artificial intelligence provides efficiency, cost-effectiveness, solutions to complex problems and decision-making. Besides, artificial intelligence limits the loss of data. While Artificial Intelligence makes our lives much simpler and saves us more time than ever, scientists predict that society may be extinguished by massive dependence on AI. Scientists claim that people are unemployed by making an AI computer. Since machines are more efficient and more effective at learning and doing things, this could be why we are extinguished.

The key benefits which obtained from AI are, cost reduction, efficiency gains, opportunities for small business, but similarly, on the other hand, it is also expected that the massive number of people will be unemployed. It is also expected that there will be an issue of accountability if AI, will be used in the financial industry, local governments and also in the military domain. Furthermore, AI is right for matching patterns and automation, making the technology suitable for many functions in big companies. A possible world can be imagined in which AI replaces several tasks performed by people today (Klaus,2017). However, in terms of security AI can be beneficial, as it can provide better surveillance and monitoring. Massive security issues can be solved by using AI. Nevertheless, on the other hand, AL can also be used in military weapon more especially for weapons of mass destruction might create issues in case of any conflicts of any power center in the world.

b) Blockchain

A blockchain is essentially a distributed database of records or a public directory of all transactions or digital events carried out and shared between the parties (see figure 2). The consent of most of the participants in the process verifies each transaction in the public ledger. Furthermore, data can never be deleted once it is entered. A specific and verifiable record of each transaction is contained in the Blockchain. Blockchain technology itself is therefore undisputed and over the years operates well and is widely applied to both financial and non-financial applications worldwide. One of the icons of the digitization period in which we exist is Blockchain. Blockchain is seen as disruptive to traditional business structures like other emerging innovations and would potentially affect our organization in various ways(Crosby, et al, 2015). Bitcoin is the most well-known example of blockchain technology inherently related. It is also the most contentious one, as it helps allow an open global multi-billion-dollar transaction market without state intervention. It must also tackle a range of regulatory problems affecting national governments and financial institutions one of the most harmful, effects which can be observed Blockchain technology more especially in terms of virtual currency, is a high possibility of severe crimes, for example, organized crimes such as Money laundering and terrorist financing. It will allow virtual currency value to be transferred or traded all over the world, without the requirement of a central bank or any other institutional authority. Thus, as in 2009, the Bitcoin ecosystem was developed as the cryptographic protocol to transfer value through the peer-to-peer network, without depending on central banking network. On the other hand, the world financial system slowly regulates its financial system and accepting the virtual currency as well. Similarly, in terms of regulation, the European Union working on their AML direction, which will result shortly will applicable, and then the majority of countries from the European Union will accept as a financial instrument. One of the most critical concern arises by blockchain technology is, international trade or exchange, thus what is an exchange or trading for what? By whom it is traded? Furthermore, who is the ultimate beneficiary? Furthermore, it will affect both trades in goods and services as well as have an impact on intellectual property rights (Nowak and Kluź, 2020).

c) Internet of Things

During 1990 the Internet brings a revolution in this world. Thus world connectivity increased by dramatically. Similarly, the presence of Internet also become the primary factor in local growth as we international growth for the corporate world. The Internet allows corporate to work internationally. Thus it increased the overall factor of globalization. Internet considers as catalyst agent for economic growth. A high degree of communication between people and processes enables the automated and contextual delivery of multiple services whenever and wherever appropriate, contributing to Connected Life. Connected Life will benefit millions of people worldwide, supported by cross-industries collaboration. It will have a positive impact in many economic sectors such as automotive, shipping and logistics, healthcare and utilities (Chan, 2015).The connectivity of massive people around the world, with different kind of service provides, is called the phenomenon of the Internet of things (IoT)

Figure 2. Functioning of Blockchain Technology

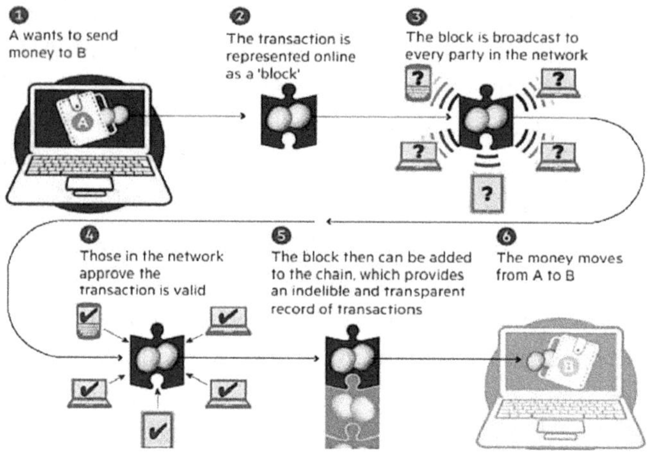

The Internet of Things is a comprehensive information society infrastructure, which enables advanced services, based on existing and changing information and communication technologies, to connect (physical and virtual) things (Patel,& Patel, 2016). In the modern world, there are massive benefits attached or attribute are indicated by (IoT) as it provides interconnectivity to the millions of people with information and communication infrastructure. The IoT devices are heterogeneous based on various hardware and networks. You can interact via different networks with other devices or service platforms. Furthermore, the state of the device changes dramatically by its self; thus, during sleeping, it can be non-functional or non-active. Similarly, on the other hand, it provides economic of sales a large number of devices can be connected with the server or different platform at the same time. Similarly, the large number of buyer or seller can be connected on any trading platform. Give figure 3; explain the phenomenon of the Internet of things (IoT).

Figure 3. Internets of Things and Business
(Patel & Patel, 2016)

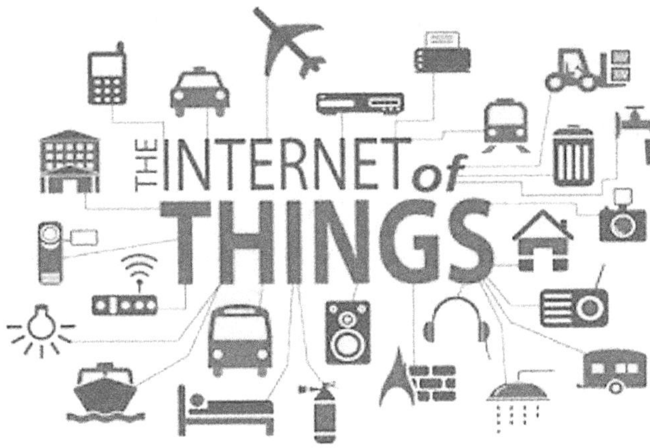

CONCLUSION

The aim of writing this chapter is to illustrate the implication of information technology as outcome of fourth industrial revolution and corporate social responsibility. Our discussion reveals that the Fourth Industrial Revolution will have a significant effect on corporate sector and furthermore, it is also a real phenomenon technology ease of our life with a greater extent. Similarly, on the other hand, majority of the people in third world countries are living with the multi-level of poverty and are not able to get benefit from recent technology but other hand technology advancement creating massive issues of governance and security as well, which are a future threat for those people who are living in poverty. Our discussion also reveals that the efficient use of technology especially fourth industrial revolution can solve massive emerging issues of the world. Nevertheless, on the hand, if we do not appropriately use technology, it might create more problems in the future. These issues are related to especially with security and technology used by wrong people as well; thus unsustainable use of technology.

Furthermore, it is also expected that due to technological revolution huge number of people of the world might lose their jobs, thus somehow technology will able to solve issue in developed economic but on the other hand it is expected that technology will not beneficial for the people of third world countries. The factor might increase income inequalities and at macro level effect on more polarized world. Similarly, it is also responsibility of world leadership to use scientific resources for betterment of the world especially for third world countries. Otherwise, the technology might create more challenges for the world rather than solving the issues.

REFERENCES

Ávila-Robinson, A., & Miyazaki, K. (2014). Assessing nanotechnology potentials: Interplay between the paths of knowledge evolution and the patterns of competence building. *International Journal of Technology Intelligence and Planning*, *10*(1), 1–28. doi:10.1504/IJTIP.2014.066709

Baldwin, R. (2016). *The great convergence*. Harvard University Press.

Baş, K. (2009). Küreselleşme ve Gelir Dağılımı Eşitsizliği. *Journal of the Cukurova University Institute of Social Sciences*, *18*(1).

Boon, W., & Moors, E. (2008). Exploring emerging technologies using metaphors–a study of orphan drugs and pharmacogenomics. *Social Science & Medicine*, *66*(9), 1915–1927. doi:10.1016/j.socscimed.2008.01.012 PMID:18308439

Bouchaud, J. P. (2008). Economics needs a scientific revolution. *Nature*, *455*(7217), 1181–1181. doi:10.1038/4551181a

Brey, P. (2009). Philosophy of technology meets social constructivism: A Shopper's guide. *Readings in the Philosophy of Technology, 98.*

Carroll, L. S. L. (2017). A comprehensive definition of technology from an ethological perspective. *Social Sciences*, *6*(4), 126. doi:10.3390ocsci6040126

Chan, H. C. (2015). Internet of things business models. *Journal of Service Science and Management*, *8*(04), 552–568. doi:10.4236/jssm.2015.84056

Chui, M. (2017). Artificial intelligence the next digital frontier? *McKinsey and Company Global Institute*, *47*, 3–6.

Crosby, M., Pattanayak, P., Verma, S., & Kalyanaraman, V. (2016). Blockchain technology: Beyond bitcoin. *Applied Innovation*, *2*(6-10), 71.

Devezas, T. C. (2012). The recent global crisis under the light of the long wave theory. *Journal of Globalization Studies*, *3*(2), 26–58.

Devezas, T. C. (2012). The recent global crisis under the light of the long wave theory. *Journal of Globalization Studies*, *3*(2), 26–58.

Kumar, V., Kumar, U., & Persaud, A. (1999). Building technological capability through importing technology: The case of Indonesian manufacturing industry. *The Journal of Technology Transfer*, *24*(1), 81–96. doi:10.1023/A:1007728921126

Nowak, B. E., & Kluź, A. (2020). Global Economic Governance and the Challenge of Technological Revolution. In *The Future of Global Economic Governance* (pp. 43–57). Springer. doi:10.1007/978-3-030-35336-0_4

Patel, K. K., & Patel, S. M. (2016). Internet of things-IOT: definition, characteristics, architecture, enabling technologies, application & future challenges. *International Journal of Engineering Science and Computing, 6*(5).

Prisecaru, P. (2016). Challenges of the fourth industrial revolution. *Knowledge Horizons. Economics*, *8*(1), 57.

Reddy, N. M., & Zhao, L. (1990). International technology transfer: A review. *Research Policy*, *19*(4), 285–307. doi:10.1016/0048-7333(90)90015-X

Schwab, K. (2016). *The fourth industrial revolution by Klaus Schwab* (K. J. Song, Trans.). Mega-study Corporation.

Skrbina, D. (2014). *The metaphysics of technology*. Routledge. doi:10.4324/9781315879581

Wahab, S. A., Rose, R. C., & Osman, S. I. W. (2012). Defining the concepts of technology and technology transfer: A literature analysis. *International Business Research*, *5*(1), 61–71.

Xu, M., David, J. M., & Kim, S. H. (2018). The fourth industrial revolution: opportunities and challenges. *International Journal of Financial Research, 9*(2), 90-95.

Chapter 5
CSR on Financial Markets:
Opportunities, Challenges, and Constraints

ABSTRACT

Financial institutions can make a substantial contribution to promoting the principles of sustainable development among their main stakeholders, namely portfolio investors and financial consumers. The challenges posed by climate change have led to the intensification of the financial innovation process and the emergence of new financial instruments such as green bonds and sustainability indices. Their success was due both to the involvement of international institutions that have developed various voluntary principles for companies and to portfolio investors who understood their role in the new context and bought new types of securities. Therefore, the efforts of both sides are bearing fruit in an environment in which confidence must be regained after the earthquake generated by the international financial crisis and the image crisis that financial institutions are facing.

INTRODUCTION

Scandals involving large transnational corporations, environmental disasters caused by oil companies and global warming were important factors that led consumers, NGOs and other stakeholders to pay attention to the impact of companies' activities on the environment and local communities. Over

DOI: 10.4018/978-1-7998-3988-0.ch005

time, companies have also focused on non-environmental issues related to working conditions, employee education, respect for human rights. In this way, we are witnessing a rethinking of the relationship between economic, social and environmental performance that any company must have. Thus, the economic, social and environmental objectives of companies are no longer in conflict and are integrated into the business strategy. Companies are not only responsible to shareholders, but also to the environment, employees and local communities (Matei, 2013, Sierra et al., 2013, Khan et al, 2019).

For several decades, we have been talking about sustainability: sustainable industry, sustainable agriculture, sustainable tourism, etc. Sustainable development is a concept that has found its rightful place in all areas. More and more companies and public authorities are pursuing environmental, social and economic issues in their work. The three P's: people, planet and profit or the "three pillars of sustainability" are elements that need to be considered in order to assess the performance of different organizations in a broader context. "Triple Bottom Line" involves the incorporation of economic, environmental and social aspects in the activity of any company or public institution.

Sustainable development is the most important goal of humanity, but its complexity involves the implementation of the principles of sustainability in all areas and the mobilization of stakeholder groups, whose activity does not necessarily have a negative impact on the environment or resource consumption. In fact, sustainable development and corporate social responsibility are two concepts that must shape the activity of each public or private entity, because any economic agent must not only limit its negative impact on the environment, but must intensify its positive effects on the society in which it acts through various tools, to protect the environment, to contribute to the development of the local community and to promote ethical business behavior and to fight corruption (Ebner, & Baumgartner, 2006; Matei, 2013).

At the international level, we are witnessing the focus of efforts by international organizations such as the UN, OECD, International Monetary Fund, World Bank, which seek to shape the sustainable and responsible behavior of various actors in the world economy, to provide multiple economic operators levers and tools through which they can meet the objectives of sustainable development (Matei, 2013). In a first phase, companies and institutions in different fields of activity became aware of the contribution they can make to sustainable development and then identified the means by which they can do so taking into account the specifics of the activity. Internationally, the activity of institutions such as the United Nations, which launched the principles of corporate social responsibility (Global Compact Principles), principles that were later adapted in collaboration with other organizations for other entities or fields of activity (for investments responsible for agriculture, for portfolio investors, etc.).

Given the four areas of interest of the social responsibility programs (environment, labor standards, human rights and the fight against corruption), the impllications of CSR activities they can be felt in all fields of activity and on different categories of stakeholders. In addition, CSR programs have some interdependencies with other areas such as management, marketing, communication and corporate governance. Having a voluntary character, these programs are initiated based on a decision of the management team that analyzes the costs of these programs and the benefits they can register (increase of market share, sales or profit). Therefore, the development of these programs also requires a detailed financial analysis and the company's management decides on the opportunity of the program. Communication plays an important role in the development of these programs because the company can better evaluate and understand the opportunity of CSR programs run by companies and depending on the publicity made when initiating and completing such programs. In addition, the annual social responsibility reports published by companies contribute to better informing the general public.

FINANCIAL SYSTEM AND CORPORATE SOCIAL RESPONSIBILITY UNDER THE PRESSURE OF CRISIS

Climate change, financial and health crises have demonstrated the fragility of the international financial system. The securities created as instruments that favored risk sharing and allowed the financing of large-scale businesses were transformed, under the pressure of financial innovation, into toxic assets that poisoned not only the activity of financial institutions and the lives of ordinary citizens who did not even know their. Financial innovation is an ongoing process, which is a reality of recent decades, being fueled by technical progress but also by intensifying competition between banks but also between banks and stock exchanges, which are trying to launch new financial products that respond to changes in the economy. financial innovation — is a regular ongoing part of a profit-maximizing economy (Tufano, 2003, Matei, 2008). Initially, financial innovation was seen as a beneficial process for the world economy as it generates reduced transaction costs, information asymmetry and agency costs but also offers multiple possibilities to hedge and make a profit (Merton, 1995). There have been researchers who have considered financial innovation as an engine of the financial system that had the role of improving the performance of the real economy (Merton, 1992). Since the early 1990s, there have been voices that have drawn attention to the dimensions of this process. For example, an American politician considers derivatives to be an electronic Ponzzi scheme, being a fad fueled only by the desire to make a profit both by financial institutions and by institutional investors, or stock exchanges, financial services companies that hope to make a profit by carrying out extensive activities. So, there are two camps - specialists who have drawn attention to the harmful effect of financial innovation, but there are also researchers who, even after the crisis, insist on the positive role of using certain financial assets on economic growth. Therefore, this nuance must be retained, namely Of course, not all financial innovations promote economic growth "(Laeven et al., 2015). In conclusions, financial innovation has the "bright" and "dark" sides (Beck et al.,2016), scientific literature being warning regarding innovation-growth and the innovation-fragility views (Matei, 2013; Kühnhausen, 2014).

The polarization of the financial world and the existence of two economic sectors - financial institutions and financial consumers (individuals with poor financial education and poor economic knowledge) eventually led to violent clashes. The irresponsible attitude of financial institutions and transnational corporations involved in numerous frauds and financial scandals has irreparably affected the social and economic life of citizens who find it difficult to save and invest, especially in developing countries (Voica & Panait, 2017). Securitization, a financing technique designed to transfer risk from the banking system to the capital market, has finally proved to be a curse of the financial market that triggered the financial crisis of 2008. The irresponsible actions of banks that overused this financing technique, continuing to grant credits to some dubious creditworthiness borrowers (Shin, 2009), the lack of responsibility of the rating agencies that did not properly evaluate the complex financial assets, the faulty supervision of the financial markets by the public authorities contributed to the triggering of the biggest financial crisis in the history of mankind (Blundell-Wignall et al., 2009).

The design of this financing technique that allowed the transfer of risk outside the banking system generated the radical transformation of credit risk management at the level of credit institutions. For this reason, at the level of commercial banks there was a relaxation of the conditions for granting loans and the way in which they reacted to the shocks on the market. Excessive use of securitization has led to changes in lending mechanisms, to easier fulfillment of certain indicators imposed by central banks. The result was a feeling of excessive flexibility in the activity of commercial banks. The determinants of the emergence and expansion of this financing technique are somewhat different in the two areas in which securitization has been practiced. In the United States, government-sponsored agencies (such as the Federal National Mortgage Association, known as Fannie Mae, and the Federal Home Loan Mortgage Corporation or Freddie Mac) have contributed to the unprecedented expansion of this technique while in Europe, the commoditization of the of loans was fueled by the introduction of the euro and the integration of the European financial market. (Altunbas et al., 2009). Therefore, different factors led to the same results.

This crisis has shaken the trust of financial consumers in both financial institutions and public authorities with powers of regulation, supervision and control of financial markets. Therefore, we are in a process of rebuilding financial markets, but the whole procedure that must be based on the responsibility of financial institutions, regaining the trust of financial consumers, attracting new categories of consumers in the financial circuit, increasing the involvement of financial consumers as of stakeholders whose role is to sanction the inappropriate behavior of financial institutions. Therefore, the metamorphosis of the international financial system is under the sign of social responsibility, financial inclusion and financial education (Ene & Panait, 2017; Voica, 2017; Zadek, 2018).

Climate change and the need to promote sustainable development have also left their mark on the international financial market. Companies and financial institutions have sought solutions for financing projects with low impact on the environment, being launched various financing schemes or specific financial instruments given the higher risks and costs of such projects. Climate change was therefore a challenge that both banks and stock exchanges that competed in fueling the process of financial innovation had to respond (Voica et al., 2015; Panait et al., 2020). Gradually, there was an education of portfolio investors who became interested in new financial products. The classic return-risk criterion traditionally used by portfolio investors has been updated and today, there are many investors who also consider ESG aspects when substantiating their decisions to sell or buy securities on the stock market. capital.

STOCK EXCHANGES – PROMOTERS OF PROFIT OF OR SUSTAINABLE DEVELOPMENT PRINCIPLES?

The activity of stock exchanges is in a continuous metamorphosis in the last decades. The process of demutualization of stock exchanges has affected almost all these institutions, and from mutual associations of brokers, stock exchanges have become joint stock companies (Akhtar, 2002; Abukari & Otchere, 2019). The new state has generated multiple consequences such as waves of mergers and acquisitions that have led to the formation of large stock exchange groups that bring together several stock exchanges from the same country or even from different countries such as Chicago Mercantile Exchange Group or NYSE Euronext (Matei et al., 2008).

Demutualisation of Sctock Exchanges and Maximizing Own Profit

We are thus witnessing the disappearance of traditional exchanges that functioned as mutual associations, that had stock exchange rings where brokers met and executed buy and sell orders received from clients. The first change regard the legal status of stock exchanges, which were transformed from brokers' associations (with one vote for one member) into joint stock companies (with one vote per share). Brokers have been deprived of decision-making power and influence over the capital market. Decision-making power and voting rights were transferred to shareholders. The transformation also led to a clear separation between owners, decision makers and customers. Thus, demutualization is a strategic change that targets governance, ownership structure, stock market objectives, and stock market attitudes toward risk (Sial et al., 2014; Otchere & Mohsni, 2016). The legal form of organization also has repercussions on the objectives of the exchanges: if initially, the exchange provides services to its members, currently, as a joint stock company, the exchange aims to maximize profits for its shareholders, its activities being guided by market economy principles.

Changing the business model has also become a reality in the stock market environment given the challenges posed by:

- technical progress that led to the emergence of electronic trading systems, new financial products and alternative trading systems;

- the liberalization of capital movements at the international level, which generated the intensification of competition between stock exchanges in attracting issuers, more and more multinational companies opting for double listing - on the national market and on a foreign market for quick access to funds available in the world economy;
- intensifying competition between stock exchanges and banks as main suppliers of financial products and services, but also between stock exchanges
- globalization and liberalization of capital movements that have generated mergers and acquisitions in the financial field but also the listing of large companies on representative stock exchanges.

Many studies conducted worldwide (Akhtar, 2002, Otchere, Abou-Zied, 2007, Serifsoy, 2008, Sial et al, 2014) have shown beneficial effects not only on the stock market as an entity, but also on the national capital market in which activates the respective stock exchange The most important advantages of demutualization are:

- increasing the size and liquidity of the respective stock exchange;
- improving stock market performance and the quality of the stock market.
- adopting bold strategies regarding window dressing, insider trading, and market abuse;
- the adoption of the principles of corporate governance by the stock exchange makes it thus become a trend setter for listed companies;
- increase the attractiveness for foreign investors and intensify their activity on the stock exchange;
- increasing the financial flexibility of the stock exchanges, which is also oriented towards financing mechanisms specific to the capital market. In addition to the beneficial effects of demutualization, we must also mention the disadvantages and risks involved in this transformation (Azzam, 2010):
- stock exchanges may be tempted to reduce the rigor of regulatory activity and to establish more permissive listing conditions in order to attract issuers;
- listing the shares of the stock exchange on the own market may generate a conflict of interests;
- the difficulties registered by the stock exchange can cause big problems to the listed companies that will no longer be able to attract the

available capitals in the economy but also to the investors that will face a decrease of the liquidity of the held securities.

Demutualization has also generated a wave of mergers and acquisitions but also of alliances between stock exchanges or various institutions specific to the stock market. Initially, this process targeted stock exchanges and other entities such as clearing companies in the same market. Subsequently, alliances and takeovers expanded, especially in the European continent, a fact favored by the existence of the European Union . European authorities had launched the Financial Service Action Plan (FSAP) which aims was to create an integrated financial market that ensures the smoothing of relations between companies and small investors with financial intermediaries in the national market or in EU markets. (Matei et al., 2008).

Unfortunately, internationally, the stock market activity is moving further and further away from its primary role, namely that of financing economic activity by launching initial public offerings that ensure both the listing of the issuing company and the mobilization of funds for business development and by launching primary public offerings for the sale of shares and bonds to attract capital available on the financial market. The intensification of the financial innovation process has led to the emergence of complex financial products, considered in some cases toxic assets that have generated particularly intense speculative operations that have nothing to do with the real economy (Matei et al, 2008). Difficulties in valuing these assets were manifested even in the case of rating agencies, which led to the misleading of portfolio investors, even institutional investors. Their confidence fueled the wave of speculative operations, and the fangs of financial crises appeared when the world expected less. Capital market institutions have shown little responsibility to investors, and the negative effects have spread throughout the world economy (Matei, 2013).

THE STOCK EXCHANGES – TREND SETTERS FOR CSR

Stock exchanges are no longer considered only engines of securities trade and financing of the real economy, but have also considerably nuanced the activity in the sense that they have also become ambassadors of sustainable development and CSR, through various instruments. Starting from the global compact principles aimed at promoting rs at the company level, the UN had the initiative to launch similar principles to address investors, which through their financial strength can shape the behavior of issuing companies. In this regard, the Principles for Responsible Investment were launched in 2006 at the New York Stock Exchange (Box No 1). The choice of this location is a recognition of the role that the US financial market plays worldwide and the importance of stock exchanges in efforts to promote sustainable development among portfolio investors.

Box 1. Principles for Responsible Investment

- **Principle 1:** We will incorporate ESG issues into investment analysis and decision-making processes.
- **Principle 2:** We will be active owners and incorporate ESG issues into our ownership policies and practices.
- **Principle 3:** We will seek appropriate disclosure on ESG issues by the entities in which we invest.
- **Principle 4:** We will promote acceptance and implementation of the Principles within the investment industry.
- **Principle 5:** We will work together to enhance our effectiveness in implementing the Principles.
- **Principle 6:** We will each report on our activities and progress towards implementing the Principles.

Source: https://www.unpri.org/pri

Principles of responsible investment (PRI) are based on the idea that environmental issues, social and corporate governance (ESG) can affect performance investment and consideration of these aspects lead to reduction risks and obtaining returns higher. The mission „a sustainable global financial system that rewards its users financially and benefits the environment and society" (PRI, 2020).

As can be seen from figure 1, investors' interest in these principles is growing. In present, there are 3,000 signatories in over 60 countries. But, the PRI cannot solve the challenges the world faces – success relies on enabling the signatories to act". (PRI, 2020).

Figure 1. The assets and signatories under PRI
Source: https://www.unpri.org

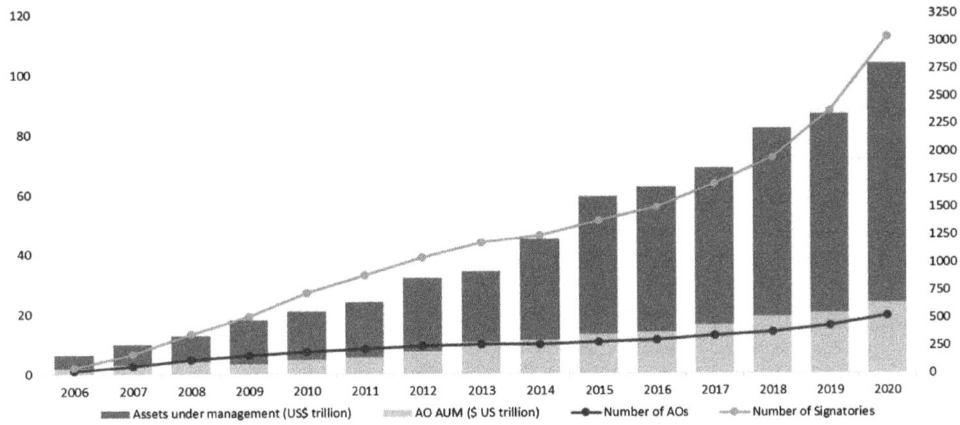

Socially responsible investments have gained ground, especially in developed countries, the reasons being multiple:

- ESG factors (table 1) could affects the activity of companies and implicitly the performances of the shares issued by them, so the profitability and the risk of the securities (Aouadi & Marsat, 2018, Siminica et al., 2019, Sichigea et al., 2020).
- Portfolio investors demand more and more transparency from the issuing companies, not only being interested in the economic aspects but also in non-financial data regarding their activity (García-Sánchez et al., 2020; Townsend, 2020).
- Mandatory or voluntary regulations oblige or encourage issuing companies to publish non-financial data on their activity, either in a special section of the annual report or in an individual report (Fatemi et al., 2018; Rosati & Faria, 2019; Zaman et al., 2020).

From the point of view of the dissemination of information on regarding the environmental impact, the oil and gas companies are also trying to improve their image among the stakeholders. At the international level, CSR reporting rates for the oil & gas sector are highest according to KPMG data released in the year 2017. Toward an average of 60%, the ratio for these companies is 81%. Most companies opt choose to present CSR information in their annual financial report. Companies that decide to provide more complex information on CSR actions are usually doing so this by publishing a sustainability report

(Markota Vukić et al., 2018; Manes-Rossi et al., 2018; Sierra-Garcia et al., 2018). At the international level, the most widely used reporting form on CSR is the GRI standard (KPMG, 2017).

Table 1. Example of ESG issue

Environmental	Social	Governance
Climate change Resource depletion Waste Pollution Deforestation	Human rights Modern slavery Child labour Working conditions Employee relations	Bribery and corruption Executive pay Board diversity and structure Political lobbying and donations Tax strategy

Source: https://www.unpri.org/download?ac=10948

Starting from specific initiatives to promote the principles of sustainable development among issuing companies, the most powerful stock exchanges in the world launched in 2009 under the auspices of international organizations like United Nations Conference for Trade and Development (UNCTAD), the UN Global Compact, United Nations Environment Programme Finance Initiative (UNEP FI) and the The UN Principles for Responsible Investment (UN PRI) an initiative called Sustainable Stock Exchanges (SSE).

This initiative aims to create a platform to provide meeting points between various capital market actors that can have significant contributions in promoting sustainable development. Specifically, the stock exchanges are involved in promoting ESG (environmental, social and corporate governance) issues and sustainable investment, given the launch by the UN of Sustainable Development Goals (SDGs). These bold, interconnected goals aim to reduce poverty, protect the environment, promote gender equality etc (box no 2). These goals must be viewed in a positive light because they provide huge business opportunities in certain industries, even if achieving them can create difficulties or additional costs for certain companies. In addition, Sustainable Development Goals can be considered a framework and common language for stakeholders (Schramade, 2017) because they offer an excellent path to value creation for society and shareholders (table 2).

Box 2. UN Sustainable Development Goals (SDGs).

> In headlines the 17 SDGs of the UN 2030 Transforming the World Agenda are the following: (1) No poverty; (2) Zero hunger; (3) Good health and wealth being; (4) Quality education; (5) Gender equality; (6) Clean water and sanitation; (7) Affordable and clean energy; (8) Decent work and economic growth; (9) Industry innovation and infrastructure; (10) Reduced inequalities; (11) Sustainable cities and communities; (12) Responsible consumption and production; (13) Climate action; (14) Life below water; (15) Life on land; (16) Peace, justice and strong institutions and (17) Partnerships for the goals (UN, 2015).

Table 2. Opportunities offered by SDGs to companies

S. No	Brief description	Estimated amount of investment opportunities			Comment on investment opportunities
		High	Medium	Low	
1	No poverty				Very few pure plays
2	Zero hunger				Very few pure plays
3	Good health & well-being	•			Many in the healthcare, staples and materials sectors
4	Quality education				Very few pure plays
5	Gender equality		•		Very company specific rather than industry specific
6	Clean water and sanitation		•		Some pure plays
7	Affordable and clean energy	•			Many producers of renewable energy or its equipment; lots of providers of energy efficiency
8	Decent work and economic growth	•			This applies to almost any viable business
9	Industry, innovation and infrastructure	•			Many innovative companies and quite a few infrastructure builders
10	Reduced inequalities		•		Very company-specific rather than industry-specific
11	Sustainable cities and communities		•		Very company-specific rather than industry-specific
12	Responsible consumption and production	•			Much of the universe meets this criterion, as most companies could make their products sustainable. Doing this is still a considerable challenge
13	Climate action				Few – formulated at government level
14	Life below water				Some opportunities in for example fish farming, marine or sledging
15	Life on land				Very few, mainly formulated as a government goal
16	Peace, justice and strong institutions		•		Not that many and not easily identified. Think of financials that complement social systems
17	Partnerships for the goals		•		Not that many and purely company-specific

Source: Schramade (2017)

In addition, achieving these ambitious goals requires considerable financial effort on the part of both private companies and public authorities, which is why they will have a significant impact on the international financial market. Specialists even consider SDGs as new ethical guidelines for responsible investments in capital markets. These objectives are an essential challenge for the capital market (Rendtorff, 2020), both for issuing companies and for portfolio investors.

The capital market can offer financing solutions considering the intensification of the financial innovation process but also the existence of 17 SDGs that,, offer a roadmap for tackling the world's most pressing societal challenges, which can be transformed into a powerful driver of growth, given the right mix of innovation and investment" (SSE, 2020 anniversary raport). The involvement of stock exchanges in promoting the principles of sustainable development is particularly complex and can take various forms such as educating participants, issuing companies and portfolio investors, the creation of financial instruments that meet the requirements of economic agents such as products aimed at the transition to low carbon economy such as green bonds or climate change related products.

Establishing mandatory recommendations or criteria for ESG disclosures (European directive), In fact, the Stock exchanges are promoters of ESG transparency (Brooks & Oikonomou, 2018, Bizoumi et al., 2019). The first stock exchanges that imposed such criteria were those in France and South Africa since 2002. After the launch of the SSE initiative, more and more stock exchanges have introduced into disclosure requirements for listed companies, which are required to either publish specific data in the annual report or in the sustainability report, or to explain why they do not. Thus, the stock exchanges from Brazil, India, Thailand and Namibia followed. (2012, B3, in 2014, BSE and NSE in India, SET in Thailand, and the Namibia Stock Exchange).

ESG INDICES THAT WERE THE FIRST SUSTAINABLE PRODUCTS LAUNCHED ON CAPITAL MARKETS

The appearance of sustainability reports is recent, specialists mentioning the the mid-1990s. Starting with the 1970s, large companies began to publish social or environmental reports to provide stakeholders with information especially in the case of environmentally sensitive industries (Bellantuono et al., 2016; Baldini et al., 2018; Caputo et al, 2020). In the last decade, the publication of sustainability reports has become a constant of economic life, this fact being favored not only by the establishment of specific requirements by stock exchanges but also by the emergence of specific regulations such as Directive 2014/95 / EU of the European Parliament and of the Council (amending Directive 2013/34 / EU). These mandatory regulations transpose into European legislation the recommendations made internationally in various forums such as the UN's Sustainable Development Goals, the provisions of the Paris Climate Change Agreement, recommendations of the Financial Stability Board regarding the voluntary publication of financial risks related to climate change. (KPMG, 2017, Banța, 2019, Caputo et al., 2020).

The Directive 2014/95 / EU of the European Parliament and of the Council (amending Directive 2013/34 / EU), imposes to companies with more than 500 employees to disclose non-financial information and diversity information in non-financial statement. The provions of this act regarding the inclusion of non-financial information in the annual management report of companies start from 2018 onwards for 2017 financial year data.

The impact of this regulation in EU countries will certainly be different for several reasons:

1. In half of EU countries, there have been delays in transposing the directive into national law by the end of 2016, as established by the European directive (KPMG, 2017)
2. The national regulations on CSR reporting are different at EU level, there are different notables between member countries, the leaders in the field being UK, Germany and Sweden,
3. Given the general nature of the information requested from companies, they usually publish data that contribute to consolidating or improving the reputation and image among stakeholders (Zaman et al., 2020).

The studies carried out for certain EU countries such as Poland, Romania, Spain suggested that the companies have a high degree of subjectivity regarding the published information, even some key performance indicators are established (table 3).The companies try to present only this kind of information that help them consolidate or improve their reputation and image among stakeholders, (Matuszak & Różańska, 2017, Szadziewska et al, 2018, Popescu, 2019). This demonstrates the importance of standardizing sustainability reports. Therefore, SSE member stock exchanges promote responsible investments on the capital market and the creation of an international sustainable financial system but issuing companies must be genuinely involved in promoting the principles of sustainable development and not use CSR programs as a tool to improve the image of stakeholders or as a greenwashing strategy (Siano et al, 2017, Rosati, 2019, Pimonenko et al, 2020).

Table 3. Key performance indicators

ID	Category	Metric
E1	Environmental	GHG Emissions
E2	Environmental	Emissions Intensity
E3	Environmental	Energy Usage
E4	Environmental	Energy Intensity
E5	Environmental	Energy Mix
E6	Environmental	Water Usage
E7	Environmental	Environmental Operations
E8	Environmental	Environmental Oversight
E9	Environmental	Environmental Oversight
E10	Environmental	Climate Risk Mitigation
S1	Social	CEO Pay Ratio
S2	Social	Gender Pay Ratio
S3	Social	Employee Turnover
S4	Social	Gender Diversity
S5	Social	Temporary Worker Ratio
S6	Social	Non-Discrimination
S7	Social	Injury Rate
S8	Social	Global Health & Safety
S9	Social	Child & Forced Labor
S10	Social	Human Rights
G1	Governance	Board Diversity
G2	Governance	Board Independence
G3	Governance	Incentivized Pay
G4	Governance	Collective Bargaining
G5	Governance	Supplier Code of Conduct
G6	Governance	Ethics & Anti-Corruption
G7	Governance	Data Privacy
G8	Governance	Sustainability Reporting
G9	Governance	Disclosure Practices
G10	Governance	External Assurance

Source: https://sseinitiative.org/esg-guidance-database/

The explosion of stock market indices is evidence of the intensification of the financial innovation process. Originally created as stock indices that calculated the performance of blue chip companies on the US market, the stock market index has seen a spectacular evolution both in terms of calculation methodology and in terms of the basket of assets underlying the index. Technical progress has allowed the creation and use of complex calculation formulas, using both arithmetic mean and geometric mean. The interest for stock indices is also demonstrated by the fact that more and more entities have been involved in launching and calculating stock indices. Many green indices have their origins in social responsibility indices or ESG indices, which were not based only on environmental or climatic factors, such as FTSE4 Good Series and Dow Jones Sustainability (Matei, 2013; Voica, Panait, Rădulescu, 2015; Boitan, 2020). Recently, other types of indices have emerged that include components with a wider range of green investments, such as energy efficiency, environmental management and others (eg FTSE Environmental Market, S&P Eco, Wilderhill New Energy Innovation). Other types of indices are limited to a single factor, such as carbon emissions (for example, S&P Carbon Efficient).

Figure 2. Evolution of Dow Jones Sustainability Index for period 2010-2020
Source: https://www.spglobal.com/spdji/en/indices/equity/dow-jones-sustainability-world-index/#overview

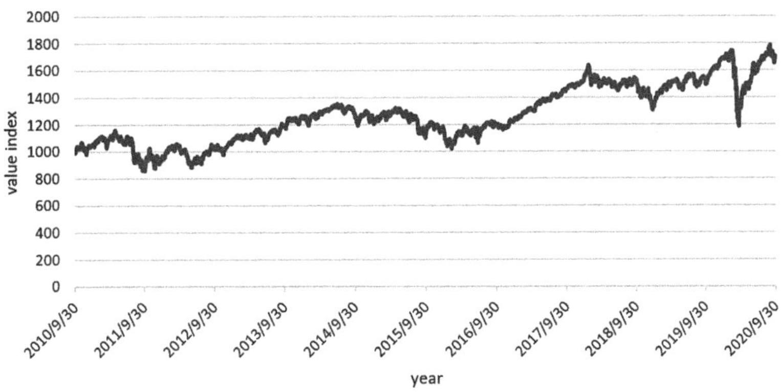

At international level, Dow Jones and MSCI are the world's largest provider of Sustainablity or Governance ESG Indexes. The indices are launched for different zones or type of economies (Dow Jones Sustainability Europe Index, Dow Jones Sustainability U.S. Composite Index, Dow Jones Sustainability Emerging Markets Index, Dow Jones Sustainability World Developed Index Composite, Dow Jones Sustainability MILA Pacific Alliance Index). There are also index focused on some aspects like climate change and the transition to a low-carbon economy. These indices are constructed taking in considerations different carbon reduction objectives used by the listed companis like carbon-efficient and fossil-fuel-free-strategies. (examples Paris-Aligned & Climate Transition - PACT, Carbon Efficient Carbon Price Risk 2030 Adjusted Global

1200 Fossil Fuel Free). There are also thematic indices that renewable energy, clean technology, water or evan Catholic Values (that index was launched for investors that want to have a proper conduit in their investing strategies and do not want to breach religious norms). The evolution of these index is encouraging taking in account the crises that affected the world economy but also the characteristics of the selected companies in the index basket (figure 2).

MSCI index have similar aproches regarding the selection of the securities used to create them. The MSC ESG Equity Indexes and MSC ESG Fixed Income Indexes are goruped on three categories – integration, values and impact like MSCI Low Carbon Target, MSCI ex Controversial Weapons, MSCI ex Tobacco Involvement, MSCI Women's Leadership or Bloomberg Barclays MSCI Socially Responsible (MSCI, 2020).

The need to reduce carbon emissions and the influence of climate change has led to the emergence of other financial instruments, namely green bonds. Bachelet et al, 2019 consider that green bonds as a "plain-vanilla" fixed income products that open sustainable doors for investors into financing green projects. So, they are debt instruments used to finance projects that are environmentally friendly:

- Alternative Energy: Wind, Solar, Geothermal, Biomass, Waste Energy, Wave Tidal, Small Hydro, Large Hydro, Biogas, Bio-fuels,
- Energy Efficiency such as Smart Grid, Other Energy Storage, Superconductors, Natural Gas Combined Heat & Power, LED Lighting, Clean Transportation Infrastructure, Industrial Automation, IT Optimization Service & Infrastructure
- Pollution Prevention & Control Environmental Remediation such as Waste Treatment Reuse & Recycling of Waste,
- Sustainable Water like Water Infrastructure & Distribution, Rainwater Harvesting, Smart Metering Devices, Drought-resistant Seeds, Desalinization, Waste Water Treatment, Water Recycling Equipment & Services, Watershed Conservation Efforts
- Green Building like Green Certified Residential and Commercial Properties based on local environmental performance standards, Green Certified Residential and Commercial Properties based on local environmental design standards,
- Climate Adaptation such as Flood protection, food security and stress-resilient agricultural systems, reforestation and watershed management, climate resiliency services.

The first issue of green bonds was done by European Investment Bank in 2007 (EU, 2019). The World Bank issued in 2009 the green bond for institutional investors. These international institutions have remained the main issuers of green bonds given the confidence it enjoys among investors and the scale of the projects it finances.

The nominal value of green bond issues has increased considerably in the last 10 years (rising from less than $50 billion in 2014 to close to $230 billion in 2018 (BIS, 2019). This fact favored by the attempts of some international or European bodies to promote principles to support issuers and institutional investors who are the main players in this market. In 2019, total green bond issuance was recorded at USD257.7bn according with Climate Bond Initiative's (CBI, 2020). The most important countries in the ranking of issuers are the USA, China followed by European countries such as France, Germany and Sweden, which is why from a regional point of view, the leader is Europe which accounted for 45% of global issuance. At EU level, sustained efforts are being made to connect finance with sustainability. In 2018 the European Commission published the Action Plan on Financing Sustainable Growth. One of the aim of the European Commission is to create standards and labels for green financial products.

The international green bond market is in a process of transformation, in the sense that in addition to supranational, more and more companies and municipalities have decided to become actively involved in the transition to the green economy and to issue such securities (table 4). The emergence of emerging market issuers, particularly from China or other asia countries like Vietnam (Anh Tu et al., 2020), has led not only to market development but also to the diversification of currencies in which green bond issues are denominated.

Accordingly with Bank of International Settlements, a key catalyst for market development was launch of the Green Bond Principles (GBPs) by the International Capital Market Association (ICMA) in 2014 (BIS, 2019) and updated in 2018. The GBPs govern: (i) the use of proceeds; (ii) the process for project evaluation and selection; (iii) the management of proceeds; and (iv) reporting. The principles offer guidelines for issuing green bonds in order to increase the level of transparency related to the issuance of such securities and increase investor confidence.An important aspect of these principles are the certification by third-party providers or Climate Bond Initiative's (CBI). In this way, the investors are sure that the securities bought environmental or climate-related benefits,and are not used as a tool of green-washing.

Table 4. Stock exchanges with a dedicated section for green or sustainable bonds

Name of Stock Exchange	Type of Dedicated Section	Launch Date
Name of Stock Exchange	Type of Dedicated Section	Launch Date
Oslo Stock Exchange	Green bonds	January 2015
Stockholm Stock Exchange	Sustainable Bonds	June 2015
London Stock Exchange	Green bonds	July 2015
Shanghai Stock Exchange	Green bonds	March 2016
Mexico Stock Exchange	Green bonds	August 2016
Luxembourg Stock Exchange	Luxembourg Green Exchange	September 2016
Borsa Italiana	Green and Social bonds	March 2017
Taipei Exchange	Green bonds	May 2017
Johannesburg Stock Exchange	Green bonds	October 2017
Japan Exchange Group	Green and Social bonds	January 2018
Vienna Exchange	Green and Social bonds	March 2018
Nasdaq Helsinki	Sustainable bonds	May 2018
Nasdaq Copenhagen	Sustainable bonds	May 2018
Nasdaq Baltic	Sustainable bonds	May 2018
Swiss Stock Exchange	Green and Sustainability bonds	July 2018
The International Stock Exchange	Green bonds	November 2018
Frankfurt Stock Exchange	Green bonds	November 2018
Santiago Stock Exchange	Green and social bonds	July 2019
Moscow Exchange	Sustainable bonds	August 2019
Euronext	Green bonds	November 2019
Hong Kong Exchange	STAGE, Sustainable and Green Exchange	June 2020
Singapore Stock Exchange	Green, Social and Sustainability bonds	n.a.

Source: https://www.climatebonds.net/green-bond-segments-stock-exchanges

Starting from the success of green bonds on the international financial market, ICMA had a new initiative and in 2017 launched Social Bonds Principles and updated its in 2020. Social bonds are securities issued to raise funds for projects with positive social outcomes. The SBP have four core components: (1) use of proceeds, (2) process for project evaluation and selection, (3) management of proceeds, (4) reporting (ICMA, 2020). Social Project categories include:

- Affordable basic infrastructure like clean drinking water, sewers, sanitation, transport, energy
- Access to essential services such as health, education and vocational training, health care, financing and financial services)
- Affordable housing
- Employment generation, and programs designed to prevent and/or alleviate unemployment stemming from socioeconomic crises, including through the potential effect of SME financing and micro finance

- Food security and sustainable food systems (e.g. physical, social, and economic access to safe, nutritious, and sufficient food that meets dietary needs and requirements; resilient agricultural practices; reduction of food loss and waste; and improved productivity of small-scale producers)

Sustainability-Linked Bonds (SLB) are debt securities used by companies and other issuers to raise funds for projects that contribute to sustainability (from an environmental and/or social and/or governance perspective). ICMA launched in 2020 principles aplicable to these types of securities. The SLBP have five core components: 1. Selection of Key Performance Indicators (KPIs) 2. Calibration of Sustainability Performance Targets (SPTs) 3. Bond characteristics 4. Reporting 5. Verification. Therefore, the need to adapt public companies and institutions to the challenges generated by climate change has led to the intensification of the financial innovation process and the emergence of financial products designed to finance green, social projects or which promote, in various forms, sustainable development.

CONCLUSION

The development of the capital market has many forms of manifestation: the process of financial innovation, the demutualization of stock exchanges, the intensification of mergers and acquisitions. In addition, the capital market has a special importance on the process of economic growth, the effects being both positive and negative. The importance of the capital market for financing companies is a recognized fact, but the innovation process makes its impact felt by diversifying the tools used to attract capital available in the economy. The capital market also offers possibilities to cover financial risks through specific hedging operations but also tools for carrying out speculative operations. Unfortunately, speculative trading has intensified sharply in recent decades, and the desire of quick-earned investors has fueled the process of financial innovation that has led to the launch of complex financial instruments that are difficult for rating agencies to assess. . Unfortunately, the origins of the international financial crisis in 2008 can be detected in the US capital market, the scale of securitization operations and the failure of rating agencies in the valuation of financial products were the basis for triggering this crisis.

The challenges generated by climate change have also generated the process of metamorphosis of the international financial system that must be rebuilt taking into account the principles of sustainable development. These general principles take various forms such as the Principle of Responsible Investment, Global Compact Principles, Green Bonds Principles, Social Bonds Principles. Their voluntary nature was not an impediment to their adoption and observance by corporations and public institutions. They rethought their behavior and business strategy not only under the pressure of stakeholders but also as a result of the emergence of new business opportunities.

Stock exchanges have also gone through a process of transformation that has targeted not only the form of organization but also their involvement in the economy. Their role in concentrating the demand and supply of financial funds has intensified in the sense that the financing of green, social or sustainable projects can be achieved on the capital market through specific instruments that are launched by both companies and public institutions or international bodies.

Stock exchanges activity is now under the sign of sustainable development, and sustainability indices are benchmarks on the international capital market for portfolio investors who want to have, through their actions, a positive contribution to the world economy.

REFERENCES

Abukari, K., & Otchere, I. (2019). Has stock exchange demutualization improved market quality? International evidence. *Review of Quantitative Finance and Accounting*, 1–34. doi:10.100711156-019-00863-y

Akhtar, S. (2002). *Demutualization of stock exchanges: problems, solutions and case studies*. Asian Development Bank.

Altunbas, Y., Gambacorta, L., & Marques-Ibanez, D. (2009). Securitisation and the bank lending channel. *European Economic Review*, *53*(8), 996–1009. doi:10.1016/j.euroecorev.2009.03.004

Anh Tu, C., Sarker, T., & Rasoulinezhad, E. (2020). Factors Influencing the Green Bond Market Expansion: Evidence from a Multi-Dimensional Analysis. *Journal of Risk and Financial Management*, *13*(6), 126. doi:10.3390/jrfm13060126

Aouadi, A., & Marsat, S. (2018). Do ESG controversies matter for firm value? Evidence from international data. *Journal of Business Ethics*, *151*(4), 1027–1047. doi:10.100710551-016-3213-8

Azzam, I. (2010). Stock exchange demutualization and performance. *Global Finance Journal*, *21*(2), 211–222. doi:10.1016/j.gfj.2010.06.007

Bachelet, M. J., Becchetti, L., & Manfredonia, S. (2019). The green bonds premium puzzle: The role of issuer characteristics and third-party verification. *Sustainability*, *11*(4), 1098. doi:10.3390u11041098

Baldini, M., Dal Maso, L., Liberatore, G., Mazzi, F., & Terzani, S. (2018). Role of country-and firm-level determinants in environmental, social, and governance disclosure. *Journal of Business Ethics*, *150*(1), 79–98. doi:10.100710551-016-3139-1

Banța, V. C. (2019). Performance evaluation of the implementation of the 2013/34/EU directive in Romania on the basis of corporate social responsibility reports. *Sustainability*, *11*(9), 2531. doi:10.3390u11092531

Beck, T., Chen, T., Lin, C., & Song, F. M. (2016). Financial innovation: The bright and the dark sides. *Journal of Banking & Finance*, *72*, 28–51. doi:10.1016/j.jbankfin.2016.06.012

Bellantuono, N., Pontrandolfo, P., & Scozzi, B. (2016). Capturing the stakeholders' view in sustainability reporting: A novel approach. *Sustainability*, *8*(4), 379. doi:10.3390u8040379

BIS. (2019). *Quarterly Review*. https://www.bis.org/publ/qtrpdf/r_qt1909z.htm

Bizoumi, T., Lazaridis, S., & Stamou, N. (2019). Innovation in Stock Exchanges: Driving ESG Disclosure and Performance. *Journal of Applied Corporate Finance*, *31*(2), 72–79. doi:10.1111/jacf.12348

Blundell-Wignall, A., Atkinson, P., & Lee, S. H. (2009). The current financial crisis: Causes and policy issues. *OECD Journal: Financial Market Trends*, *2008*(2), 1–21.

Boitan, I. A. (2020). Sustainable stock market indices: A comparative assessment of performance. *Journal of Research in Emerging Markets*, *2*(1), 7–14. doi:10.30585/jrems.v2i1.410

Brooks, C., & Oikonomou, I. (2018). The effects of environmental, social and governance disclosures and performance on firm value: A review of the literature in accounting and finance. *The British Accounting Review*, *50*(1), 1–15. doi:10.1016/j.bar.2017.11.005

Caputo, F., Leopizzi, R., Pizzi, S., & Milone, V. (2020). The Non-Financial Reporting Harmonization in Europe: Evolutionary Pathways Related to the Transposition of the Directive 95/2014/EU within the Italian Context. *Sustainability*, *12*(1), 92. doi:10.3390u12010092

Ebner, D., & Baumgartner, R. J. (2006, September). The relationship between sustainable development and corporate social responsibility. In Corporate responsibility research conference (Vol. 4, No. 5.9, p. 2006). Queens University, Belfast.

Ene, C. (2017). Current Issues Regarding The Protection Of Retail Investors On The Capital Market Within The European Union. *The USV Annals of Economics and Public Administration*, *17*(1 (25)), 35–44.

Ene, C., & Panait, M. (2017). The financial education-Part of corporate social responsibility for employees and customers. *Revista Romana de Economie*, *44*(1), 145–154.

EU. (2019). *TEG report on EU green bond standard.* https://ec.europa.eu/info/files/190618-sustainable-finance-teg-report-green-bond-standard_en

Fatemi, A., Glaum, M., & Kaiser, S. (2018). ESG performance and firm value: The moderating role of disclosure. *Global Finance Journal*, *38*, 45–64. doi:10.1016/j.gfj.2017.03.001

García-Sánchez, I. M., Rodríguez-Ariza, L., Aibar-Guzmán, B., & Aibar-Guzmán, C. (2020). Do institutional investors drive corporate transparency regarding business contribution to the sustainable development goals? *Business Strategy and the Environment*, *29*(5), 2019–2036. doi:10.1002/bse.2485

ICMA. (2020). https://www.icmagroup.org/green-social-and-sustainability-bonds/

Khan, S. A. R., Yu, Z., Golpîra, H., & Sharif, A. (2019). The nexus between corporate social responsibility and corporate performance: An empirical evidence. *LogForum, 15*.

KPMG. (2017). The road ahead. *Survey of Corporate Responsibility Reporting 2017*. https://home.kpmg/uk/en/home/insights/2017/11/kpmg-international-survey-of-corporate-responsibility-reporting-2017.html

KühnhausenF. (2014). Financial innovation and fragility. Available at SSRN 2404881.

Laeven, L., Levine, R., & Michalopoulos, S. (2015). Financial innovation and endogenous growth. *Journal of Financial Intermediation, 24*(1), 1–24. doi:10.1016/j.jfi.2014.04.001

Manes-Rossi, F., Tiron-Tudor, A., Nicolò, G., & Zanellato, G. (2018). Ensuring more sustainable reporting in Europe using non-financial disclosure—De facto and de jure evidence. *Sustainability, 10*(4), 1162. doi:10.3390u10041162

Markota Vukić, N., Vuković, R., & Calace, D. (2018). Non-financial reporting as a new trend in sustainability accounting. *Journal of Accounting and Management, 7*(2), 13–26.

Matei, M. (2013). *Responsabilitatea socială a corporaţiilor şi instituţiilor şi dezvoltarea durabilă a României*. Expert Publishing House.

Matei, M., Stancu, A., Enescu, G., & Geambaşu, C. (2008). Burse de mărfuri şi valori. *Editura Universităţii din Ploieşti.*

Matei, M., & Voica, M. C. (2013). Social Responsibility in the Financial and Banking Sector. *Economic Insights - Trends and Challenges, 65*(1).

Matuszak, Ł., & Różańska, E. (2017). CSR disclosure in Polish-listed companies in the light of Directive 2014/95/EU requirements: Empirical evidence. *Sustainability, 9*(12), 2304. doi:10.3390u9122304

Merton, R. C. (1992). Financial innovation and economic performance. *Journal of Applied Corporate Finance, 4*(4), 12–22. doi:10.1111/j.1745-6622.1992.tb00214.x

Merton, R. C. (1995). Financial innovation and the management and regulation of financial institutions. *Journal of Banking & Finance, 19*(3-4), 461–481. doi:10.1016/0378-4266(94)00133-N

MSCI. (n.d.). https://www.msci.com/esg-indexes

Otchere, I., & Abou-Zied, K. (2008). Stock exchange demutualization, self-listing and performance: The case of the Australian Stock Exchange. *Journal of Banking & Finance, 32*(4), 512–525. doi:10.1016/j.jbankfin.2007.07.011

Otchere, I., & Mohsni, S. (2016). Changing organizational form in the stock exchange industry and risk-taking. *Financial Markets and Portfolio Management, 30*(4), 427–451. doi:10.100711408-016-0276-6

Panait, M., Radulescu, I., & Brezoi, A. (2020). Financial Markets–Under the Sign of CSR. Some Evidences Regarding Financial Education. *LUMEN Proceedings, 11*, 96-106.

Panait, M., Voica, M. C., & Radulescu, I. (2014). The activity of capital market actors: Under the sign of social responsibility. *Procedia Economics and Finance, 8*, 522–528. doi:10.1016/S2212-5671(14)00123-3

Pimonenko, T., Bilan, Y., Horák, J., Starchenko, L., & Gajda, W. (2020). Green Brand of Companies and Greenwashing under Sustainable Development Goals. *Sustainability, 12*(4), 1679. doi:10.3390u12041679

Popescu, C. R. G. (2019). Corporate social responsibility, corporate governance and business performance: Limits and challenges imposed by the implementation of directive 2013/34/EU in Romania. *Sustainability, 11*(19), 5146. doi:10.3390u11195146

Rendtorff, J. D. (2020). Corporate citizenship, stakeholder management and Sustainable Development Goals (SDGs) in financial institutions and capital markets. *Journal of Capital Markets Studies.*

Rosati, F., & Faria, L. G. (2019). Addressing the SDGs in sustainability reports: The relationship with institutional factors. *Journal of Cleaner Production, 215*, 1312–1326. doi:10.1016/j.jclepro.2018.12.107

Schramade, W. (2017). Investing in the UN sustainable development goals: Opportunities for companies and investors. *Journal of Applied Corporate Finance, 29*(2), 87–99. doi:10.1111/jacf.12236

Serifsoy, B. (2008). Demutualization, outsider ownership, and stock exchange performance: Empirical evidence. *Economics of Governance, 9*(4), 305–339. doi:10.100710101-007-0037-0

Shin, H. S. (2009). Securitisation and financial stability. *Economic Journal (London), 119*(536), 309–332. doi:10.1111/j.1468-0297.2008.02239.x

Sial, A., Tahir, A. Q., Zulfiqar, S., Iqbal, M., & Naqvi, S. A. A. (2014). Demutualization of stock exchanges and stock market Growth: Broader economic investigation of demutualized Exchanges. *Journal of Economics. Finance& Accounting, 1*(4), 285–294.

Siano, A., Vollero, A., Conte, F., & Amabile, S. (2017). “More than words”: Expanding the taxonomy of greenwashing after the Volkswagen scandal. *Journal of Business Research, 71*, 27–37. doi:10.1016/j.jbusres.2016.11.002

Sichigea, M., Siminica, M. I., Circiumaru, D., Carstina, S., & Caraba-Meita, N. L. (2020). A Comparative Approach of the Environmental Performance between Periods with Positive and Negative Accounting Returns of EEA Companies. *Sustainability*, *12*(18), 7382. doi:10.3390u12187382

Sierra, L., Zorio, A., & García-Benau, M. A. (2013). Sustainable development and assurance of corporate social responsibility reports published by Ibex-35 companies. *Corporate Social Responsibility and Environmental Management*, *20*(6), 359–370. doi:10.1002/csr.1303

Sierra-Garcia, L., Garcia-Benau, M. A., & Bollas-Araya, H. M. (2018). Empirical analysis of non-financial reporting by Spanish companies. *Administrative Sciences*, *8*(3), 29. doi:10.3390/admsci8030029

Siminica, M., Ionascu, C., & Sichigea, M. (2019). Corporate Social Performance versus Financial Performance of the Romanian Firms. *Prague Economic Papers*, *28*(1), 49–69. doi:10.18267/j.pep.687

Szadziewska, A., Spigarska, E., & Majerowska, E. (2018). The disclosure of non-financial information by stock-exchange-listed companies in Poland, in the light of the changes introduced by the Directive 2014/95/EU. *Zeszyty Teoretyczne Rachunkowości*, *2018*(99 (155)), 65–95. doi:10.5604/01.3001.0012.2933

Taliento, M., Favino, C., & Netti, A. (2019). Impact of environmental, social, and governance information on economic performance: Evidence of a corporate 'sustainability advantage' from Europe. *Sustainability*, *11*(6), 1738. doi:10.3390u11061738

Townsend, B. (2020). From SRI to ESG: The Origins of Socially Responsible and Sustainable Investing. *The Journal of Impact and ESG Investing*, *1*(1), 10–25. doi:10.3905/jesg.2020.1.1.010

Tufano, P. (2003). Financial innovation. In *Handbook of the Economics of Finance* (Vol. 1, pp. 307–335). Elsevier.

UNPRI. (2020). https://www.unpri.org/

Voica, C., & Panait, M. (2017). Foreign Banks' Activity in Romania - Under the Sign of Ethics and CSR or Under the Profit's Sign? *Journal of Financial and Monetary Economics*, *4*, 439–447.

Voica, M. C. (2017). Financial inclusion as a tool for sustainable development. *Romanian Journal of Economics, 44*(1 (53)), 121-129.

Voica, M. C., Panait, M., & Radulescu, I. (2015). Green investments–between necessity, fiscal constraints and profit. *Procedia Economics and Finance*, *22*, 72–79. doi:10.1016/S2212-5671(15)00228-2

Zadek, S. (2018). Aligning the Financial System with Sustainable Development. *Financing Sustainable Development*, 102.

Chapter 6
The Financial Education:
Part of CSR, of Financial Institutions, and Public Authorities

ABSTRACT

Financial education is a process that must take place throughout the life of consumers, given the intensification of the process of financial and technological innovation materialized in the emergence of new financial products and ways of accessing them. The financial education programs must focus on capitalizing on and use of financial knowledge and skills by children, young people, and women. The education can create responsible financial behavior within consumers to efficiently manage resources throughout life, including periods of the current health crisis. COVID has demonstrated the importance of economic resilience and the ability of consumers to adapt to the turbulence specific to this period. The financial fragility faced by certain categories of consumers during this period demonstrates the need to implement financial education programs. There is a need to adopt radical changes that are taking place in the financial market under the impact of fintech.

INTRODUCTION

In recent decades, the financial sector has been shaken by multiple scandals and crises that have shown weak oversight by public authorities with responsibilities in the field, poor valuation of complex products by rating

DOI: 10.4018/978-1-7998-3988-0.ch006

agencies, the pursuit of profit by credit institutions that set unrealistic targets for employees or who do not have rigorous risk management systems. The effects of financial crises and scandals have been felt economically and socially by many categories of stakeholders such as individuals and legal clients, public institutions. Financial consumers - individuals were among the most affected categories because the relationship with credit institutions usually involves contracting real estate loans with a mortgage that generates the purchase of a home (Matei, 2013. Andrei et al., 2018, Starešinić et al., 2019). The impossibility of paying the instalments to the credit institution entails the execution of the mortgage and the loss of the house, which can generate multiple personal dramas, especially if the clients have a family and dependent children.

The results of the financial crises have led to a dramatic decline in consumer confidence and some reluctance on the part of credit institutions and other market operators. Therefore, financial institutions are currently in a complex process of rebuilding the image and regaining the confidence of consumers and investors in the banking market, the insurance market and the capital market. Efforts must be supported by both the encouraging attitude of financial supervisors and consumer behavior, given the role of the financial market in promoting sustainable development and achieving their objectives SDGs (Matei, 2013; Botis, 2017; Ene, 2017, Stoian, & Iorgulescu, 2019).

The financial market is in a full revolution generated by the digitalization of banking products and services. Fintech is a trend that generates new business models, processes or products but also challenges for companies, financial institutions, individual consumers and public authorities (Gabor& Brooks, 2017; Ionescu & Rădulescu, 2019; Marara et al., 2019). Public authorities need to meet the new challenges posed by fintech and create the regulatory, supervisory and control framework for new financial products and services such as payment instruments and services or alternative forms of financing (crowdfunding and individual lending). the person). At EU level, the FinTech Action Plan was launched, through which the European institutions created the necessary framework for the implementation of „support measures designed to contribute to the introduction of FinTech solutions, as well as proactive measures to encourage and stimulate new solutions and to address decidedly emerging risks and challenges,, (EU, 2018).

Thus, the management of financial institutions initiated a series of measures such as:

- promoting codes of ethics among employees,

- transparency in the relationship with customers who must be well informed about the commissions charged by banks,
- promoting cybersecurity culture,
- more rigorous management of the risks,
- promoting a culture of risk,
- adopting a healthy remuneration policy for specialized staff and management staff
- caution in launching new financial products, which should be done only after a rigorous assessment of their risks
- more rigorous evaluation of financial products in order to be rated by rating agencies,
- promoting the principles of CSR by carrying out specific programs on the four general directions established by the United Nations through the Global Compact Initiative, namely the environment, human rights, the fight against corruption,
- development of Financial Inclusion Programs that aim at the access of certain categories of people such as women or the rural population to modern financial services
- promoting the principles of financial education among different categories of stakeholders.

Therefore, the financial institutions like any companies must manifest social responsibility directly in relation to its customers, by promoting an ethical behavior towards all categories of stakeholders and not only through CSR programs (Ciutacu et al., 2005, Matei, 2013, Palazzo et al, 2020). Many studies focused on the cameleonic behaviour of financial insitutions,which on the one hand, runs various CSR programs or promotes the principles of sustainable financing in the case of lending to large companies, but on the other hand, in relation to individual consumers, practices abusive contractual clauses or uses fraudulent promotion programs (Shaban et al., 2017; Voica & Panait, 2017).

This situation is similar to the greenwashing strategy specific to companies in the industry that through CSR programs focused on environmental protection try to promote a positive image among stakeholders, even if they have no real concerns in this area (Vollero et al, 2011; Vollero et al et al, 2016; Siano et al, 2017). So, stakeholders will have the certainty that CSR programs promoted by financial institutions are not simple marketing tools that try to create a false positive image among consumers. Patiño, & Gutiérrez, 2019 draw attention to the phenomenon by saying that, , financial education programs have become a marketing tool rather than an activity that helps to solve financial problems.,,

This chapter is the structure on several sections. In the first section, the specific situation of the financial market is presented, insisting on the metamorphosis process that the financial market goes through under the impact of several challenges generated by the international financial crisis, COVID health crisis, innovation and fintech. In section two, the author presents the importance of the process of financial inclusion on sustainable development. The high level of financial exclusion that mainly affects the population of developing countries but also certain categories of consumers can be diminished with specific tools such as financial education programs or mobile financial services.

FINANCIAL INCLUSION - SIZE AND IMPORTANCE

Financial exclusion is a reality of the millennium, being present especially in developing countries. The phenomenon is also present in developed countries, but its size is much smaller, and the tools are more numerous and more sophisticated. Financial exclusion is a reality that affects the unemployed, women, people with disabilities who do not have their own earnings, or retired ethnic groups who have emigrated to developed countries. The causes of the phenomenon are multiple and consist in the lack of access, difficult access to banking products and services and high costs (Yue et al.2019).

The exacerbation of competition between banks that has generated intensified financial innovation and the emergence of very complex products, banks' desire to increase profits. has led, in some cases, to a reduction in the number of agencies. As Sinclair, 2001 considered „exclusion can come about as a result of problems with access, conditions, prices, marketing or self-exclusion in response to negative experiences or perceptions." So, the financial exclusion in generated by inappropriate behavior of financial institutions and consumers alike (figure 1). The multitude of determining factors from both the demand and the supply, make the solutions for reducing this phenomenon to be complex, numerous.

Figure 1. The determining factors of financial exclusion
Source: Authors representation

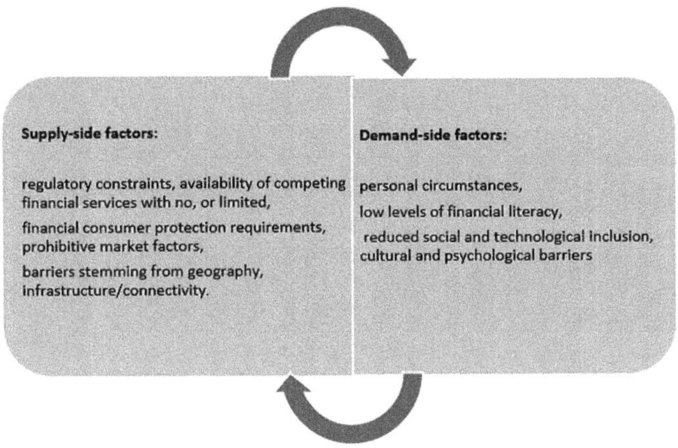

The degree of financial inclusion varies greatly at the global level, with statistical data published by the World Bank demonstrating notable regional differences (Global Fintex data). The indicators calculated by this international institution are numerous, below are some of them, namely the share of people who have a bank account, the share of men who have such a financial product and the share of women who have opened an account at a banking institution (in all three cases, taking into account only people over 15 years). As can be seen from Figure 2 and 3, there are notable differences even between the countries of Central and Eastern Europe, which were part of the communist bloc, as well as between men and women.

So, the gender gap in financial inclusion is a reality at the international level. The financial freedom is still elusive for women from many countries, but important steps were done in this respect. According to Global Findex database published by Word Bank for 2017, a global gender gap of 7 percentage points still persists since 2011 (when these statistical indicators were published for the first time). There are also exceptions that are registered in countries such as Bolivia, Cambodia, the Russian Federation and South Africa where there are no notable differences between the sexes or in countries like Argentina, Indonesia, and the Philippines, where women have more accounts than men.

Figure 2. Indicators of financial inclusion for some Central and Eastern European countries
Source: Global Findex database, (2017)

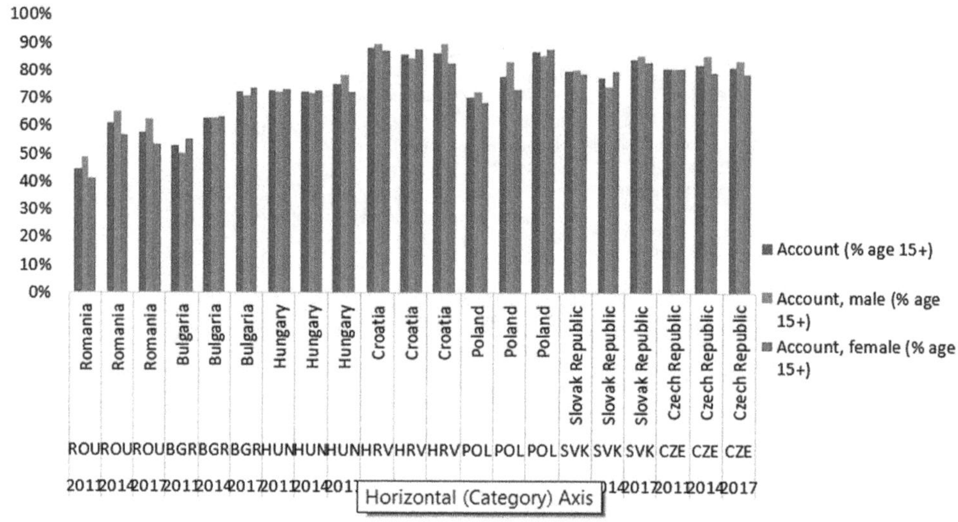

Figure 3. Made or received digital payments (2014, 2017)
Source: Global Findex database, (2017)

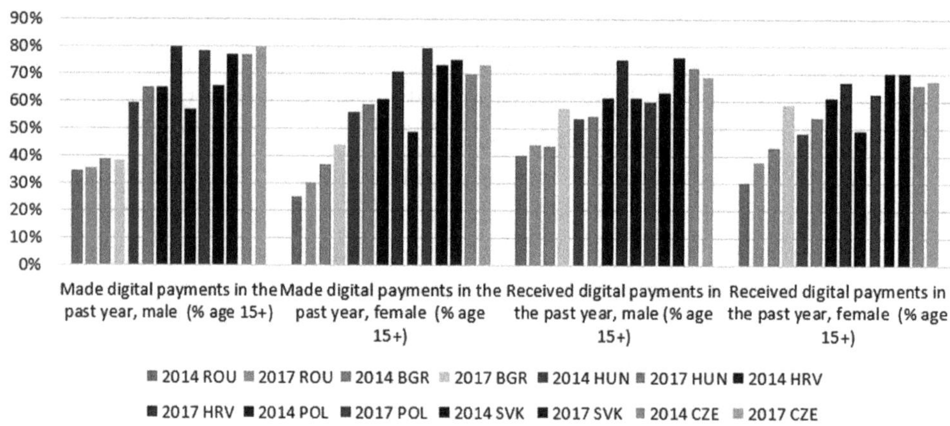

The high degree of financial exclusion that is characteristic of women is generated by certain factors such as lower wages earned by women or a lack of income from work, social norms that generate less mobility from women and reduced demand for banking services, financial dependence on the life partner, the low level of education of women compared to parteners, lower access of women to technology (more precisely to mobile telephony which is considered a tool of financial inclusion).

However, at the level of a household, women are responsible for budget and savings. This paradox must end given the women's ability to spend and invest family money but also the benefits that can increase the degree of inclusion among families. Investing in the financial inclusion of women will generate benefits not only for current generations (by increasing the well-being of women and their families, but also for future ones). Mothers and parents in general play an important role in transmitting financial values, attitudes and in creating financial to their children. OECD study on youth literacy mentions the importance of Discussing money matters with parents (OECD PISA, 2015)

Statistical data provided by international institutions prove the important role that migrant women play in the transfer of money earned to their countries of origin (UNWomen, 2017). Migrant women usually have lower wages than men (they find jobs in domestic and care sectors, manufacturing and agriculture, so called feminized sectors of work, a fact generated thousands of times by sex stereotypes.

Despite this situation, they transfer larger amounts and longer periods of time. The feminization of international migration (Chammartin, 2002; Le Goff, 2016; Olayiwola, 2020) demonstrated by statistical data thus generates positive effects on the financial inclusion of women because they are forced to make various financial operations to transfer money to countries of origin.

In a first phase, migrants face certain psychological barriers in accessing banking systems from developed countries (distrust in complex banking systems, compared to those in the country of origin, lack of financial education specific to developing countries or the time horizon). Their financial behaviour is generated by their desire to save money to be sent to families left in the country. So, migrants have a specific saving process that generate periodic sending of large sums of money to the family that need of a bank account. The frequency of remittances is different, being influenced by the needs of the family, the sex of the migrant, the prospects of opening a business in the country of origin or the prospects of buying a home, the intention to reunite the family in the destination country. The regular sending of money to the family determines the increase of the financial inclusion for the other members of the family.

FINANCIAL EDUCATION PROGRAMS - BETWEEN NECESSITY AND EFFICIENCY

Financial education is defined as "the process by which financial consumers / investors improve their understanding of financial products, concepts and risks and, through information, instruction and / or objective advice, develop the skills and confidence to become more aware of financial risks and opportunities, to make informed choices, to know where to go for help, and to take other effective actions to improve their financial well-being" (OECD, 2005). Therefore, financial education presupposes:

- understanding of products, mechanisms and concept specific to the financial market,
- accumulation of knowledge regarding loans, how to calculate interest, inflation, bank guarantees, portfolio and risk diversification, etc.,
- developing skills for responsible spending of funds and for making safe investments with a high degree of profitability,
- making informed choices, given the multitude of financial products,
- awareness of the risks and opportunities offered by financial products and services,
- confidence in one's own knowledge and instincts,
- adjusting the attitudes of overconfidence that are manifested in the case of consumers who have certain knowledge in the financial field,
- the ability to ask for help from competent people, in case of important decisions or if you want to make investments in products with a high degree of complexity.

Financial education, financial consumer protection and financial inclusion are considered by OCDE as three essential ingredients for the financial empowerment of individuals and the overall stability of the financial system, as highlighted through three sets of high-level principles endorsed by G20 leaders: Innovative Financial Inclusion (2010); Financial Consumer Protection (2011); and National Strategies for Financial Education (2012)" (OCDE, 2020)

Financial education programs must target another important category, namely children and young people. According with OECD Principles and Good Practices for Financial Education and Awareness. „Financial education should start at school. People should be educated about financial matters as early as possible in their lives". For this reason, it is necessary to implement long-term solutions to increase the degree of financial inclusion. This can be achieved through a combination of tools such as financial education strategy and consumer protection policies that differentiate the multiple categories of stakeholders that can support the financial education process (figure 4). Internationally, this approach has been approached differently, in the sense that either a financial inclusion strategy based on a sustained financial education policy has been chosen, or for the simultaneous implementation of the financial education strategy and the inclusion financial strategy.

Figure 4. Importance of education on financial inclusion 2011, 2014, 2017
Source: Global Findex database, (2017)

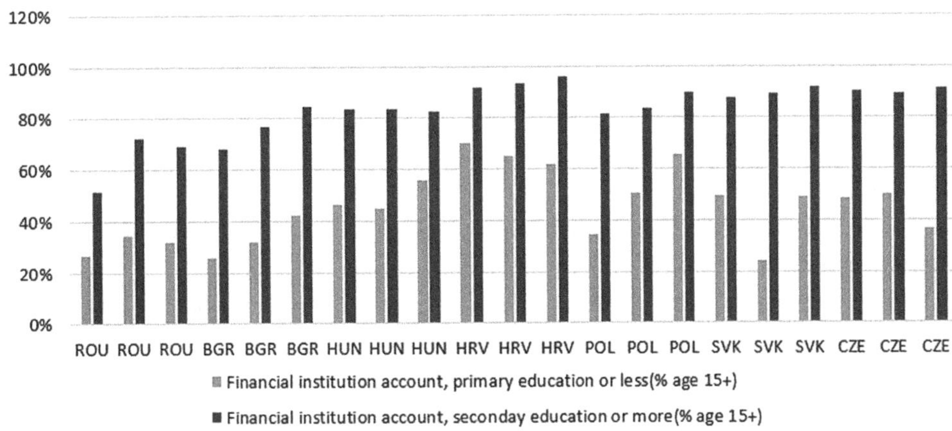

Financial inclusion programs run by banks or even national financial inclusion strategies aim at the access of certain categories of people such as women or the rural population to modern financial services. The ultimate goal is to create a "sustainable financial system rests on two pillars: well-functioning, competitive and sound financial institutions, and financially literate consumers, investors and entrepreneurs" (EBF, 2020). Through the right decisions that investors and consumers make, they contribute to the stability of the financial system and to the growth of their well-being and their families, which ultimately contributes to poverty reduction, human development, economic growth and even sustainable development (Matei, 2013; Raimi et al, 2015; Voica, 2017; Abor 2018 et al. ; Kim et al., 2018; Manta et al., 2020; Matekenya et al., 2020). For these reasons, financial inclusion is considered a catalyst for achieving sustainable development (Soyemi, Olowofela, 2019), econometric studies conducted supporting the relationship between the two variables. But there are also voices challenging the significant impact of financial inclusion on development (Mader, 2018).

The phenomenon of financial inclusion is particularly complex, and financial inclusion is a multidimensional concept (Sahay et al, 2015). So, its evaluation must be done taking into account the specificities of each country. Financial inclusion presupposes both the existence of numerous financial products and services, the dispositions of consumers at reasonable prices, easy access to these products and services but also consumer awareness of the available financial services. For this reason, in developing countries, the national financial inclusion policy also involves adults who aim to make investments in physical and communication infrastructure. (Sarma & Pais, 2011; Matekenya et al., 2020) to allow the movement and rapid access of individuals to banking products and services. The technic progress that takes the form of mobile telephony offers safe and easy solutions for increasing the degree of financial inclusion in developing countries where physical crime is not very developed and the physical movement of consumers involves time and high costs. In African countries, the degree of financial inclusion has increased considerably as mobile telephony has penetrated households. (Gabor, & Brooks, 2017).

The existence of employees who know how to spend money responsibly and initiate investment plans for the post-retirement period, of consumers who know how to choose from the multitude of financial products offered by credit institutions is essential for both public authorities and financial institutions. For this reason, more and more entities initiate and carry out financial education programs either individually or in collaboration with other entities such as schools, universities or the ministry of education (Ene & Panait, 2017;Iacovoiu, 2018).

The tools for increasing financial education among individuals and entrepreneurs are many, and the actions taken worldwide by international organizations are essential because they set the general framework for action, in the sense that they have developed general principles and encouraged Member States to develop and to publish national strategies or to carry out various Financial Education Programs. In parallel, public authorities have been involved in an extensive process of consumer protection in the financial sector, conducting both information campaigns and thematic checks at financial institutions in their attempt to limit the unethical practices of banks, namely misleading advertising campaigns or abusive contractual clauses (Iacovoiu, & Stancu, 2017; Andrei et al., 2018).

Table 1. The financial education and well being

The Intended Pathway
Financial Education + Financial Therapy
Financial Literacy + Financial Mental Health knowledge & skills + motivation & confidence
Good Financial Behavior: decisions & actions society requires
Household Financial Well-Being

Source: Willis, (2011)

Starting from the need to protect financial consumers, individuals who have faced the effects of the international financial crisis and numerous financial scandals, in 2009, the OECD launched a comprehensive financial education program, and one of the tools considered were the strategies in order to increase the financial literacy of the population and increase the degree of financial inclusion.OECD (2020) considers that Financial literacy has components: Financial knowledge or Financial behaviors, Attitudes to longer-term financial planning. The complexity of the financial education process generates certain problems in the development and successful completion of these.

Financial education programs must not only consist in the transmission and assimilation of economic knowledge but also in learning psychology techniques so that people can make a decision in the least stressful conditions. Consumers must learn to manage the emotions that may accompany certain financial decisions and to minimize irrational influences that may affect the purchase of a financial product or service. Consumers must be taught to carefully manage their prejudices about financial problems. Consumers need to be confident that they are able to use the new concepts, which is why we are talking about a financial therapy that will help motivate individuals to access financial products and services (Table 1).

Consumers should regularly participate in Financial Education Programs given both the evolution of the financial market in terms of increasingly complex products, but also because of the evolution of each individual throughout life (events such as the appearance of a child can change the financial behavior of an individual) and the emergence of new financial decisions that must be made (job loss determines the need for a reset of financial behavior, changing financial priorities for an individual).

Therefore, financial education programs must be accessed periodically by interested consumers considering the following considerations the consumer financial marketplace is dynamic, financial education has a short shelf life, consumers must make almost daily financial decisions and periodically major decisions are needed. of important events in the life of individuals such as starting a family, changing or losing a job (Willis, 2011, Lusardi, 2019).

Scientific studies and the analysis of the situation by public authorities have shown that certain groups must be considered because they are vulnerable or because their influence on the process of financial inclusion is manifested in the long run. For this reason, in most countries, the national strategy focused on target groups like young people, women, low income groups, elderly people, entrepreneurs (micro-, small- and medium-sized enterprises), migrants and, people living in rural areas.

The researchers noted that in higher education „The limited attention given to financial education in the development of student competencies can undermine the decision making of individuals in their adulthood. Financial education is not considered as a key subject in the development of student competencies" (Abad-Segura & González-Zamar, 2019).

This has negative long-term consequences because it does not bear fruit and develop the entrepreneurial potential that young people have and reduces their chances of starting a business or having responsible investment plans for retirement. (Akhuemonkhan et al., 2013, Raimi, 2020)., For this reason, the financial education program must primarily target young people (Lucey, 2018). They have to make many financial decisions during life and in this way they turn into a better economic decision maker, in addition, the programs of financial education could develop the anterenorial spirit of young people. In this way, they could start businesses and by becoming parents, they contribute to the creation of their children's financial behavior.Financial education acquires new values in the conditions given the increase in life expectancy. This is particularly important given that on average, women live longer than men, have shorter working lives and earn less and thus need to make sound financial plans for their immediate and longerterm financial security from a young age.

The complexity of the phenomenon of financial education requires a sustained approach from several entities such as financial institutions, financial supervisors and international organizations (Panait et al, 2020). Studies conducted worldwide that have shown the limitations of financial education programs. Financial knowledge is not enough to make good decisions, and other issues such as the attitude, opinions or values that each investor believes in are important. Investors' confidence in their knowledge and skills are essential for starting financial market transactions. For this reason, financial education must also be done from the perspective of behavioral finance (figure 5).

Figure 5. Components of financial capability
Source: Authors representation

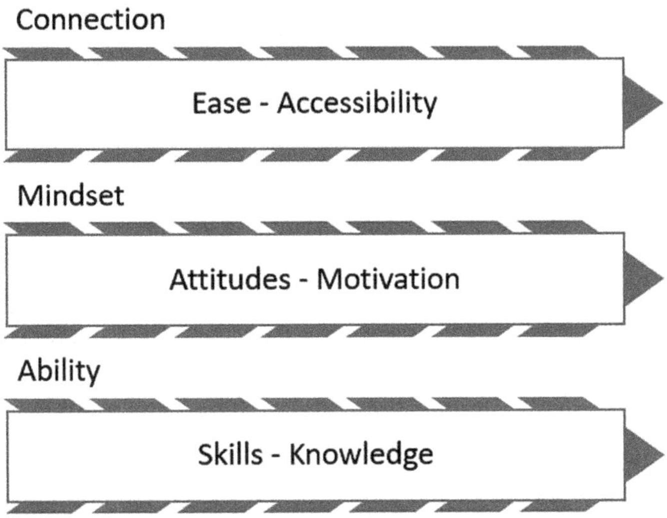

Figure 6. Responsible Financial Behaviour
Source: OCDE and authors representation

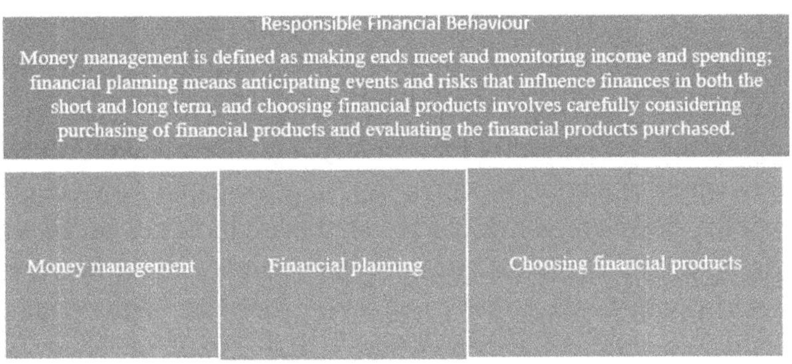

In the international scientific literature, financial capability is a new concept, and attitudes and motivations are essential in this process. Consumers must have confidence in their ability to make decisions, they must have confidence in financial institutions and have access to the right financial services and products. For this reason, the OECD has a trilogy approach for the financial empowerment of consumers based on financial inclusion, financial consumer protection and financial education. In this way, financial well-being can be achieved (figure 6).

Financial education must not only focus on the investment process, but also on the saving process. On the one hand, financial education programs must aim to increase the savings rate and, on the other hand, they must aim to attract low-income and vulnerable people into the financial system. (Klapper, Lusardi, Panos, 2012; Ene & Panait, 2017).

Financial education is a complex process that involves a two-way relationship between financial consumers and investors (on the one hand) and financial institutions, public authorities, international financial bodies, on the other. Financial consumers need to become aware of the importance of financial education in the context of the intensification of financial innovation that has led to the emergence of financial products for speculative or hedging operations. Thus, consumers must be able to make savings, correctly assess the risk of financial products, be aware of losses that may occur, identify investment opportunities offered by different compartments of the financial market, be aware of possible fraud and potentially cybersecurity (Dzomira, 2016). The complexity of this process also consists in the need to adapt consumers and investors to the challenges generated by the digitalization of the financial sector. Therefore, financial education requires the adaptation of consumers and investors to the paradigm shifts that take place in the international financial system, the change of attitude and the improvement of behavior.

Financial education is a complex process because financial decisions are present at any time in an individual's life such as opening a current account to receive a salary, taking out a loan to buy a home, obtaining a consumer loan to buy a car or redecorating the house, financing one's own or children's studies, placing the savings made. Financial education is a process that has long-term consequences given that, since the period of active life, consumers as employees must make decisions when saving for retirement. For this reason, financial education should be everywhere (EBA, 2020).

The Organization for Economic Co-operation and Development (OECD) defines financial literacy not only the „knowledge and understanding of financial concepts and risks but also the skills, motivation, and confidence to apply this knowledge and understanding in order to make effective decisions across a range of financial contexts, to improve the financial well-being of individuals and society, and to enable participation in economic life". Specialists draw attention to the limited positive effects that these programs have, there are even negative effects. Hurdle for the effectiveness of financial education programs:

- the low level of consumers 'financial literacy
- complexity of financial decisions and the heterogeneity of consumer financial circumstances and values
- the speed of financial innovation
- the voluntary nature of financial education programs and lack of interest from consumers (participation in these programs requires time and effort, which is why most individuals show lack of interest).

In addition to financial education programs, a tool used in the fight to increase financial literacy are dedicated platforms that are created either by financial institutions or by public authorities, in order to provide consumers with various information on financial products and services. To determine the effectiveness of this platform, we identified five financial education platforms in Europe (Italy, Greece, Romania, Slovakia, Bulgaria). We chose these platforms to see if the level of development of the country has implications on the interest of consumers for these tools and if the traffic is appropriate.

To analyse traffic on these platforms, the SEMRUSH web page analysis tool was used. The analyzed is focused on Traffic analysis from the country of origin (organic traffic) for period 2012-2020.

The selected platforms are:

- "Fondazione per l'Educazione Finanziaria e al Risparmio" (Italy) managed by the Italian Banking Association (graphic 6.1). The activity on this platform is quite intense compared to the other countries, an explanation being the large number of migrants from Central and Eastern Europe who work in this country and who want to get information in order to establish the most efficient savings plans (figure 6.7).
- In Romania, the Fluentinfinante platform offers multiple information sections for Romanian consumers. The traffic on this platform is intense, compared to other countries in the region (figure 6.8).
- FINQ platform. In Slovakia, consumers' interest in financial information is declining, as the current health crisis and its impact on the financial market are inexplicable (figure 6.9).

Figure 7. Traffic on feduf.it
Source: https://www.semrush.com/

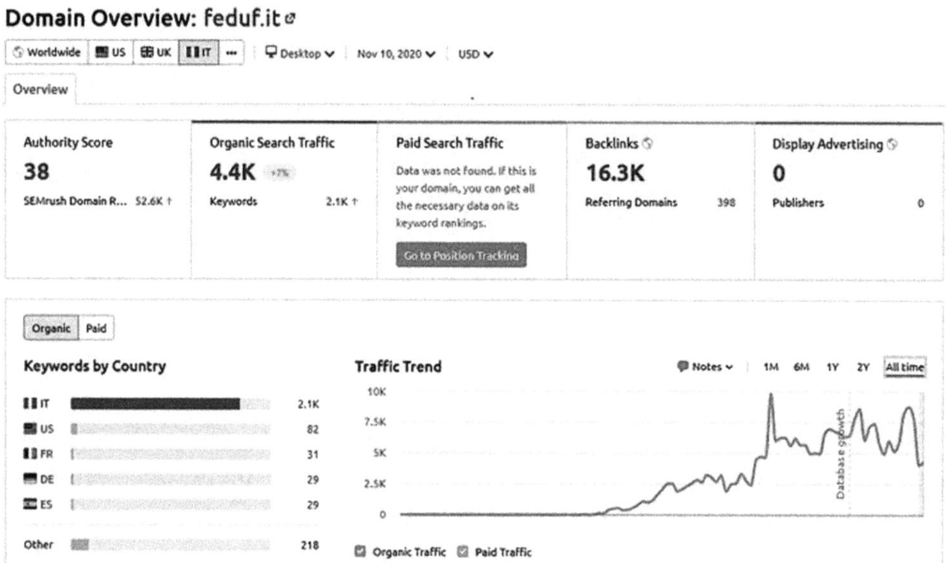

Figure 8. Traffic on fluentinfinante.ro
Source: https://www.semrush.com/

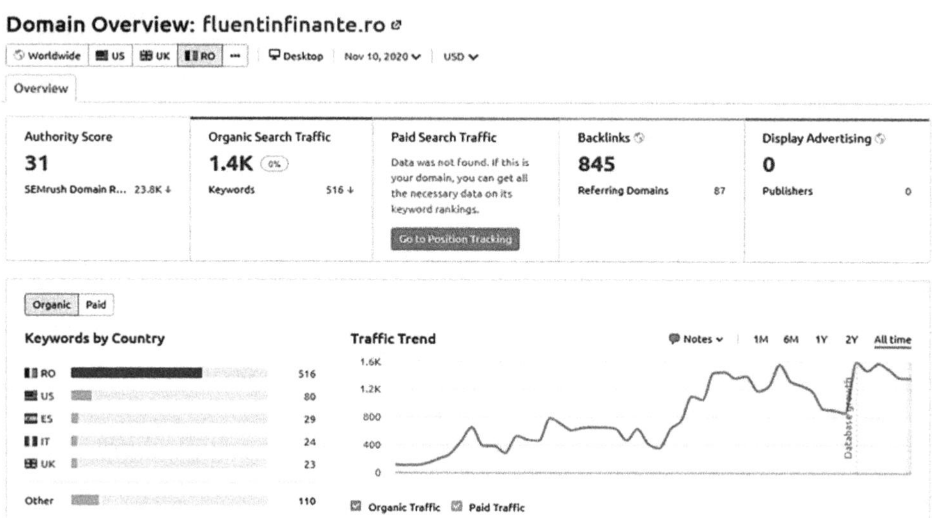

Figure 9. Traffic on finq.sk
Source: https://www.semrush.com/

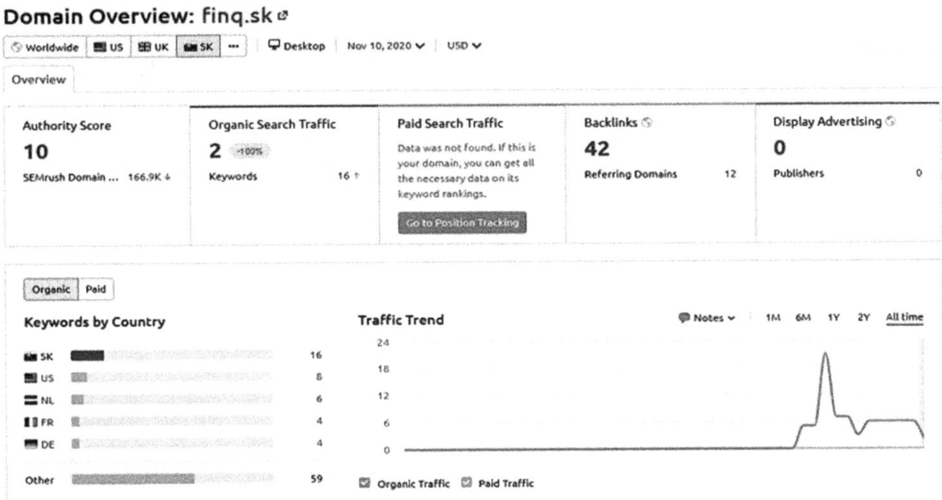

Figure 10. Traffic on gfli.gr
Source: https://www.semrush.com/

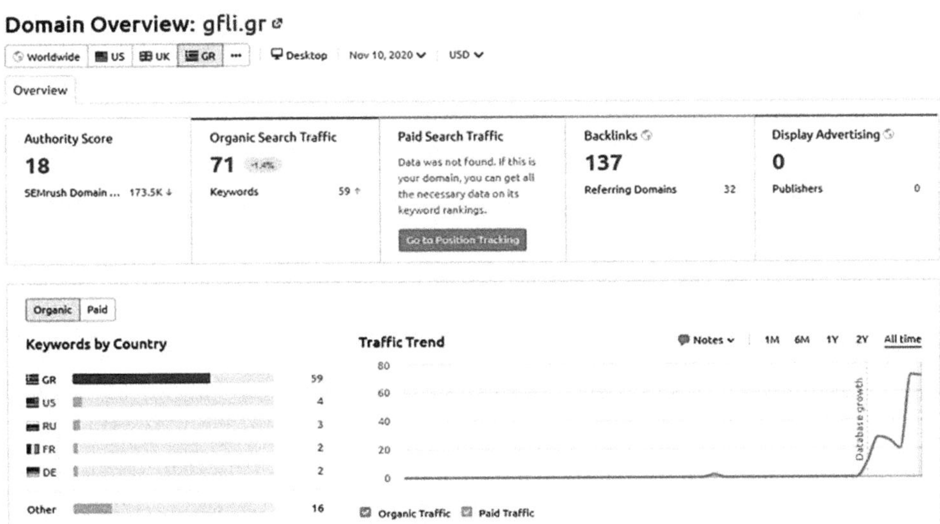

- The GFLI platform administered by the Hellenic Financial Literacy Institute established in February 2016. The consumers 'interest for financial subjects is low (figure 6.10).

- In Bulgaria, a certain interest of consumers can be identified in accessing the platform dedicated to financial education (figure 6.11).

Considering the evolution of the financial education phenomenon at international level and the specific situation of the selected countries in order to carry out the analysis, most platforms of this type appeared after 2012.

Figure 11. Traffic on semeinfinansi.bg
Source: https://www.semrush.com/

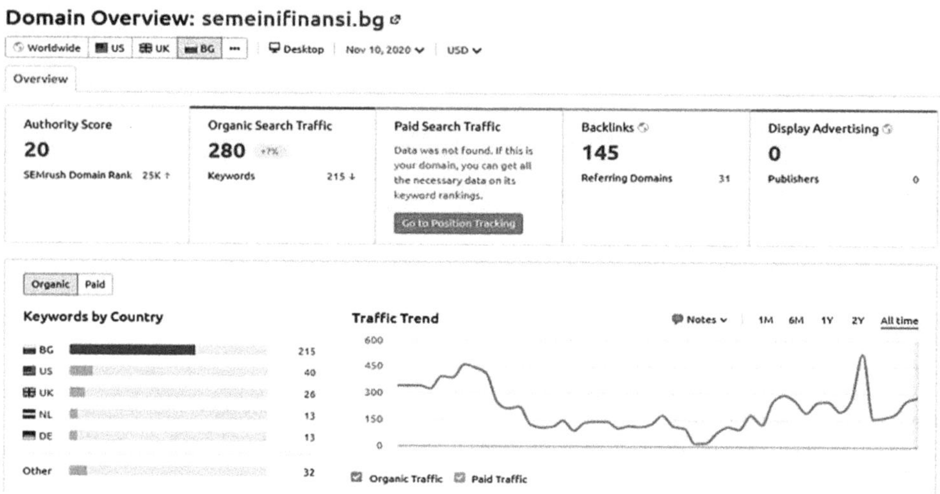

In conclusion, the interest of consumers to access platforms dedicated to financial education is quite low. The efficiency of these financial education tools is quite low because it involves efforts by financial consumers to identify platforms, understand concepts and train specific skills in the financial market.

Decades ago, American companies realized that having employees with sound financial knowledge and making the right decisions about taking out a bank loan, buying a home, or initiating an investment plan for the post-retirement period is an essential asset for the efficient functioning of these companies (Bayer, 1996, Garman, 1997, Bernheim, B. D., & Garrett, 2003). The efforts of these companies were also supported by the public authorities, who wanted to have, on the financial market, informed consumers who would make the right decisions considering the risks and costs of financial products and who would not fall prey to financial fraud. In the United States, the financial education at work movement emerged in the 1960s and expanded in the next decades. (Lusardi, A., & Mitchelli, 2007).

Since last couple of years, more and more financial market supervisor authorities are turning their attention to employees as a target group for financial education programs. Thus, financial education programs are initiated at the workplace, and the advantages seem to ensure the success and efficiency of these programs. The financial education courses take place during the working hours, so the free time of the employees is not consumed, and the knowledge and skills acquired by them are used both in their personal interest and as employees. Therefore, the positive effects are felt at the level of both employees and employers

CONCLUSION

Financial education is a complex process by which consumers try to keep up with the specific challenges of the financial market. The intensification of the financial innovation process generated by the increase of the competition between banks but also between banks and stock exchanges has resulted in the appearance of more and more complex products, difficult to evaluate even by the rating agencies. In this complex universe, financial consumers sometimes feel embarrassed, overwhelmed by information but also by the fears and anxieties generated by an investment on the financial market, especially on the capital market.

Studies and reports of financial supervisors and central banks and consumer protection authorities draw attention to the unethical behavior of institutions that either practice abusive contractual clauses or have misleading promotional campaigns, which try to benefit from the asymmetry of specific information. financial market. The level of reduced financial education has its say, and consumers fall into the trap of credit institutions by signing contracts that are not beneficial to them.

The scandals that have affected financial institutions have led to a decline in consumer confidence in the effectiveness of the risk management tools used by these entities. The frauds generated by the inventive employees of these institutions left negative marks not only on the consumers' finances but also on their psyche, because the losses registered by them were large and consisted even in the loss of life savings accumulated for buying a house or providing a live decently after retirement.

In addition, international crises such as the 2008 financial crisis or the health crisis caused by COVID have brought new challenges for consumers. Thus, not only the financial education becomes important, but also the financial resilience that the consumers show at the market shocks. During this period, when some employees have lost their jobs or gone from an 8-hour program to a part-time program, the existence of savings is essential for maintaining a short-term standard of living. In addition, financial education must allow these individuals to reset their financial behavior given that the prospects for alleviating the crisis are not in sight.

These considerations support the statement regarding the complexity of the financial education phenomenon. This feature is also fueled by the large number of categories of stakeholders who need and are targeted by financial education programs. Among them, the importance of young people and women stands out. Financial education is essential for young people because they will make important decisions in the period immediately following the completion of their studies that can affect their entire existence - buying a home through a mortgage loan. In addition, they are the future parents who will be responsible for forming a senator financial behaviour for the companies. The second important category is women because on the one hand for cultural or religious reasons they are not very involved in the financial market. Their involvement in the household and the lack of a job that generates salary can be a motivation for the small number of accounts opened and used by women. Instead, in the process of managing a family's budget, most of the time, women have the main role, which makes it necessary to increase literacy among this category. In addition, as mothers, they form and pass on to future generations the pattern of responsible and resilient financial behaviour. The process of financial education supposed the involvement of many entities such as financial institutions, public authorities, schools and universities.

REFERENCES

Abad-Segura, E., & González-Zamar, M. D. (2019). Effects of Financial Education and Financial Literacy on Creative Entrepreneurship: A Worldwide Research. *Education Sciences*, *9*(3), 238. doi:10.3390/educsci9030238

Abor, J. Y., Amidu, M., & Issahaku, H. (2018). Mobile telephony, financial inclusion and inclusive growth. *Journal of African Business*, *19*(3), 430–453. doi:10.1080/15228916.2017.1419332

Akhuemonkhan, I. A., Raimi, L., & Sofoluwe, A. O. (2013). Entrepreneurship education and employment stimulation in Nigeria. *Journal of Studies in Social Sciences*, *3*(1).

Andrei, J. V., Panait, M., & Voica, C. (2018). Challenges and Approaches for the Corporate Social Responsibility and Human Resource Management in the Financial Sector. *Economics. Management and Financial Markets*, *13*(3), 415–431.

Bayer, P. J., Bernheim, B. D., & Scholz, J. K. (1996). The effects of financial education in the workplace: Evidence from a survey of employers (No. w5655). National Bureau of Economic Research.

Bernheim, B. D., & Garrett, D. M. (2003). The effects of financial education in the workplace: Evidence from a survey of households. *Journal of Public Economics*, *87*(7-8), 1487–1519. doi:10.1016/S0047-2727(01)00184-0

Botiş, S. (2017). The Impact of Financial Education on Banking Behavior. *Acta Universitatis Danubius. Œconomica, 13*(6), 292-302. http://journals.univ-danubius.ro/index.php/oeconomica/article/view/4498/4368

Chammartin, G. (2002). The feminization of international migration. International Migration Programme: International Labour Organization, 37-40.

Ciutacu, C., Chivu, L., & Preda, D. (2005). The social responsibility of the company–a challenge for the contemporary world. *The Romanian Economics Magazine*, *2*, 79.

Di Salvatore, A., Franceschi, F., Neri, A., & Zanichelli, F. (2018). Measuring the financial literacy of the adult population: the experience of Banca d'Italia. *Bank of Italy Occasional Paper*, (435).

Dzomira, S. (2016). Financial consumer protection: Internet banking fraud awareness by the banking sector. *Banks and Bank Systems*, *11*(4), 127–134. doi:10.21511/bbs.11(4-1).2016.03

EBA. (2020). https://eba.europa.eu/consumer-corner/financial-education

EBF. (2020). https://www.ebf.eu/ebf-media-centre/european-platform-for-financial-education-launched/

Ene, C. (2017). Current Issues Regarding The Protection Of Retail Investors On The Capital Market Within The European Union. *The USV Annals of Economics and Public Administration*, *17*(1 (25)), 35–44.

Ene, C., & Panait, M. (2017). The financial education-Part of corporate social responsibility for employees and customers. *Revista Romana de Economie, 44*(1), 145–154.

EU. (2018). Communication From The Commission To The European Parliament, The Council, The European Central Bank, The European Economic And Social Committee And The Committee Of The Regions *FinTech Action plan: For a more competitive and innovative European financial sector*, COM/2018/0109 final. https://eur-lex.europa.eu/legal-content/EN/TXT/?uri=CELEX:52018DC0109

Gabor, D., & Brooks, S. (2017). The digital revolution in financial inclusion: International development in the fintech era. *New Political Economy*, *22*(4), 423–436. doi:10.1080/13563467.2017.1259298

Garman, E. T. (1997). Personal finance education for employees: Evidence on the bottom-line benefits. *Financial Counseling and Planning*, *8*(2), 1.

Iacovoiu, V., & Stancu, A. (2017). Competition and Consumer Protection in the Romanian Banking Sector. *Amfiteatru Economic*, *19*(45), 381.

Iacovoiu, V. B. (2018). An Empirical Analysis of Some Factors Influencing Financial Literacy. *Economic Insights - Trends and Challenges*, *70*(2).

Ionescu, R., & Rădulescu, I. D. (2019). Behavioral Finance and the Fast Evolving World of Fintech. *Economic Insights – Trends and Challenges, 8*(71), 47-57.

Kim, D. W., Yu, J. S., & Hassan, M. K. (2018). Financial inclusion and economic growth in OIC countries. *Research in International Business and Finance*, *43*, 1–14. doi:10.1016/j.ribaf.2017.07.178

Klapper, L., Lusardi, A., & Panos, G. A. (2012). *Financial literacy and the financial crisis*. The World Bank. doi:10.3386/w17930

Le Goff, M. (2016). Feminization of migration and trends in remittances. *IZA World of Labor: Evidence-Based Policy Making*.

Lucey, T. (2018). A critically compassionate approach to financial literacy: A pursuit of moral spirit. *Education Sciences*, *8*(4), 152. doi:10.3390/educsci8040152

Lusardi, A. (2019). Financial literacy and the need for financial education: Evidence and implications. *Schweizerische Zeitschrift für Volkswirtschaft und Statistik*, *155*(1), 1. doi:10.118641937-019-0027-5

Lusardi, A., & Mitchelli, O. S. (2007). Financial literacy and retirement preparedness: Evidence and implications for financial education. *Business Economics (Cleveland, Ohio)*, *42*(1), 35–44. doi:10.2145/20070104

Mader, P. (2018). Contesting financial inclusion. *Development and Change*, *49*(2), 461–483. doi:10.1111/dech.12368

Manta, O., Gouliamos, K., Kong, J., Li, Z., Ha, N. M., Mohanty, R. P., Yang, H., Pu, R., & Yue, X. G. (2020). The Architecture of Financial Networks and Models of Financial Instruments According to the "Just Transition Mechanism" at the European Level. *Journal of Risk and Financial Management*, *13*(10), 235. doi:10.3390/jrfm13100235

Marrara, S., Pejic-Bach, M., Seljan, S., & Topalovic, A. (2019). FinTech and SMEs: The Italian Case. In *FinTech as a Disruptive Technology for Financial Institutions* (pp. 14–41). IGI Global. doi:10.4018/978-1-5225-7805-5.ch002

Matei, M. (2013). *Responsabilitatea socială a corporaţiilor şi instituţiilor şi dezvoltarea durabilă a României*. Expert Publishing House.

Matekenya, W., Moyo, C., & Jeke, L. (2020). Financial inclusion and human development: Evidence from Sub-Saharan Africa. *Development Southern Africa*, 1–18. doi:10.1080/0376835X.2020.1799760

OECD. (2005). *Recommendation on Principles and Good Practices for Financial Education and Awareness re commendation of the Council*. OECD. https://www.oecd.org/finance/financial-education/35108560.pdf

OECD. (2015). *PISA 2015 Results (Volume 4): Students' Financial Literacy*. OECD.

OECD. (2020). *OECD/INFE 2020 International Survey of Adult Financial Literacy*. www.oecd.org/financial/education/launchoftheoecdinfeglobalfinancialliteracysurveyreport.htm

Olayiwola, E. (2020). Migration and the Feminization of Power: A Reading of Mike Bamiloye's Transnational Films. *African Journal of Gender and Religion*, *26*(1).

Palazzo, M., Deigh, L., Foroudi, P., & Siano, A. (2020). How to boost place branding leveraging on community relations. An exploration of the banking sector in Ghana. *Qualitative Market Research, 23*(1).

Panait, M., Radulescu, I., & Brezoi, A. (2020). Financial Markets–Under the Sign of CSR. Some Evidences Regarding Financial Education. *LUMEN Proceedings, 11*, 96-106.

Patiño, O. A., & Gutiérrez, L. M. P. (2019). Financial Education and Inclusion: The Role of Banks. *International Journal of Sustainable Entrepreneurship and Corporate Social Responsibility, 4*(1), 57–72. doi:10.4018/IJSECSR.2019010104

Raimi, L. (2020). Breaking the Formal Financing Barriers Facing Entrepreneurs: Crowdfunding as an Alternative Financing for Enterprise Development in Nigeria in the Digital Era. In Handbook of Research on Social and Organizational Dynamics in the Digital Era (pp. 218-234). IGI Global.

Raimi, L., Saibu, A., & Shokunbi, M. O. (2015). *An exploratory study of Zakat and Waqf for financial inclusion in Nigeria*. Academic Press.

Sahay, R., Čihák, M., N'Diaye, P. M. B. P., Barajas, A., Mitra, S., Kyobe, A., ... Yousefi, S. R. (2015). *Financial inclusion: can it meet multiple macroeconomic goals?* Academic Press.

Sarma, M., & Pais, J. (2011). Financial inclusion and development. *Journal of International Development, 23*(5), 613–628. doi:10.1002/jid.1698

Shaban, O. S., Abdallah, A. A., & Al-Ibbini, O. A. (2017). Financial Crisis between Personnel Misbehavior, Corporate Governance and Absence of Ethics and Values. *International Research Journal of Applied Finance, 8*(5), 264–272.

Siano, A., Vollero, A., Conte, F., & Amabile, S. (2017). "More than words": Expanding the taxonomy of greenwashing after the Volkswagen scandal. *Journal of Business Research, 71*, 27–37. doi:10.1016/j.jbusres.2016.11.002

Sinclair, S. P. (2001). Financial exclusion: An introductory survey. CRSIS, Edinburgh College of Art/Heriot Watt University.

Soyemi, K. A., Olowofela, O. E., & Yunusa, L. A. (2019). Financial inclusion and sustainable development in Nigeria. *Journal of Economics & Management, 39*, 105–131.

StarešinićB.OmazićM. A.AleksićA. (2019). Reputation as a Key Resource for Market Success in the Banking Sector. *Available at* SSRN 3490616.

Stoian, A., & Iorgulescu, F. (2019). Sustainable Capital Market. In *Financing Sustainable Development* (pp. 193–226). Palgrave Macmillan. doi:10.1007/978-3-030-16522-2_8

UN Women. (2017). https://www.unwomen.org/en/digital-library/publications/2017/7/women-migrant-workers-and-remittances

Voica, C., & Panait, M. (2017) Foreign banks` activity in Romania – under the sign of ethics and csr or under the profit`s sign? *Journal of Financial and Monetary Economics, 4*, 439-447. http://www.icfm.ro/jfme.icfm.ro/JFME2017.pdf

Voica, M. C. (2017). Financial Inclusion as a tool for sustainable development. *Revista Romana de Economie, 44*(1).

Vollero, A., Palazzo, M., Siano, A., & Elving, W. J. (2016). Avoiding the greenwashing trap: Between CSR communication and stakeholder engagement. *International Journal of Innovation and Sustainable Development, 10*(2), 120–140. doi:10.1504/IJISD.2016.075542

Vollero, A., Siano, A., Palazzo, M., & Elving, W. (2011). Corporate Communication and CSR; comparing Italian and Dutch energy companies on anti-greenwashing strategies. *CSR Communication conference 2011: The 1st international CSR Communication conference.*

Willis, L. E. (2011). The financial education fallacy. *The American Economic Review, 101*(3), 429–434. doi:10.1257/aer.101.3.429

Willis, L. E. (2013). Financial education: Lessons not learned & lessons learned. *Life-Cycle Investing: Financial Education and Consumer Protection, 125.*

World Bank. (2017). *Global Findex database*. Author.

Yue, X. G., Cao, Y., Duarte, N., Shao, X. F., & Manta, O. (2019). Social and Financial Inclusion through Nonbanking Institutions: A Model for Rural Romania. *Journal of Risk and Financial Management, 12*(4), 166. doi:10.3390/jrfm12040166

Chapter 7
Transational Corporations:
Under the Sign of Profit or Sustainable Development?

ABSTRACT

The money transfer internationally has generated a metamorphosis of the world economy under the supremacy of transnational corporations. The inflows of foreign capital into the host countries' economies is considered a solution to the multiple problems faced, especially by developing countries – unemployment, lack of monetary funds, or high-performance technology. The presence of transnational corporations in the economies of the host countries has proved to be not always beneficial for them, as there are significant discrepancies between their interests as economic agents and national interests. For this reason, the attitude of the public authorities towards foreign direct investments has been nuanced, and differentiated financial and fiscal incentives have been established to maximize their positive impact. Over time, specialists have drawn attention to the negative externalities generated by transnational corporations. International organizations like the UN or the OECD are involved in improving the global corporation's workings to promote corporate social responsibility.

DOI: 10.4018/978-1-7998-3988-0.ch007

INTRODUCTION

The sustainable development is a major goal of mankind, and global, regional, national and local efforts are huge. The concept of sustainable development is based on the ecosystem-eco-efficiency dualism, the efficient use of natural resources, energy and information materials being achieved responsibly taking into account the requirements of current society but also of future generations. This ensures intergenerational equity in the use of resources, which is one of the important principles of sustainable development (figure 1).

The launch of the UN's Sustainable Development Goals in 2015 created not only new responsibilities but also business opportunities. The launch of the SDGs brought an international premiere in the sense that for the first time, private sector representatives participated in negotiations to establish a global sustainable development agenda. For this reason, SDGs could be used as framework for improving CSR engagement of TNCs. The existence of the 17 SDGs (figure 2) with their 169 targets can help transnational companies both to establish concrete objectives of economic, social and environmental involvement but also to properly report on the impact of their activity on different categories of stakeholders, thus ensuring the comparability of data published by to companies.

Figure 1. 5Ps (people, planet, prosperity, peace and partnership)
Source: Authors representation

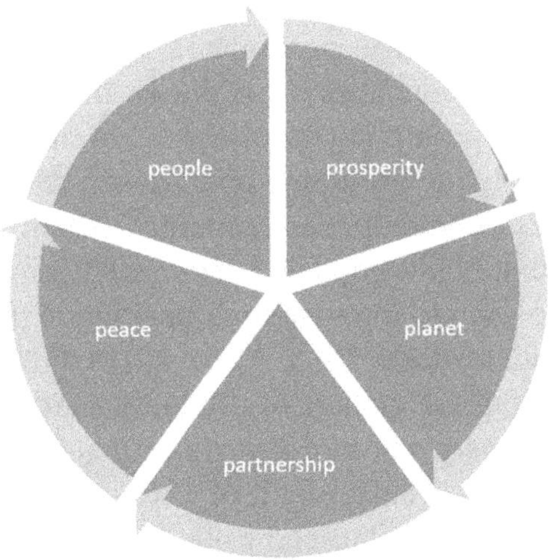

Figure 2. The Sustainable Development Goals
Source: Authors representation

In addition, achieving the goals of sustainable development and the complexity of this issue requires public-private partnerships between public institutions, companies, NGOs and other stakeholders but also cooperation between states, which have common responsibilities, but different approaches depending on the specific level of development. Developed countries need to be much more involved, given the relevance of the "polluter pays" principle, but also the expertise they have in this area, for which they even provide assistance to developing countries. In addition, transnational corporations can play a central role in promoting the principles of sustainable development and social responsibility in developing countries in which they operate.

The TNCs motives for initiating and running CSR programs are complex, such as building reputations as good global citizens, the personal motivations of the managers who want to improve their position in the corporate system (Matei, 2013, Jammulamadaka, 2015, Ahen, 2019) through indirect support from activists, signaling the quality of products, reducttion of conflicts of interest between managers and non-investing stakeholders (Harjoto & Jo, 2011, Panait et al., 2020). The strength of TNCs to promote the principles of sustainable development and to carry out CSR programs is considerable not only due to the financial situation presented by these entities but also due to interdependencies with stakeholders along the value chain. In addition, TNCs can act on several levels (figure 3), in different countries.

Figure 3. The levels of TNCs implication
Source: Schönherr et al. (2017)

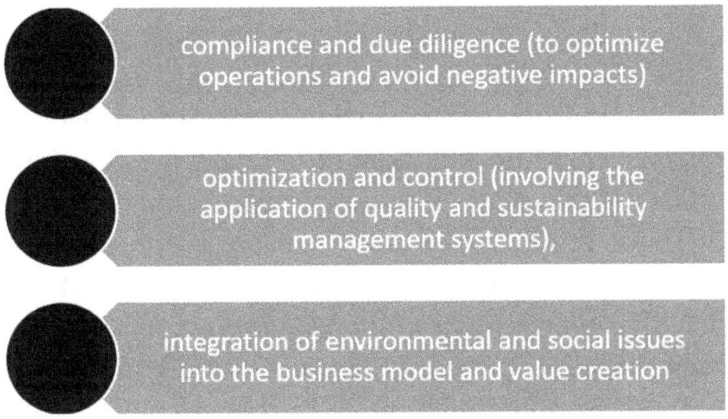

Corporate social responsibility has become increasingly important given the limits of action of public authorities, globalization, intensification of consumerism and environmentalism, but also the challenges posed by the crisis of natural resources, environmental issues, global economic crisis and health crisis generated of COVID. The opposition to TNCs, negative consequences of trade and globalization generated a reconsideration of the image of these entities among stakeholders who began to have higher and higher expectations regarding the involvement of those in the economic, social and environmental fields (Schönherr et al. 2017).

More and more companies, constrained or not by the rules imposed by banking institutions, stock exchanges or public authorities, have become increasingly responsible and aware of the role they must play for the sustainable development of mankind. So, "*giving back to society some of the proceeds of commercial activity and engaging in voluntary, philanthropic activities*" they are no longer considered to be a sufficient reason why ST involvement must be done at another level (Schönherr et al. 2017, p.36).

Large transnational corporations have developed and implemented sustainable development policies, being concerned both with the protection of the environment and with the long-term safety and well-being of employees and local communities. The objectives of maximizing the profit and dividends paid to shareholders must be correlated with respect for the rights of stakeholders, and the development of the company's activity must not affect the interests and aspirations of future generations. Part of companies' efforts to act sustainably consist of social responsibility programs that target local communities, the environment or humanitarian action. In this way, transnational corporations have moved to a higher level in terms of their business objectives, from maximizing profit for shareholders to maximizing value for stakeholders.

However, the analysis of the specialized literature reveals a high level of scepticism towards TNCs as sustainability leaders taking in account the relative ineffectiveness of voluntary corporate social responsibility programs in the last two decades. More and more researchers are questioning whether TNCs could offer proper solutions to the problems they themselves generate (Matei, 2013; Folke et al., 2019) and there are sceptics who believe that these entities are incompatible with sustainable development. Some of them consider that CSR report" misleading, *incomplete, and self-serving, that is, simply public relations gimmicks that are not a true reflection of their business practices*" (Rondinelli, 2006, p. 3). The researchers draw attention to greenwashing strategies practiced by TNCs that only seek to improve the image of their environmental involvement.

This chapter is organized on specific sections. In the introduction section, the author presents the implication of TNCs in promoting sustainable development principles. The the importance of TNCs in world economy in analysed in a specific part of the chapter. The next section is dedicated to analyse of relation between transitional corporations and their stakeholders. For a better understanding of the many possibilities for promoting the principles of sustainable development, the strategies of the transnational society are presented in a separate section. In a separate section, the author focuses on the role of TNCs as promoters of CSR. The chapter ends with a section of conclusions in which the main results of the analysis are presented.

TRANSITIONAL CORPORATIONS AND THEIR STAKEHOLDERS

Transnational corporations are a force that dominates and shapes the international economy, through the FDI flows they generate and through the multiple effects they have on both host and home countries. The complexity of foreign direct investments generates a spectacular increase of interdependencies at the international level, the negative externalities but also their positive effects being felt by different categories of stakeholders. The statistical data published by UNCTAD reveal the economic strength of the large TNCs (table 1) which in some cases are more powerfully than even the public authorities of the host countries. For this reason, their involvement in promoting the principles of sustainable development is essential, especially since their influence is not only exerted within the corporate system but throughout the global value chain, with major training effects at the level of companies in host countries.

Table 1. Selected indicators of international production

Item	Value at current prices ($ billions)				
	1990	2005–2007 (pre-crisis average)	2017	2018	2019
Sales of foreign affiliates	929	24 610	29 844	30 690[a]	31 288[a]
Value added (product) of foreign affiliates	1 297	5 308	7 086	7 365[a]	8 000[a]
Total assets of foreign affiliates	6 022	55 267	101 249	104 367[a]	112 111[a]
Employment by foreign affiliates (thousands)	27 729	58 838	77 543	80 028[a]	82 360[a]

[a] - Data for 2018 and 2019 are estimated based on a fixed-effects panel regression of each variable against outward stock measured in book value and a lagged dependent variable for the period 1980–2017.

Source: WIR 2020, UNCTAD (2020)

Taking in account the important financial, material, human resources of TNCs, "*global presence and ability to share best practices across borders*" (Witte, Dilyard, 2018, p. 2) these entities also have an important potential in maximizing the value created for different categories of stakeholders, not only for shareholders. The mission of a company can be explained by different theories such as agent theory (or shareholder model) or participatory theory (or stakeholder model).

According to the agent theory, within a company there are several interest groups, the company not being a unitary or homogeneous whole. This theory presupposes the delegation of authority, through which the principal entrusts to a certain person named agent the management of financial resources, interests, assets, etc. Such relationships are established between shareholders and managers or between creditors and debtor companies. The result of these delegations is the conflict of interests between principals and agents. Proponents of this theory - Jensen and Meckling (1976) - believe that managers do not always pursue the goals of shareholders as principals, but try to make their own gains. Shareholders have the ability to monitor and supervise their business, but this leads to additional costs generically called agent costs. So these costs generated by conflicts of interest between shareholders and managers determine and finally, the structure of the company's capital. This theory is supported by Milton Friedman (1970) who believes that the only responsibility of companies is to make a profit and thus increase the wealth of shareholders.

The participatory theory of the company is considered the most popular and most influential of the theories developed in business ethics. The foundations of this theory were laid at the beginning of the last century, when American researchers such as A. Berle, G. Means, R. Coase developed studies that argued that the purpose of a company is to serve society. And the activity of American companies demonstrates certain concerns in this field. Thus, during the economic crisis of the 1930s, General Electric identified four major groups with which it interacts: shareholders, employees, customers and the public. The literature notes 1963 as the reference year for participatory theory, when the Standford Research Institute defined in a report the notion of stakeholders as "those groups without whose support the organization would cease to exist."

Over time, the development of participatory theory has been supported by many researchers such as Henry Mintzberg, Russel Ackoff, William Dill and Edward Freeman who have given various definitions of the notion of stakeholders. The best known definition is given by Freeman who considers that "an interested party (or participant) in an organization is any group or individual that may affect or is affected by the achievement of the organization's objectives." This definition given by Freeman is considered to be a broad definition, and there are also narrower definitions, such as that given by Clarkson (1994), who considers stakeholders as people who voluntarily or involuntarily bear a risk from an organization. Therefore, this theory is based on two principles:

The principle of embedded rights (thus, a company must not violate the rights of others); The principle of embedded effect (according to which one corporation is responsible for the effects of its actions on others). The international literature retains numerous definitions of the notion of stakeholders. The analysis of this multitude of definitions allows us to formulate a conclusion, namely the fact that a company has at least four groups of stakeholders or participants: shareholders, suppliers, employees, consumers. There are other participants that differ from one company to another or that, in the case of the same company, differ depending on the environment in which the company operates at a given time or the projects it carries out.

The most well-known stakeholders of corporations are:

- management: CSR programs are most often initiated by the management team;
- the representatives of the employees (trade unions) get involved in the CSR programs, without being the initiators of such programs, because they do not have the necessary skills, information and means of promotion;
- employees may be involved in CSR actions, as a result of either a managerial decision or their own decision; in some situations paradoxes can also appear, because a person can be simultaneously the representative of a company, consumer and member of the local community;
- public authorities act either as a promoter of CSR by ensuring the legal and institutional framework, or as a simple stakeholder that is affected by the actions of companies that promote CSR activities;
- the local community, which is most often the beneficiary of CSR programs, allows the company to run its business, sell its products and employ the local workforce;
- suppliers - the social involvement of companies, especially of large corporations, is not limited to their own activity but also to that of suppliers and subcontractors who are checked if they act in a responsible manner;
- consumers - the influence exerted by consumers on companies has a high potential, there are certain notable differences depending on the intensity of needs, traditions, etc.
- shareholders who have invested certain amounts of money and who expect an adequate remuneration of the invested funds depending on the risk assumed, through decisions taken, they have a major influence on the economic and financial performance of the company, which depend to some extent considerable and the economic environment in which the company operates;
- creditors who make available to the company, in the short or long term, financial resources under certain conditions (interest, guarantees, the method of payment of interest and principal);
- competing companies that influence and are influenced by the decisions of the respective company.

Therefore, participatory theory is a theory of the company that takes into account the environment in which the company operates and the ways in which the company influences and is influenced by this environment.

Stakeholders are involved differently in the life of a company, and their importance and role are different, they can be explained either by a static model of the "bicycle wheel" type (which involves the representation of stakeholders in the form of concentric circles, the importance given by the distance from the center of the wheel) or through a dynamic model such as the one proposed by Mitchell, Agle and Wood in 1997. These researchers propose three criteria for identifying stakeholders:

- power - "the relationship between the social actors, in which the social actor A can determine the social actor B to do something that B would not have done",
- legitimacy - "a general perception or hypothesis that an entity's actions are desirable, close to systems of constructed social norms, values, beliefs and definitions."
- urgency - "is defined as the degree from which applications require immediate action"

The first two criteria - power and legitimacy - are static, while urgency gives a dynamic character to the model built by the three. However, all three criteria are variable, in the sense that they can change depending on the context in which the company operates. Using these three criteria, the three specialists identify three types of stakeholders:

- Latent stakeholders that are defined by only one criterion;
- Moderate stakeholders who are characterized by two criteria and who expect or hope for something from the company, which is why they are also called waiting stakeholders;
- Authoritative stakeholders - stakeholders who meet all three criteria.

Regardless of the criteria used to classify stakeholders, their number and involvement / impact differ depending on the type of organization to which they belong: transnational corporation, small or medium enterprise, etc. but also the economic, social, and cultural environment in which the company operates. Thus, large companies are much more visible, and their activity is intensively monitored by external stackers. So, the stockholder perspective (Friedman, 1970) of corporate social responsibility is not longer valid in a world of globalization, multiple crisis, interconnections between economies and companies. The TNCs should manifest as global citizens which must show responsibility to stakeholders and be involved in achieving sustainable development goals.

Initially seen as a universal panacea that would solve all the problems facing developing countries, foreign direct investment (FDI) has shown its dark side over time. Initially considered an agent of development and progress considering the positive effects on employment, contributions to the state budget, involvement in privatization and restructuring of local companies, export expansion, TNCs generate, voluntarily or not, multiple negative externalities like unemployment, environmental pollution, tax evasion, fuelling corruption (Matei, 2004; Brown et al., 2009; Iacovoiu, 2015).

TRANSNATIONAL CORPORATIONS AND INTEGRATION STRATEGIES

Transnational corporations adopt different production integration strategies to keep up with the important changes taking place in the world economy: the development of information technology, the intensification of global competition, the challenges posed by the 2008 international financial crisis and the COVID health crisis. Thus, TNCs can opt either for the establishment in the host country only of a distribution subsidiary, which implies a minimum capital and a reduced training of the local labor force, or for the application of a complex integration strategy.

Advances in the field of information technology facilitate and create new forms of organizing productive activity. The high speed and low cost of communication influences the system of hierarchical reporting, increasing the possibilities of horizontal communication between units with different and geographically dispersed functions. Due to this factor, TNCs can develop flexible reporting and organization systems, the most targeted areas being research-development and financial management.

Increasing demand and convergence of consumer requirements for certain products (such as clothing, electronics) have led manufacturing TNCs to adopt a complex integration strategy. For many products, however, the differences are maintained due to cultural, economic considerations and regulations specific to each country, determining the adaptation of products to the requirements of each market.

Figure 4. The strategy of the branch with functional autonomy
Source: authors based on World Investment Report (1993); UNCTAD, (1993)

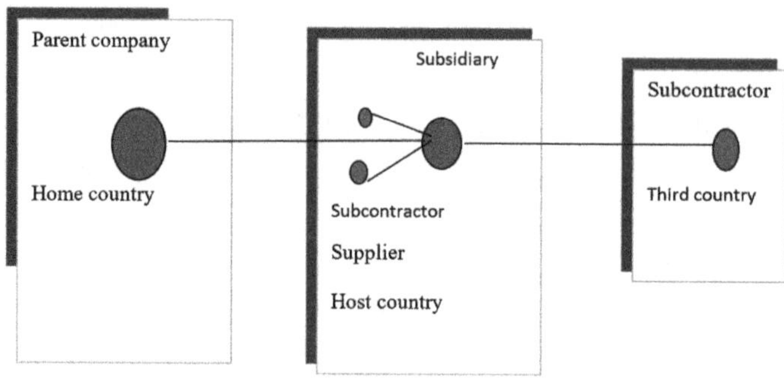

The intensification of competition determines the location of subsidiaries abroad and the integration of the activities of the value chain in order to reduce costs and increase efficiency. The development of information technology makes it possible to integrate supply activities. Studies indicate that TNCs that have integrated these activities have achieved long-term reductions in production costs.

The international literature retains three types of strategies adopted by TNCs for the functional organization of productive activities: the strategy of the branch with functional autonomy - standalone strategy, simple integration strategy and the complex integration strategy.

1. The Strategy of the Branch with Functional Autonomy

In this case, the TNCs subsidiaries have a great autonomy, their relations with the parent company being reduced to issues related to ownership, technology transfer and capital goods. These subsidiaries independently develop links with the various economic segments of the host country (with local suppliers and subcontractors), employ local managers and workers, borrow from the local financial market, conduct foreign trade operations with companies from other countries and are responsible for carrying out the production activity (figure 4).

TNCs opts for such a strategy for reasons of trade barriers, low cost of technology in the host country, (financial) restrictions that may arise in the movement of resources, changing host country policy or increasing the powers of that branch due to increased efficiency. Such a subsidiary can be seen as a small-scale version of the parent company.

Figure 5. Simple integration strategy
Source: Author based on World Investment Report (1993); UNCTAD, (1993)

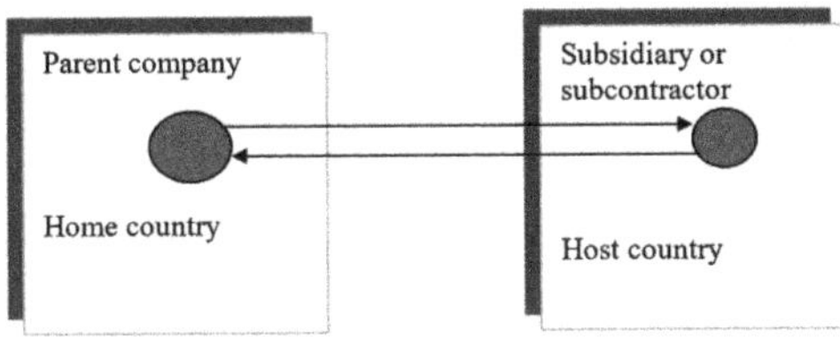

This type of strategy is suitable in the industrial sector, but it is also common in the tertiary sector, due to the fact that the services are consumed at the place of production, the subsidiary being a replica, from a functional point of view, of the parent company. The orientation of FDI in countries in transition to a market economy, mainly in the field of consumer goods, demonstrates their choice for such a strategy. This category includes ST producers of soft drinks (Coca Cola and Pepsi Cola), food products (Philip Morris through Kraft Jacobs Suchard and Unilever), cosmetics and detergents (Procter & Gamble and Henkel).

2. Simple Integration Strategy

Many TNCs have moved from strategies of transferring a complete business to a foreign market, the so-called registered cloning in the case of subsidiaries with functional autonomy to a greater specialization by location. Thus, the aim was to place certain operations of the chain of value-added creative activities in countries that offer certain locational advantages, such as low labor costs. This trend is supported by the growth of intra-firm trade since the 6th decade of the twentieth century. The growth rate is higher for Europe, reflecting the importance of intra-regional trade as economic integration between European countries. Another indicator is the extent to which trade is "captive" within the corporate system (intra-firm trade). Thus, more than a third of US trade in goods is captive. For the US and Japan, the share is even higher in the case of research-intensive industries and professional skills.

In the host countries, a limited range of economic operations is developed, in close interdependence with the activity of the parent company (figure 5). The links between the subsidiary and TNCs are not limited to those related to ownership and technology transfer, but also to issues related to the market, financing and the provision of inputs. This strategy is also favored by technological progress which has led to a reduction in transport and communication costs. The result is the intensive development of labour-intensive production units in emerging markets (especially in China) to achieve certain components of the final product.

Figure 6. Complex integration strategy
Source: World Investment Report (1993); UNCTAD, (1993)

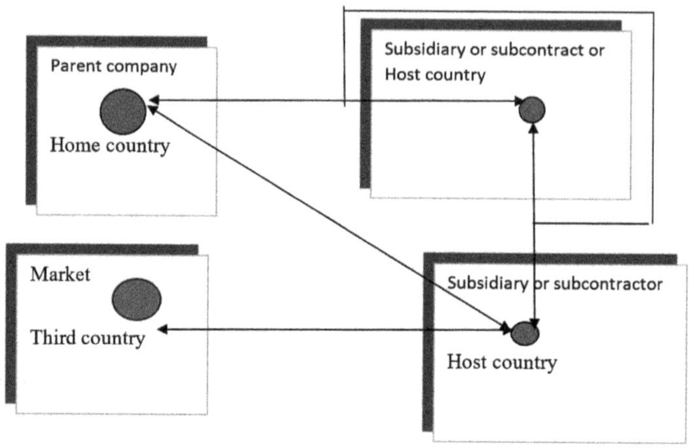

This type of strategy is adopted by TNCs which operates in price sensitive industries such as textiles, footwear, toys and sports equipment. In the case of technology-intensive industries, such a strategy is practiced, the most eloquent example being the semiconductor industry which has taken on a special scale in Asian countries. The development of information and communication technology has increased the degree of marketing of services, companies in the tertiary sector can also adopt such a strategy (eg: data processing, software). In the case of European countries, where TNCs opted for this type of strategy, the motivations being the low price level for certain production factors and the superior training of the labor force.

3. Complex Integration Strategy

The need to maximize profits, correlated with the changes in the world economy (intensification of competition, development of information and communication technology, increasing demand) make TNCs to locate certain activities in the countries that ensure their greatest efficiency. Thus, the subsidiaries located in a certain country, can fulfil, alone or in collaboration with other subsidiaries or with the parent company, certain functions of the entire corporate system. It considers not only the production function but also other activities such as research, development, finance and accounting, supply and staff training (figure.6).

TRANSNATIONAL CORPORATIONS AS PROMOTERS OF CSR

The new scientific approaches in the field of stakeholder theory consider that the company-stakeholder relationship is an essential asset that must be used properly by managers. While CSR determines what a company's responsibilities are, stakeholder theory designates those entities for whom the company is responsible and who can influence or are influenced, positively or negatively, by the actions of a company. For this reason, the two notions - CSR and stakeholders are interdependent. Thus, certain researchers (Longo et al., 2005) measured the performance or social behavior of corporations by the degree of stakeholder satisfaction. Moreover, researchers have noticed an increasing involvement of transnational corporations trying to balance the interests of many stakeholders, shaping a new field of analysis, namely stakeholder management.

The initiation of CSR programs involves in a first phase the determination of stakeholders' expectations, which imply certain stages:

- identification of stakeholders;
- determining the legitimacy of stakeholders;
- quantitative and qualitative measurement of their expectations.

CSR tools are quite diverse, but the trend is to turn them into standards that can be recognized and replicated to measure and improve the social performance of companies. In addition, these standards allow to reach a minimum level of performance and ensure a certain quality of the CSR activity carried out by the company. CSR standards can be grouped into five categories:

- Adoption of CSR principles by a company or a group of companies;
- Implementation of codes of good practice at branch level;
- Adoption of CSR standards developed by the International Organization for Standardization;
- The conventions of the World Labor Organization that establish minimum performance criteria in the field of labor;

- Creation of a general internal framework for measuring and reporting CSR (Process frameworks) to demonstrate the social involvement of corporations.

Studies conducted at European and international level have shown a stronger inclination of companies in more developed areas to promote CSR programs, as well as a link between the size of the company and its social involvement. Thus, in the study conducted at European level - Observatory of European SMEs, 2002 - it was observed that the most intense social involvement of SMEs is in the most economically advanced countries - Norway, Denmark, Sweden, while, in the less developed EU countries - Spain and Greece - involvement was much lower.

Although it has been observed that CSR programs are carried out by both large companies and SMEs, the size of the company still has a differentiated impact in certain situations. It has thus been shown that while transnational corporations make sustained efforts to report their social involvement, SMEs do not have sufficient financial and human resources neither for CSR actions, nor for reporting and informing the public in this respect, which is why their social performance is considered to be lower.

In addition, at the level of SMEs, the relationship with stakeholders is often intuitive and informal. Given the low financial strength of SMEs, public authorities can play an important role in promoting CSR among SMEs and in reporting their social involvement. Thus, in Italy, a social responsibility project was initiated in 2002 - called CSR-SC, in order to disseminate the culture of CSR and good practices of social involvement among SMEs and to support these companies in the development their social responsibility strategies.

The involvement of public authorities in supporting SMEs in this area is also necessary given the role of SMEs at national and international level. Empirical research has shown that all firms - both large and small - give equal importance to the ethical, social and environmental principles that social responsibility entails. Certain differences are observed in the case of their application of principles in certain specific situations. Most of the time, SMEs are sensitive to activities related to close stakeholders such as employees, customers and suppliers and try to promote loyalty in relation to them.

In some cases, the differences regarding the social involvement can also be explained by the perception regarding the probable magnitude of the consequences of one's own activities (the perceived Probable Magnitude of Consequences). For example, small companies consider that they have a low impact on the environment, which is why they are not heavily involved in CSR actions targeting the environment, although managers are aware of the importance of protecting the environment and natural resources. The clients of these companies who are not interested in the concerns of SMEs in this field also contribute to this situation because they consider that the activity of these companies has a negligible impact on the environment.

Given the environment in which they operate, SMEs can be divided into three categories:

- companies that act as subcontractors in international production chains, being suppliers of transnational companies; the pressures exerted by consumers, transnational corporations and the general public are strong and lead them to adopt certain minimum standards on employee remuneration, environmental conditions and environmental protection;
- companies operating independently in the international economy promote CSR actions if national and international regulations require it or if consumers exert pressure in this regard;
- companies serving national markets or national production chains are socially involved only insofar as there are normative acts or pressures exerted by consumers who impose this; these companies predominate in developing countries where regulations are not very strict and consumer pressure is low, which is why the social involvement of these companies is low.

The expansion of the subcontracting activity at European and international level is due to the intensification of competition which is based not only on considerations related to the price of the final product, but also on the quality and characteristics of the product and the satisfaction of customer needs. More and more transnational companies from all economic sectors have decided to outsource certain activities such as research, development, product design, assembly or marketing, given certain considerations such as increasing the sophistication of consumer preferences, reducing the life cycle of product, intense making changes in technological processes, the need for specialization.

For SMEs, outsourcing is an opportunity that has many advantages such as:

- Increasing the efficiency by using the competencies generated by the specialization, the final result being the obtaining of economies of scale and the improvement of the advantages generated by the lower costs;

- Increasing the utilization rate of the production capacities available to SMEs;
- Intensifying the transfer of technology and knowledge.

The intensification of subcontracting activities also presents certain obstacles such as those generated by the legislative differences that appear in the case of companies from different countries. For this reason, at EU level, the European Parliament Resolution on the social responsibility of subcontractors in production chains has been adopted, which seeks to create legal instruments to:

- Better transparency of subcontracting activities, respecting the legislative differences specific to European countries,
- Improving the social dialogue between companies and unions;
- Providing facilities to companies that make efforts so that subcontractors do not violate labor law by imposing certification systems or codes of conduct;
- Exclusion of companies as suppliers of public institutions in case they violated the rights of employees;
- The creation at international level of a legal framework targeting transnational companies and trade union federations that establish certain labor standards and the protection of workers regardless of the country where they work;
- The creation at national level of liability systems (similar to those in Austria, Belgium, Finland, France, Germany, Italy, the Netherlands and Spain) concerning the rights and obligations of subcontractors as employers.

In addition to the efforts made by public authorities to support SMEs, the efforts made by various governmental or international agencies and transnational corporations to initiate and conduct partnership programs to strengthen business links with subcontractors (Unilever in Viet Nam, Toyota in Thailand, Intel in Malaysia or Motorola in China).

CONCLUSION

Transnational corporations and foreign direct investment have numerous effects on the economies of the host countries both through the productive activity carried out and through the social responsibility programs developed. Over time, we have witnessed a reshaping of the state's role in the economy and a redefinition of the role of the public and private sectors in economic development. It has become increasingly clear that businesses, through their voluntary actions, must manage their economic, social and environmental impact so as to contribute to the sustainable development of the world economy.

The objectives and motivations of the programs and the approach to the concept of social responsibility (SR) is different for the multitude of actors involved: transnational corporations (ST), small and medium enterprises (SMEs) and portfolio investors. In addition to ST, a special role in promoting the concept of SR belongs to public authorities, as evidenced by the work of governments in developed countries that has resulted in numerous legislative initiatives and even the establishment of a Ministry of Social Responsibility in the UK.

Given the four areas of interest of social responsibility programs (environment, labor standards, human rights and the fight against corruption), RS programs have some interdependencies with other areas such as management, marketing, business ethics, communication and corporate governance. Being voluntary, these programs are initiated based on a decision of the management team that analyzes the costs and risks of taking these programs, but also the benefits they can have (increasing market share, sales or profit). Therefore, the development of these programs involves a detailed financial analysis that will decide on the opportunity of the program, but also a risk management, given the possibility of recording failures or negative effects even by the initiating company. Communication plays an important role in the development of these programs because the company can better evaluate and understand the opportunity of RS programs developed by companies and depending on the advertising made during the initiation and completion of such programs. In addition, the annual social responsibility reports published by companies contribute to better informing the general public.

The social responsibility of transnational corporations acquires very special values and characteristics, taking into account the fact that they are part of a globalizing economic and social environment, at the confluence of certain levels of responsibility. obligations as well as rights determined by both the economic and social environment of the country of origin and that of the host countries.

REFERENCES

Agwu, E. M., & Taylor, A. R. (2014). CSR as a strategic management tool: Expectations and realities of two MNCs in Nigeria. *International Journal of Civic Engagement and Social Change*, *1*(1), 27–43. doi:10.4018/ijcesc.2014010103

Ahen, F. (2019). Globalisolationism and its implications for TNCs' global responsibility. *Humanistic Management Journal*, *4*(1), 33–54. doi:10.100741463-019-00057-7

Chang, V., Zhang, W., & Xiong, C. (2019). The strategic view and development of corporate social responsibility: The case study of Samsung. *International Journal of Strategic Decision Sciences*, *10*(1), 105–130. doi:10.4018/IJSDS.2019010107

Clarkson, M. (1994, May). A risk based model of stakeholder theory. In *Proceedings of the second Toronto conference on stakeholder theory* (pp. 18-19). Academic Press.

Freeman, R. E. (2010). *Strategic management: A stakeholder approach.* Cambridge university press. doi:10.1017/CBO9781139192675

Friedman, M. (1970). The social responsibility of business is to increase its profits. In *Corporate ethics and corporate governance* (pp. 173–178). Springer.

González, M. D. L. C., & Martinez, C. V. (2004). Fostering corporate social responsibility through public initiative: From the EU to the Spanish case. *Journal of Business Ethics*, *55*(3), 275–293. doi:10.100710551-004-0994-y

Harjoto, M. A., & Jo, H. (2011). Corporate governance and CSR nexus. *Journal of Business Ethics*, *100*(1), 45–67. doi:10.100710551-011-0772-6

Iacovoiu, V. B. (2015). Considerations about foreign direct investments and economic development. *International Business, 15*(1), 173-22.

Jammulamadaka, N. (2015). Responsibility for the third world factory: Limits of eurocentric CSR and making room for the state. *Decision (Washington, D.C.)*, *42*(1), 71–82.

Jensen, M. C., & Meckling, W. H. (1976). Theory of the firm: Managerial behavior, agency costs and ownership structure. *Journal of Financial Economics*, *3*(4), 305–360. doi:10.1016/0304-405X(76)90026-X

Latif, K. F., & Sajjad, A. (2018). Measuring corporate social responsibility: A critical review of survey instruments. *Corporate Social Responsibility and Environmental Management*, *25*(6), 1174–1197. doi:10.1002/csr.1630

Latif, K. F., Sajjad, A., Bashir, R., Shaukat, M. B., Khan, M. B., & Sahibzada, U. F. (2020). Revisiting the relationship between corporate social responsibility and organizational performance: The mediating role of team outcomes. *Corporate Social Responsibility and Environmental Management*, *27*(4), 1630–1641. doi:10.1002/csr.1911

Longo, M., Mura, M., & Bonoli, A. (2005). Corporate social responsibility and corporate performance: the case of Italian SMEs. *Corporate Governance: The International Journal of Business in Society*.

Matei, M. (2004). *Foreign direct investments. Functions and evolutions.* Expert Publishsing House.

Matei, M. (2013). *Responsabilitatea socială a corporaţiilor şi instituţiilor şi dezvoltarea durabilă a României.* Expert Publishing House.

Mitchell, R. K., Agle, B. R., & Wood, D. J. (1997). Toward a theory of stakeholder identification and salience: Defining the principle of who and what really counts. *Academy of Management Review*, *22*(4), 853–886. doi:10.5465/amr.1997.9711022105

Ojo, M. (Ed.). (2016). *Analyzing the Relationship Between Corporate Social Responsibility and Foreign Direct Investment*. IGI Global. doi:10.4018/978-1-5225-0305-7

Panait, M., Erokhin, V., & Andrei, J. V. (2020). Implication of TNCS. In *Agri-Food Sector–Challenges*. Constraints and Limits-Profit or CSR.

Pérez, A., del Mar García de los Salmones, M., & Liu, M. T. (2019). Maximising business returns to corporate social responsibility communication: An empirical test. *Business Ethics (Oxford, England)*, *28*(3), 275–289. doi:10.1111/beer.12221

Pérez, A., López, C., & García-De los Salmones, M. M. (2017). An empirical exploration of the link between reporting to stakeholders and corporate social responsibility reputation in the Spanish context. *Accounting, Auditing & Accountability Journal*, *30*(3), 668–698. doi:10.1108/AAAJ-11-2013-1526

Rondinelli, D. A. (2007). Globalization of sustainable development: Principles and practices in transnational corporations. *Multinational Business Review*, *15*(1), 1–24. doi:10.1108/1525383X200700001

Schönherr, N., Findler, F., & Martinuzzi, A. (2017). Exploring the interface of CSR and the Sustainable Development Goals. *Transnational Corporations*, *24*(3), 33–47. doi:10.18356/cfb5b8b6-en

Virkar, S. (2016). Can Codes of Ethical Conduct Work? Evaluating the Effectiveness of Privatised Corporate Governance in a World of Political and Economic Convergence. In Handbook of Research on Global Indicators of Economic and Political Convergence (pp. 206-236). IGI Global.

Wrana, J., & Diez, J. R. (2018). Multinational enterprises or the quality of regional institutions–What drives the diffusion of global CSR certificates in a transition economy? Evidence from Vietnam. *Journal of Cleaner Production*, *186*, 168–179. doi:10.1016/j.jclepro.2018.03.113

Chapter 8
International Initiatives Regarding CSR

ABSTRACT

Sustainable development is a continuous and very complex process, which is why it requires considerable effort from different categories of stakeholders. Given the primary focus of companies on profit maximization, international or regional organizations have had various initiatives to promote the principles of sustainable development and create a general framework for CSR. These initiatives have taken various forms such as the Global Compact Principles for companies or portfolio investors. Most such initiatives imply the voluntary involvement of companies or other entities in promoting social responsibility through specific mechanisms. The impact of these initiatives is appreciable considering that various entities, like transnational companies, SMEs, universities, or portfolio investors, have been involved in the process of promoting sustainable development. The launch of the Sustainable Development Goals has generated an even more intense involvement of the United Nations, the principles of the Global Compact being a tool to promote these goals internationally.

INTRODUCTION

Social responsibility is a concept that has attracted the attention of international organizations such as the United Nations or the OECD, but has also led to the intensification of private initiatives by corporations or other organizations.

DOI: 10.4018/978-1-7998-3988-0.ch008

Among the most important private initiatives are the Caux Round Table (MRC), which was founded in 1968 on the initiative of Frederick Philips, President of Philips, and Olivier Giscard D`Estaing, Vice President of the Insead Business School. from Fontainebleau, in order to alleviate the tensions generated by the trade war between the European Community and Japan. The activity of MRC is particularly intense, the main objective being the promotion of moral values in the decision-making process of corporations.

In addition to these private initiatives, the social involvement of companies has intensified considerably in recent decades as a result of the involvement of international or regional organizations in the process of developing principles or guidelines that have been rapidly embraced by companies around the world. Moreover, the success of these principles is demonstrated not only by the large number of companies that apply them but also by the translation of these principles to other entities such as universities, cities or portfolio investors.

United Nations Global Compact and CSR

The Global Compact is an initiative of former United Nations Secretary-General Kofi Annan, launched at the World Economic Forum in 1999, which became operational in 2000. The UN Secretary-General started with the idea of creating a partnership between the institution he represented and companies around the world in order to achieve the goals of sustainable development that this organization has.

Given the complexity of sustainable development goals and the possibilities of involving companies in this long-term process, the initiative is supported by six UN agencies:

- High Commissioner for Human Rights,
- United Nations Environment Program,
- International Labor Organization,
- United Nations Development Program,
- United Nations Industrial Development Organization,
- United Nations Office on Drugs and Crime.

In practice, the Global Compact is a network that brings together various entities that have concerns in the field of social responsibility: companies, unions, government institutions, cities, civil society organizations, business associations, academic organizations, etc. and the principles are according with other international documents (figure 1).

Figure 1. The basis documents for the elaboration of the Global Compact principles
Source: Matei (2013)

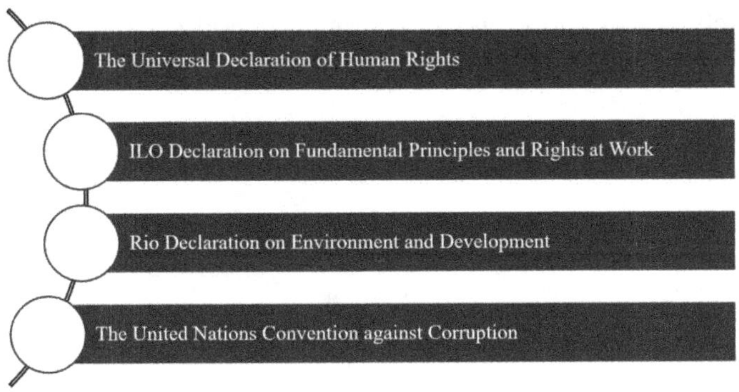

Through this initiative, companies have the opportunity to get involved in promoting the principles of sustainable development given the impact that economic activity has on social and environmental levels. The launch and promotion of these principles ensures a public-private partnership, public institutions not being the only entities that must ensure environmental protection, fight against corruption and bureaucracy, harmonious development of local communities or ensure the protection of human rights or employees. We are thus witnessing a paradigm shift in the objectives of companies that have moved from maximizing value for shareholders to maximizing value for stakeholders. Stakeholders have thus become important because they provide the environment in which companies operate, and entities such as customers or suppliers have gained major importance, without them can not ensure the much desired profit of shareholders (Matei, 2013, Volosevici, 2013; Palazzo et al., 2020; Raimi & Isiaka, 2020;Yang et al., 2020).

This public-private initiative is important from the perspective of developing, implementing and promoting the principles of sustainable development at the level of companies targeting the four major areas of interest: human rights, labor, environment and the fight against corruption. These areas of interest are important because companies are aware of the risks and opportunities of these four issues, having the opportunity to create long-term value, not only for shareholders but also for other categories of stakeholders (Matei, 2013; Munro, 2020; Raimi, 2020; Zemanová & Druláková, 2020). This paradigm shift registered at the level of companies that no longer focus only on shareholders but also consider other stakeholders, is beneficial both for companies and for society in general (table 1). In this way, companies have become aware not only of the negative externalities they generate in the economy, environment and society but are also involved in solving global problems such as climate change, water and food crises, poverty, conflict and inequality (Zaman et al., 2020).

Table 1. Principles of Global Compact

Items	Description
Human Rights	Principle 1: Businesses should support and respect the protection of internationally proclaimed human rights; and
	Principle 2: make sure that they are not complicit in human rights abuses.
Labour	Principle 3: Businesses should uphold the freedom of association and the effective recognition of the right to collective bargaining;
	Principle 4: the elimination of all forms of forced and compulsory labour;
	Principle 5: the effective abolition of child labour; and
	Principle 6: the elimination of discrimination in respect of employment and occupation.
Environment	Principle 7: Businesses should support a precautionary approach to environmental challenges
	Principle 8: undertake initiatives to promote greater environmental responsibility; and
	Principle 9: encourage the development and diffusion of environmentally friendly technologies.
Anti-Corruption	Principle 10: Businesses should work against corruption in all its forms, including extortion and bribery.

Source: The Ten Principles | UN Global Compact

These principles are voluntary in terms of adoption and application, but their assumption involves a commitment to implementation and promotion by companies that consider the following issues (table no 1). GC principles are integrated into (1) business strategy and organizational culture, being pursued for application in daily operations, (2) the decision-making process, the management team also establishing the concrete application measures.

Adherence to Global Compact principles involves signing a Letter of Commitment by the CEO of the members to express support for the ten principles. Annually, the company has the obligation to submit a Communications on Progress (COP) report. For monitoring, the Compact relies on "fire alarms," not "police patrols" (McCubbins & Schwartz 1984; Berliner& Prakash, 2012).

Moreover, in order to help the various companies that have adhered to the principles of the Global Compact, the United Nations in collaboration with other international organizations has developed documents through which businesses are supported in their implementation efforts given the diversity generated by the field of activity, the size of the entity or the area of economic activity:

- Guide for Integrating Human Rights into Business Practices (UNGC / BLIHR / OHCHR, 2009)
- Labor Principles A Guide for Business (ILO / UNGC, 2008)
- Environmental Stewardship Strategy - Overview and Resource for Corporate Leaders (UNGC / Duke University, 2010)
- Business Against Corruption - A Framework for Action (UNGC / IBLF / Transparency International, 2005).

Therefore, the Global Compact's efforts are appreciable given its involvement at different levels (local, regional or international) and through various tools such as developing models, best practices, initiating and facilitating partnerships or establishing critical issues such as climate change, water and women's empowerment. A Global Compact Management Model has been developed to ensure the correct application of the corporate sustainability strategy regardless of the company's field of activity or its size (figure 2).

The elaborated model is characterized by flexibility and has the role of guiding the efforts of planning and executing the CSR strategy of the companies, being able to be used for various implementation periods or even punctually for certain cases (figure 3).

UNGC is of utmost importance in promoting CSR internationally for several reasons:

- It is the social network which allows dialogue and interaction between participants, ensures the awareness of companies about their role in the economy and society, guiding them towards greater transparency and accountability (Ortas, et al., 2015; Claver-Cortés et al., 2020; Gurtu, 2020). Other specialists also emphasize the role of co-learning platform of UNGC, as a result of the information exchanged between the participants and the sharing of the best practices in the field.

Figure 2. Global Compact Management Model
Source: UNGC, Guide to Corporate Sustainability, (2015)

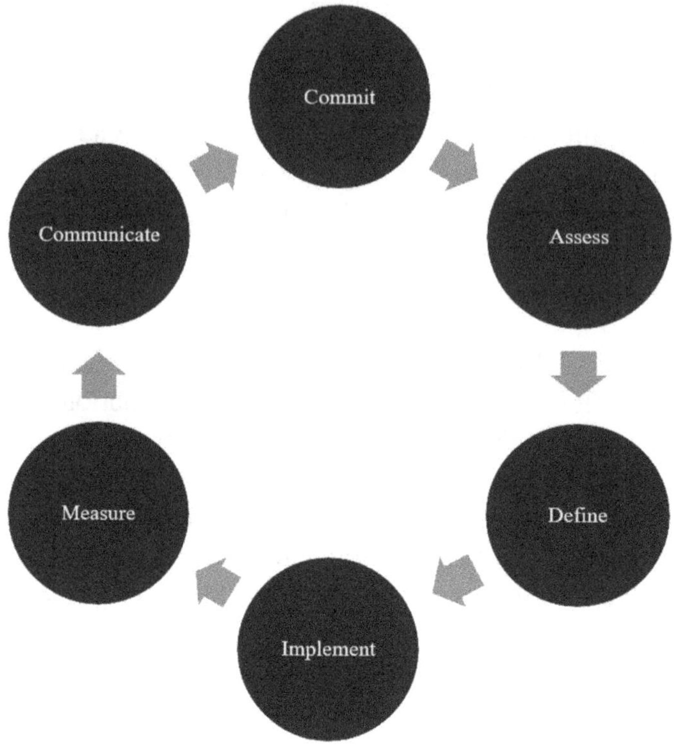

Figure 3. Steps of Global Compact Management Model
Source: UNGC, Guide to Corporate Sustainability, (2015)

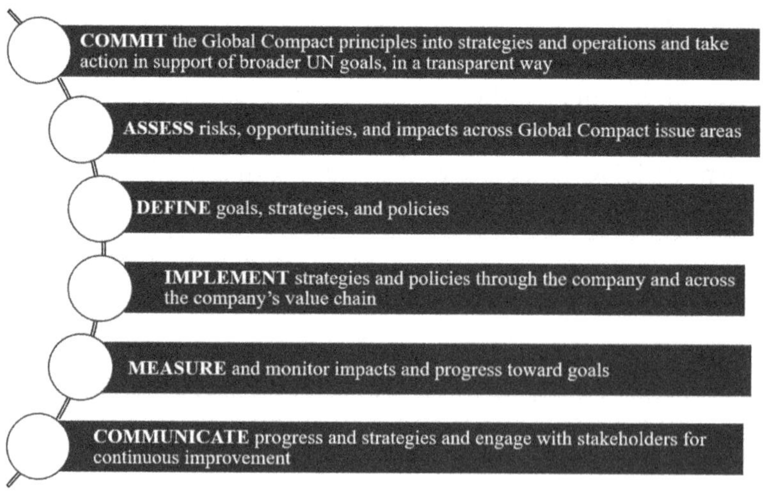

Despite the United Nations' efforts to promote these principles at international level, companies involvement can take the form of a "blue-wash phenomenon" or "ceremonial adoption", - "participation to acquire public legitimacy without any real intention to adhere to the Ten Principles of the UN Global Compact "(Martínez-Ferrero et al., 2020; Zemanová & Druláková, 2020). Specialists draw attention to this phenomenon (Matei, 2013), the companies' motives being numerous, namely protection from criticism, improvement of reputation. Many experts discuss other aspects that reveal the limits of UNGC's involvement in the process of promoting CSR, namely a few obligations imposed on participating firms, no employability of third-party monitors, and rarely imposes sanctions.

UNIVERSITIES AND UN GLOBAL COMPACT

Given the role of education in training future managers and specialists in areas such as social responsibility, business ethics or social marketing, academia has become very important in the process of promoting the principles of sustainable development at international level. Thus, universities, economic faculties and business schools have become an essential component of the Global Compact platform.

These entities can be involved in promoting the Global Compact principles through various mechanisms such as:

- incorporating the universal values of CSR into the curricula and research activoties,
- carrying out specific SR actions in various fields such as supporting local communities,

Moreover, the academic environment has brought some constructive criticism regarding the operations carried out by Global Compact, and through its resources and infrastructure, this sector contributes to knowing and understanding the notions of corporate citizenship and social responsibility, but also to promoting GC activity locally and globally

Social responsibility is not the exclusive prerogative of companies, which is why Global Compact has promoted, since 2007, **The Principles for Responsible Management Education – PRME** (table 2). Universities can make a remarkable contribution to the promotion of SR and the principles of sustainable development and sustainable development goals through individual or collective measures such as:

- align curricula and scientific research activities to the SDGs agenda,
- create practical solutions for companies be more sustainable,
- encourage students and teachers to commit to and act in support of the SDGs,
- support the public authorities in the elaboration of specific documents like SDGs National Plans,
- support the local authorities in the process of identification of regional needs for building sustainable regions,
- act as leaders of public opinion,
- act as mediators among companies, public authorities, NGOs,
- organized specific events like scientific conferences, webinars to disseminate, information and to raise awareness among stakeholders,
- organized training meetings for different types of stakeholders,
- share good practices and results of own activities.

Table 2. The Principles for Responsible Management Education - PRME

Principle 1 | Purpose	We will develop the capabilities of students to be future generators of sustainable value for business and society at large and to work for an inclusive and sustainable global economy.
Principle 2 | Values	We will incorporate into our academic activities, curricula, and organisational practices the values of global social responsibility as portrayed in international initiatives such as the United Nations Global Compact.
Principle 3 | Method	We will create educational frameworks, materials, processes and environments that enable effective learning experiences for responsible leadership.
Principle 4 | Research	We will engage in conceptual and empirical research that advances our understanding about the role, dynamics, and impact of corporations in the creation of sustainable social, environmental and economic value.
Principle 5 | Partnership	We will interact with managers of business corporations to extend our knowledge of their challenges in meeting social and environmental responsibilities and to explore jointly effective approaches to meeting these challenges.
Principle 6 | Dialogue	We will facilitate and support dialog and debate among educators, students, business, government, consumers, media, civil society organisations and other interested groups and stakeholders on critical issues related to global social responsibility and sustainability.

Source: https://www.unprme.org/what-we-do

The importance of the promotion of these principles in academic environment is very important because the future specialists, managers" frequently commands more resources and employs more people than governments of smaller nations" (Waddock et al., 2010, p. 5). The future leaders of companies and public institutions must have a broader understanding of the economy in terms of ethics, responsibility, and accountability than was needed in the past. So, the economic education is consider powerful force that could reshape the world economy over years (Tavanti, 2012; Matei, 2013; Parkes et al., 2017).

The future managers must think globally and must meet additional increasing societal demands for a responsible economy besides the shareholders wishes. They must initiate and continue the complex process of paradigm shift in the global economy that aims to metamorphose the role played by companies that must move from maximizing value for shareholders to maximizing value for stakeholders.

The adoption of these principles had to be done in view of the numerous corruption scandals in which large transnational companies such as Enron or Parmalat were involved, and which affected a considerable number of stakeholders from different countries and fields. Managers need to be aware of the power they have and the implications of their actions. Other negative externalities generated by companies such as environmental pollution raise the issue of manager responsibility, which must have additional capabilities to understand complex phenomena from international economy and must be able to apply the new values like ecological sustainability or social justice (Godemann et al., 2014).

Future managers must understand the new business philosophy, have an appropriate attitude towards the new concepts and challenges imposed by the promotion of sustainable development and apply these concepts and principles.

The involvement of universities in this complex process requires considerable efforts that must target several levels of action like curricula, research activities, teaching methodologies and institutional strategies (Godemann et al., 2014; de Paula Arruda Filho, 2017; Storey et al., 2017)

By the end of 2020, more than 800 academic institutions training economists, a third of which are in Western Europe and North America, have adhered to these principles. As in the case of companies, the universities involved in promoting these principles are also concerned with reporting on the activities undertaken, which is why the Sharing Information on Progress (SIP) report is published annually.

The publication of this kind of report is considered a powerful catalyst that will encourage university stakeholders to support academic organizations in the complex process of promoting the principles of sustainable development. The prestige of universities is fueled by their social involvement. The publication of this type of report ensures the fulfillment of two objectives - universities have access to information on the actions and good practices undertaken by other entities in the academic field and the different categories of stakeholders can observe the progress made by universities in the process of promoting the principles of sustainable development through their own mechanisms.

Figure 4. Five Pillars of Education
Source: Delors, (2006)

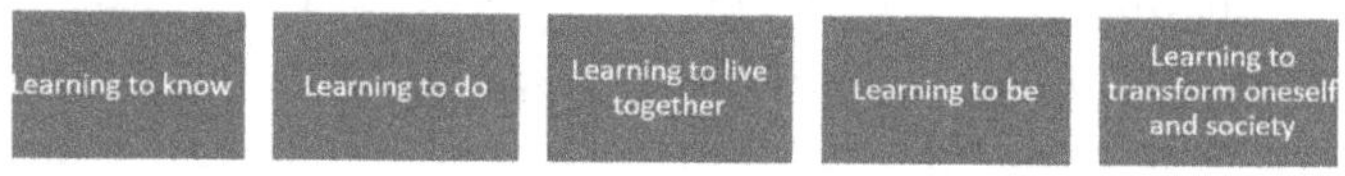

Figure 5. Impact of business schools on the Sustainable Development Goals
Source: Kolb et al. (2017).

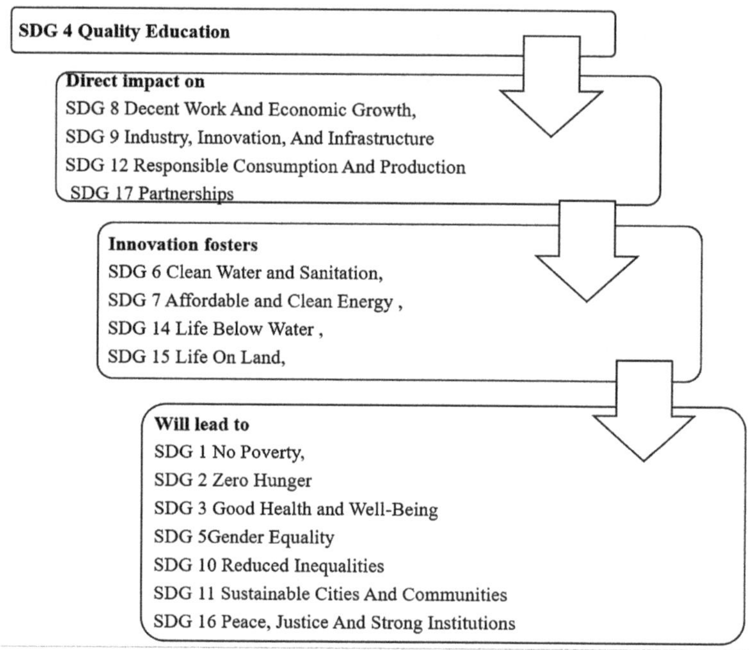

The role of universities is becoming increasingly important and complex (figure 4) with the launch of Sustainable Development Goals (de Paula Arruda Filho, 2017, Storey et al., 2017). Efforts to adapt to the new realities of the economy must be made even by teachers who must move from the role of transmitting information to a more complex mission aimed at shaping personalities, promoting responsible behaviour by students both as consumers, investors or future managers (figure 8.5).

Table 3. Melbourne Principles for Sustainable Cities

1 Vision	Provide a long-term vision for cities based on: sustainability; intergenerational, social, economic and political equity; and their individuality.
2 Economy and Society	Achieve long-term economic and social security
3 Biodiversity	Recognise the intrinsic value of biodiversity and natural ecosystems, and protect and restore them.
4 Ecological Footprints	Enable communities to minimise their ecological footprint.
5 Model Cities on Ecosystems	Build on the characteristics of ecosystems in the development and nurturing of healthy and sustainable cities.
6 Sense of Place	Recognise and build on the distinctive characteristics of cities, including their human and cultural values, history and natural systems.
7 Empowerment	Empower people and foster participation.
8 Partnerships	Expand and enable cooperative networks to work towards a common, sustainable future.
9 Sustainable Production and Consumption	Promote sustainable production and consumption, through appropriate use of environmentally sound technologies and effective demand management.
10 Governance and Hope	Enable continual improvement, based on accountability, transparency and good governance.

Source: Melbourne Principles for Sustainable Cities - 2002 | US EPA ARCHIVE DOCUMENT

CITIES AND GLOBAL COMPACT

Sustainable development of society can be achieved by involving all categories of stakeholders, which is why cities can make an important contribution to creating a sustainable society because they provide the framework for economic and social activities for citizens and companies, but they act as economic agents. . For this reason, the integration of economic, social, political and environmental aspects has become stringent in the activity of these entities, and the GC principles developed for corporations have been adapted for specific activities on cities in terms of governance and urban management.

The program Global Compact for Cities was launched in 2003 and aims for cities to adopt the 10 principles originally developed for companies. In order to adopt the 10 principles in the case of cities, a close collaboration between companies, public authorities, universities and civil society was developed taking in account the particularly complex problems facing cities, so that they also have a positive contribution. to the sustainable development of national economies. By applying these principles (table 3) daily and integrating them into urban management, cities seek to minimize negative externalities and enhance the positive ones in joint efforts to promote sustainable development by both private companies and local and national public authorities (Teller, 2003; Newman & Jennings, 2012; Matei, 2013). The program has been designed on three levels of engagement, in order to achieve a progressive involvement of cities in terms of engagement, recognition and tools used.

The methodology on which these principles are based involves intersectoral relations between companies, public authorities and civil society. The authorities of Melbourne city wrote a letter in 2001 to the initiator of the UN Global Compact - Kofi Annan in order to express their support for the ten principles developed for companies and to join the platform. The city of Melbourne's request was rejected, an Utility Debt Spiral Project has been launched to demonstrate the usefulness of involving cities in promoting social responsibility. Following the discussions among numerous specialists in urban governance, planning, sustainable development and community involvement, the principles for sustainable cities were developed during an international Charrette, sponsored by the United Nations Environment Programme (UNEP) and the International Council for Local Environmental Initiatives. This meeting was held in Melboune (Australia) in 2002.

Figure 6. Melbourne model
Source: UNGC, Sustainable Cities, vol.1, Global Compact Cities Programme, 2010, p.21

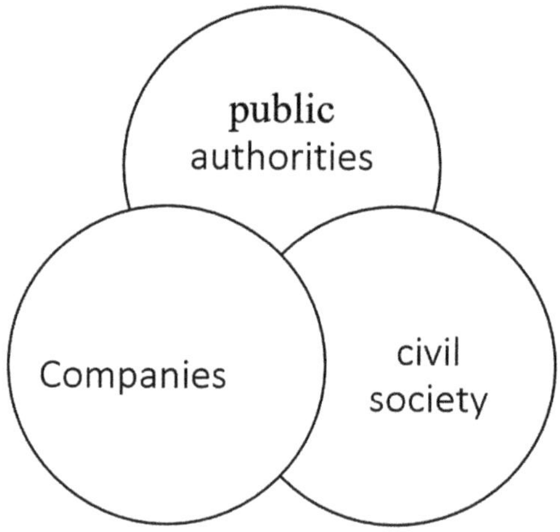

The Melbourne Principles were launched by the city's mayor in September 2002 at the United Nations World Summit on Sustainable Development in Johannesburg. The importance of these principles is also demonstrated by the interest of the participants in this event, which included the ten principles in Local Agenda 21, an international framework for sustainable development specific to local public authorities (originally developed at the 1992 United Nations Conference on Environment and Development - Earth Summit ‘).

UN GLOBAL COMPACT AND INSTITUTIONAL INVESTORS. SUSTAINABLE STOCK EXCHANGES INITIATIVE

The portfolio investors are a force that can shape the behavior of the issuers of securities. The selective behavior of portfolio investors is well known from centuries ago, when certain church institutions remove from the list of potential issuers of securities the companies from certain sectors with negative connotation of their activity – firms from arms industry or the tobacco industry. In time, besides the ethical values, new aspects are taken in account in order to make an investment: social, environmental and governance (ESG) risks. The Principles for Responsible Investment (PRI) Initiative belongs to the United Nations Global Compact and United Nations Environment Programme Finance Initiative (UNEPFI) and they have the goal to improve the sustainability of global financial system.

The principles of responsible investment (PRI), launched in 2006, are based on the idea that environmental, social and corporate governance (ESG) issues can affect investment performance and taking these aspects into account leads to reduced risks and yields. Superior (table 4).These principles are voluntary and the actors from the capital market are encouraged to incorporate ESG issue in their investment`s decisions. The specialists (*PRI Annual Report 2015*) consider that these principles are an instrument that can be useful to cope with market challenge:

- Increasingly frequent governance failures;
- Corruption;
- Misbelief that responsible investment is a thematic niche;
- Misperceptions and ambiguity in the fiduciary duty debate;
- Cimate change;
- Misperception that responsible investment damages returns
- Human rights;
- Ambiguous regulation;
- Insufficient influence for long-term investors;
- Misperception that responsible investment damages returns;

- Lack of ESG training.

Table 4. The Principles for Responsible Investment (PRI)

Principle	description
Principle 1	We will incorporate ESG issues into investment analysis and decision-making processes.
Principle 2	We will be active owners and incorporate ESG issues into our ownership policies and practices
Principle 3	We will seek appropriate disclosure on ESG issues by the entities in which we invest.
Principle 4	We will promote acceptance and implementation of the Principles within the investment industry
Principle 5	We will work together to enhance our effectiveness in implementing the Principles.
Principle 6	We will each report on our activities and progress towards implementing the Principles.

Source: About the PRI | Other | PRI (unpri.org) Adapted from Bridges Ventures (2012)

The official data are encouraging 1,350 signatories like asset owners (pension funds, insurance companies, foundations and endowments, development finance institutions and sovereign wealth funds), investment managers and service providers, from more than 50 countries, managing more than US$45 trillion. These six principles are important not only from the perspective of stakeholders implicated in their promotion and implementation but also for the consistency with the Sustainable Development Goals - SDGs.

The stock exchanges are a force in international economy if we take in account the influence exerted on listed companies, individual and institutional, brokerage companies. Activities in the stock markets directly affect several stakeholders if we take in account:

- funding operations of economic activity through the issue of securities like shares and bonds;
- speculative operations on the stock market mainly achieved through derivatives which in some cases proved to be toxic and have had a negative impact on the world economy;
- hedging operation through which the companies try to reduce some financial risks such as currency, interest rate or price risk.

The valences of exchanges` implication in economy must be analyzed in the context of organizational and operational changes that have affected the life of these financial organisms. In the past, the exchanges were floor-based exchanges with limited space and a limited number of seats available only for its members. So, these exchanges were monopoles on the national market. The development of electronic trading systems led to increased competition because local companies may list on exchanges abroad and investors may initiate transactions from anywhere in the world. In addition, in order to cope with the technological challenge, the exchanges need additional funds that could be raised from financial market and the access to financial recourses is easier for companies, especially for listed ones . So, in order to improve the flexibility of structures and to meet the actual financing needs, the exchanges decided to transform from mutual organizations to companies, even public listed companies (many exchanges decided to be listed on their own market or on other markets).

A major change is the focus on the organisational structure of exchanges: the converse from non-profit and member owned organizations to for-profit and investor-owned corporations (Aggarwal 2002). The Nordic stock exchanges initiated this process of *demutualization* (Stockholm Stock Exchange in 1993, Helsinki Stock Exchange in 1995, Copenhagen Exchange in 1996 and Amsterdam Exchange in 1997) and now many commodities and stock exchanges have suffered this transformation. This process determined by the intensification of competition among exchanges and technological transformations have determined the separation between trading rights and ownership (Steil, 2002). In contrast, a demutualized exchange is a limited liability company owned by its shareholders. Trading rights and ownership can be separated; shareholders provide capital to the exchange and receive profits, but they need not conduct trading on the exchange. The shareholders of exchanges have the vital function to provide capital and must receive profits, but they are not in power to conduct trading on the exchange. This transformation has many consequences like the establishment of different governance structures and a more rapid access to financial funds.

This transformation regarding the legal status of exchanges has many implications for these entities, investors, listed companies, regulations bodies etc. Now, the exchanges are join stock companies that must obtain profit for their shareholders and must established proper corporate governance's structure in order to meet the meet the investor expectations. For this reason, many *mergers and acquisitions* have taken place between exchanges from the same country or continent and even from different continents (New York Stock Exchange and Euronext have merged a form an intercontinental group named NYSE Euronext).

In addition, the exchanges face new constraints. The listing criteria must be well analysed, so companies and investors are not discouraged to delist or to choose another exchange. For this reason, the self-regulatory role played by exchanges diminished and public authorities have additional power in order to impose criteria in this field. However, at international level, given that the process of demutualization occurred mainly after 2000, there are situations in which the regulatory role splits in different proportions between exchanges and capital market institutions. (UNCTAD 2014a, UNCTAD 2014b).

The specialists draw attention to the negative impact that certain legal regulations can have on issuers and investors on the capital market. The major financial scandals that rocked American corporations like Enron, WorldCom, Health South, Global Crossing, Cendant, Adelphia, and Tyco led US authorities to pass a normative act to strengthen the corporate governance, to reduce the risk of new frauds and to protect small shareholders. Sarbanes-Oxley Act or SOX law is considered the most important piece of legislation specific to US equity market which was adopted by the securities regulations of 1933 and 1934. This act is important because it sets up new rules to protect auditor independence, established increased penalties for financial frauds, and imposed the certification of internal controls by the auditors (Section 404) and certification of the company's financial statements by the CEOs and CFOs. So, the companies faced with additional costs, considered disproportionately higher especially for small companies. The results consist of converting from public to private companies, listing to foreign exchanges and the reduction in the number of IPOs on American stock exchanges. This situation demonstrates that some legal criteria imposed on public companies, correlated with other factors such as the global financial crisis and increasing competitiveness between stock exchanges under different national jurisdictions could be transformed into strong constrains for public companies.

To avoid creating major differences between listed companies and those with private character, at least, in certain areas such as sustainability reporting, the initiatives may impose identical requirements for both companies' types, given that many transnational companies are not publicly traded but their work shows great interest to many stakeholders and in some cases, investors such as private equity funds want to increase their access to sustainability information.

The involvement of stock exchanges and their impact of their activity on global economy can be analyzed in the light of **The World Federation of Exchanges` activity which brings together 64 regulated exchanges across the world.**

Given this force represented by stock exchanges, they can contribute through more leverage to promote sustainable development of companies that listing their issued securities on the regulated market of the capital (Chen & Komal, 2016). The final goal is to create a more *sustainable and inclusive economy* at national and international level. The success of stock exchanges` involvement in this area is almost guaranteed given.

- The quality of their self-regulatory bodies with power to impose to certain conditions to participants (like listing criteria);
- specific transparency of regulated capital markets that provide good information to investors and issuers and offer the possibility of comparability of the data published by issuers regardless of their field of activity;
- The progress on promoting corporate governance principles within listed companies.

To ensure a higher success rate at international level, the most important exchanges in the world and international organizations had the idea to launch in 2009 *Sustainable Stock Exchanges* ***Initiative(SSEI)*** **considered** by Forbes magazine as **one of the "World's Best Sustainability Ideas".** *"For a company, sustainability imposes the use of three instruments: environmentally responsible practices, sound social policies and exceptional governance structures; the company has as immediate goals: minimize risk, decrease of volatility to increase of the long-term development impact of corporate activities".*

Given these considerations of sustainability, the stock exchanges are offered more tools for investors that intend to promote social responsible investment and for companies that must demonstrate their sustainable behaviour. The first and most widely used instrument is launching and promoting ***sustainability indices***, calculated based on the prices of the securities issued by companies that are integrating economic, environmental and social factors into the operations and management.

The first global sustainability index was launched in 1999 and is Dow Jones Sustainability World Index that is considered a benchmark in this field. Until now, the Dow Jones Sustainability Index family increase and many sustainability-related investment indices are available for zones like Europe, Asia Pacific, North America and USA and Korea. In time, this initiative was followed by other index companies and stock exchanges and now the universe of sustainability indices are huge. The exchanges like NYSE Euronext, London

Stock Exchange and NASDAQ OMX listed the most relevant sustainability indices around the world until 1999. NYSE Euronext and Vigeo, an index provider with expertise in corporate social responsibility, launch in 2013 a range of equity indices focusing on the environment, social issues and governance (ESG). These indices select companies from Europe, France, United Kingdom, USA and Benelux that meet ESG criteria.

Another instrument used by stock exchanges is ***CSR guidelines*** or best practice recommendations. The implication of exchanges in this field is different. Some of the major stock exchanges established CSR framework or asked the listed companies to present information regarding their CSR performance in the annual report. So, sustainability reporting initiatives have two main instruments: mandatory and voluntary. In practice, these tools can be used simultaneously or gradually. For example, certain mandatory reporting requirements are imposed for the largest or most traded companies on the stock market or for state-owned companies (France, Denmark and Sweden). In other cases, in a first phase, voluntary reporting criteria were established for all companies following that after a period of adjustment, all listed companies to release sustainability information.

The main stock exchanges like London Stock Exchange set up special market segments where ***green bonds*** are traded. The concept of Green Bond was created by Skandinaviska Enskilda Banken (SEB) and the World Bank in 2007/2008 in order to offer the investors the appropriate instrument for financing and gain profit from climate-related opportunities. Green bonds are issued in order to finance or re-finance different projects like energy efficiency, biodiversity conservation sustainable waste management, renewable energy sustainable land use, clean transportation, climate change adaption, clean transportation that are considered green projects. The segment of green bonds is powerful if we take into account the issuers of these securities that decided to list their bonds: World Bank, International Financial Corporation, European Bank for Reconstructions and Development, European Investment Bank and Nordic Investment Bank. Other issuers are companies, municipalities like City of Gothenburg or Isle de France and even academic institutions like Arizona State University and University of Virginia. Many of the green bonds issued by international organisations are listed on London Stock Exchange. The green bond market is growing fast: the value of issues was $36bn in 2014, almost triple to 2013 and for 2-15, the expectations are optimistic: $100bn. (SEB the Green Bond Report 18/08/2015).

At international level, we can see different ways of stock exchanges` implication (Naseem et al., 2019a), even those that are part of the

Sustainable Stock Exchanges Initiative. The stock exchanges implicated in SSEI, we observe that the main instruments used in promoting sustainable development among issuing companies and investors are communications to stakeholders, environmental and social reporting, sustainability guidance or training for companies, sustainability guidance or training for investors and launch sustainability related indices.

Taking into account the challenges of our time: climate change, globalization and food insecurity, the actions must be organised and coordinated at an international level. The results of the effort made by different stakeholders that intended to cope these challenge are *United Nations Sustainable Development Goals (SDGs)* and every effort made by public or private organisations and citizens in contributing to the success of these 17 goals and 169 targets is welcome. The stock exchanges can involve achieving ***Sustainable Development Goals***, they can have a significant contribution to support the objectives like: Gender Equality (Goal 5), Sustainability Information (Goal 12), Climate Change (Goal 13) and Global Partnerships (Goal 17).

The stock exchanges have different types of instruments that can be used in order to have a contribution to the achievement of *Sustainable Development Goals* (Naseem et *al., 2019b). T*he most popular type of sustainability initiative used by stock exchanges is sustainability indices. The universe of these indices is huge and the main hosts for them are stock exchanges like NYSE Euronext and London Stock Exchange. In the analyses made, we have noticed the establishment of new financial instruments like exchange-traded funds (ETFs) that used the Sustainability indices as underlying assets. So, through these index-linked investment products, the investors have the possibility to diversify the risk and to avoid the investment in individual sectors, such as clean energy, climate or water from one country. The stock exchanges have the possibility to promote sustainable development among issuers and investors through sustainability reporting initiative, imposing ESG listing criteria and training and guidance offered for investors.

An important force in shaping the universe of social responsible investment is public authorities and securities commissions. The securities regulators actions in the field of sustainability reporting through voluntary or mandatory initiatives regarding social and or environment reporting for all companies, for companies listed on a regular market or for targeted companies in specific industry or sector.

The companies are interested in sustainability reporting because the publishing of the data regarding the CSR activities demonstrate the resilience to environmental and social change. The reported data regarding the social responsible actions of companies convince the investors that business has a future. In present, this information is presented in the sustainability of CSR report or in the annual report.

The trends are the identification of the megaforces (ex: Climate change, energy and fuel, material resource scarcity) that affect the companies`activity and the set up of the risks and opportunities linked with these megaforces. (RobecoSAM 2014). Another important aspect in the sustainability reporting is to ensure the consistency with international standards and guidelines in order to improve comparability of information. In this field, the stock exchanges could help the companies to know the sustainability reporting frameworks set up at national, regional or international level. In this respect, many exchanges offer training workshops in collaboration with Global Reporting Initiative. The multiplicity of regulations and guidelines regarding CSR and sustainability frameworks (UN Global Compact principles and the OECD *Guidelines for Multinational Enterprises,* Global reporting initiative) raises problems not only for investors but also for public authorities in measuring the efforts of companies and meaningful comparisons between various entities in different countries.

THE ACTIVITY OF OECD ON CSR FIELD

Given the importance of foreign direct investment and transnational corporations in the world economy, the OECD took the initiative to adopt the Declaration on International Investment and Multinational Enterprises in 1976, which also includes the OECD Guidelines on Guidelines for Multinational Enterprises. Through these guidelines, a general, non-binding framework of practices and standards has been created for governments and corporations. All OECD member countries and four other countries - Argentina, Brazil, Chile and Slovakia - have joined the statement.

The Declaration on International Investment and Transnational Corporations involves four instruments of international cooperation:

- Guidelines on multinational corporations which represent a code of conduct on the behavior of these companies;
- The National Treatment Instrument through which the host countries provide CT the same treatment as the local companies;

- The Conflicting Requirements Instrument requires acceding countries to eliminate or minimize the requirements imposed on the TC by various governments;
- International Investment Incentives and Disincentives tool that ensures improved cooperation on measures with an impact on foreign direct investment.

At the beginning of this century, as a result of the intensifying economic, social and environmental challenges posed by globalization, the OECD took the initiative to update guidelines to guide the work of multinational corporations in the world economy. The OECD Guidelines provides multinational companies with certain practices and standards that can be applied voluntarily and that:

- harmonize the activity of the multinational companies with governmental policies,
- strengthen mutual trust between the multinational companies and the economies in which it operates,
- improve the climate for foreign direct investment,
- enhance the contribution that multinational companies have on sustainable development.

The OECD Guidelines for Multinational Corporations focus not only on general practices but also on areas of major importance for action of these entities in the world economy.

- Employment and industrial relations - the most important aspects of corporate behavior in this field are taken into account, namely the work of minors, forced labor, non-discrimination and the right to employee representation and constructive negotiations.
- Environment - Corporations are encouraged to improve their performance in protecting the environment, including performance on the impact on health and safety. In addition, there are recommendations on environmental management systems and the imposition of precautions when serious threats for the environment are observed.
- Fighting corruption - both private and state sector corruption, both passive and active corruption, are covered.
- Consumer interests - companies must act in accordance with good business, marketing and advertising practices, respecting measures

to ensure the safety and quality of services or products provided to consumers.

- Science and technology - transnational corporations are encouraged to promote the dissemination of research results and development activities in the countries in which they operate, thus contributing to enhancing the innovative capacities of host countries.
- Competition - emphasizes the importance of an open and competitive business climate.
- Taxation: Companies must comply with the letter and spirit of the law and cooperate with the tax authorities.

In carrying out their productive activities in various countries, multinational corporations must first of all comply with the regulations in force, take into account the views of stakeholders and promote the general policies established by the OECD. Thus, enterprises should (OECD, 2008, p. 14):

- To contribute to economic, social and ecological progress for the sustainable development of the host country;
- To respect the human rights of persons who are involved in their activities, which must be carried out in accordance with national and international commitments and obligations;
- To improve the local capacity through intense cooperation with the local communities, but also the company's activities on the domestic or foreign markets, respecting the adequate commercial practices;
- Encourage the formation of human capital, in particular by creating employment opportunities and facilitating training opportunities for employees;
- Refrain from seeking or accepting exceptions that do not comply with regulations on the environment, health, safety, work, taxation, tax incentives, etc.
- Support and apply the principles of corporate governance and develop and apply appropriate corporate governance practices;
- To develop and effectively apply management practices that improve the relationship of mutual trust between the corporation and the company in which it operates;
- To promote employees' awareness and compliance with company policies through the appropriate dissemination of these policies, including through training programs;

- Refrain from discriminatory actions or discipline against employees who make bona fide reports to the company's management or to the competent public authorities regarding practices that contravene the law, OECD guidelines or company policies;
- Encourage, where possible, business partners, including suppliers or subcontractors, to apply corporate governance principles that are compatible with these guidelines;
- Refrain from any inappropriate involvement in local political activities.

By developing the Guidelines for Multinational Corporations, the OECD has made an important contribution to raising awareness and encouraging companies operating in the world economy to promote certain principles of social responsibility, which bear multiple similarities to those developed by the UN Global Compact for Corporations.

CONCLUSION

We note the efforts made by the United Nations that took the initiative to launch a public-private partnership called the ***Global Compact*** which brings together various entities such as companies, state institutions, academic organizations, portfolio investors and non-governmental organizations that have realized the importance of supporting the sustainable development of economies in that they act.

The efforts made by United Nations Global Compact have resulted in a first phase in the development of ten principles of social responsibility for companies grouped on four major areas of interest, namely: the fight against corruption, labor standards, environmental protection and human rights (Matei 2013). The success of adopting these principles by large corporations encouraged UN officials to adapt and to launch similar principles to certain entities such as universities, cities and portfolio investors or applicable in certain fields such as agriculture:

- *The Global Compact Program* for cities through the municipalities become a signatory to the Global Compact Principles and promote sustainable development of areas where they operate;
- *Principles for Responsible Management Education (PRME)* – academic institutions incorporate specific topics like corporate sustainability,

social responsibility or climate change into curricula and run research programs in these fields;

- *Principles for Responsible Investment in Agriculture and Food Systems* aplicable to the main stakeholders implicated in agricultural field and food system like governments, the private sector, civil society organizations, UN agencies, development banks, foundations, research institutions and academia;
- *Principles for Investors in Inclusive Finance* that set up some guideline for financial institution that offer financial support to individuals and organisations such as micro enterprises and small and medium-sized enterprises that have difficulties to access funds for current or development need;
- *Principles for Responsible Investors* that promote the development of a more sustainable global financial system.

REFERENCES

Aggarwal, R. (2002). Demutualization and Corporate Governance of Stock Exchanges. *Journal of Applied Corporate Finance*, *15*(1), 4. doi:10.1111/j.1745-6622.2002.tb00345.x

Akhtar, S. (2002). *Demutualization of stock exchanges*. Asian Development Bank.

Berliner, D., & Prakash, A. (2012). From norms to programs: The United Nations Global Compact and global governance. *Regulation & Governance*, *6*(2), 149–166. doi:10.1111/j.1748-5991.2012.01130.x

Chen, S., & Komal, B. (2016). Impact of stock market development on economic growth: Evidence from lower middle income countries. *Management and Administrative Sciences Review*, *5*(2), 86–97.

Claver-Cortés, E., Marco-Lajara, B., & Poveda-Pareja, E. (2020). CSR in the Spotlight: Location and Gender as Drivers of Its Development. In Knowledge Management for Corporate Social Responsibility (pp. 185-206). IGI Global.

de Paula Arruda Filho, N. (2017). The agenda 2030 for responsible management education: An applied methodology. *International Journal of Management Education*, *15*(2), 183–191. doi:10.1016/j.ijme.2017.02.010

Delors, J. (2006). Education: A treasure to discover. UNESCO.

Godemann, J., Haertle, J., Herzig, C., & Moon, J. (2014). United Nations supported principles for responsible management education: Purpose, progress and prospects. *Journal of Cleaner Production*, *62*, 16–23. doi:10.1016/j.jclepro.2013.07.033

Gurtu, A. (Ed.). (2020). *Recent Advancements in Sustainable Entrepreneurship and Corporate Social Responsibility*. IGI Global. doi:10.4018/978-1-7998-2347-6

Kolb, M., Fröhlich, L., & Schmidpeter, R. (2017). Implementing sustainability as the new normal: Responsible management education–From a private business school's perspective. *International Journal of Management Education*, *15*(2), 280–292. doi:10.1016/j.ijme.2017.03.009

Martínez-Ferrero, J., Eryilmaz, M., & Colakoglu, N. (2020). How Does Board Gender Diversity Influence the Likelihood of Becoming a UN Global Compact Signatory? The Mediating Effect of the CSR Committee. *Sustainability*, *12*(10), 4329. doi:10.3390u12104329

Matei, M. (2012). Involvement of United Nations Organization in Promoting Corporate and Institutional Social Responsibility. *Economic Insights - Trends and Challenges*, *64*(2).

Matei, M. (2013). *Responsabilitatea socială a corporaţiilor şi instituţiilor şi dezvoltarea durabilă a României*. Expert Publishing House.

McCubbins, M. D., & Schwartz, T. (1984). Congressional oversight overlooked: Police patrols versus fire alarms. *American Journal of Political Science*, *28*(1), 165–179. doi:10.2307/2110792

Munro, V. (2020). Changing the boundaries of expectations: MNE uptake of universal principles and global goals. In Sustainable Business: Concepts, Methodologies, Tools, and Applications (pp. 881-905). IGI Global.

Naseem, M. A., Ahmad, M. I., Rehman, R. U., Khan, M. A., & Ali, R. (2019). The Trend and Development of CSR Disclosure in Chinese Listed Firms. *Agathos*, *10*(1), 267–279.

Naseem, M. A., Lin, J., Rehman, R. U., Ahmad, M. I., & Ali, R. (2019). Moderating role of financial ratios in corporate social responsibility disclosure and firm value. *PLoS One*, *14*(4), e0215430. doi:10.1371/journal.pone.0215430 PMID:30998740

Newman, P., & Jennings, I. (2012). *Cities as sustainable ecosystems: principles and practices*. Island Press.

OCDE. (2007). *The UN principles for responsible investment and the OECD guidelines for multinational enterprises: complementarities and distinctive contributions*. https://www.oecd.org/investment/mne/38783873.pdf

Ortas, E., Álvarez, I., & Garayar, A. (2015). The environmental, social, governance, and financial performance effects on companies that adopt the United Nations Global Compact. *Sustainability*, *7*(2), 1932–1956. doi:10.3390u7021932

Palazzo, M., Vollero, A., & Siano, A. (2020). From strategic corporate social responsibility to value creation: An analysis of corporate website communication in the banking sector. *International Journal of Bank Marketing*, *38*(7), 1529–1552. doi:10.1108/IJBM-04-2020-0168

Parkes, C., Buono, A. F., & Howaidy, G. (2017). The principles for responsible management education (PRME). the first decade–what has been achieved? The next decade–responsible management education's challenge for the sustainable development goals (SDGs). *International Journal of Management Education*, *15*(2), 61–65. doi:10.1016/j.ijme.2017.05.003

Raimi, L. (2019). Leveraging CSR as a 'Support-Aid' for Triple Bottom-Line Development in Nigeria: Evidence From the Telecommunication Industry. In Corporate Social Responsibility: Concepts, Methodologies, Tools, and Applications (pp. 860-877). IGI Global.

Raimi, L., & Isiaka, A. S. (2020). Regional Review: Africa: CSR in Sub-Saharan Africa: Emerging Trends, Perspectives, and Debates. The Palgrave Handbook of Corporate Social Responsibility, 1-26.

Robeco, S. A. M. (2014). *The Sustainability Yearbook 2014*. Academic Press.

Steil, B. (2002). *Changes in the ownership and governance of securities exchanges: causes and consequences*. Warton Financial Institution Center, Working Papers.

Storey, M., Killian, S., & O'Regan, P. (2017). Responsible management education: Mapping the field in the context of the SDGs. *International Journal of Management Education*, *15*(2), 93–103. doi:10.1016/j.ijme.2017.02.009

Tavanti, M. (2012). Responsible management education in practice: The principles and processes for educating socially responsible and world engaged leaders. In *Handbook of research on teaching ethics in business and management education* (pp. 546–563). IGI Global. doi:10.4018/978-1-61350-510-6.ch031

Teller, D. (2003). United Nations Global Compact cities programme: the Melbourne model: solving hard urban issues together. *Journal of Corporate Citizenship*, *2003*(11), 133–142. doi:10.9774/GLEAF.4700.2003.au.00014

UN Global Compact Guide to Corporate Sustainability, Shaping A Sustainable Future. (2015). UN.

UNCTAD. (2010). *Sustainable Stock Exchanges Real Obstacles, Real Opportunities*. https://www.sustainalytics.com/sites/default/files/responsible_research___sustainable_stock_exchanges_2010.pdf

UNCTAD. (2014a). *Best practice guidance for policymakers and stock exchanges on sustainability reporting initiatives*. https://unctad.org/en/PublicationsLibrary/diaeed2013d6_en.pdf

UNCTAD. (2014b). *Sustainable Stock Exchanges (SSE) Report: A Report on Progress, 2014*. http://www.sseinitiative.org/wp-content/uploads/2012/03/SSE-2014-ROP.pdf

UNEPFI. (2015). *UN Global Compact, PRI Annual Report*. FROM AWARENESS TO IMPACT.

UNGC. (2010). *Sustainable Cities* (Vol. 1). Global Compact Cities Programme.

Ventures, B. (2012). *Sustainable & Impact Investment. How we define the market*. http://bridgesventures.com/wp-content/uploads/2014/07/BV004-Bridges-Ventures-report-UPDATE.pdf

Volosevici, D. (2013). Corporations-between Governance and Social Responsibility: The European Commission Approach. *Economic Insights - Trends and Challenges*, 2(2), 125. http://www.upg-bulletin-se.ro/archive/2013-2/13.Volosevici.pdf

Waddock, S., Rasche, A., Werhane, P. H., & Unruh, G. (2010). The principles for responsible management education. *Towards assessing business ethics education*, 13-28.

Yang, M., Bento, P., & Akbar, A. (2019). Does CSR Influence firm performance indicators? evidence from Chinese pharmaceutical enterprises. *Sustainability*, *11*(20), 5656. doi:10.3390u11205656

Zaman, G., Panait, M. C., Voica, M. C., & Ene, C. (2020). Corporate Social Responsibility in the Agri-Food Sector. In *Recent Advancements in Sustainable Entrepreneurship and Corporate Social Responsibility* (pp. 37–68). IGI Global. doi:10.4018/978-1-7998-2347-6.ch003

Zemanová, Š., & Druláková, R. (2020). Mainstreaming Global Sustainable Development Goals through the UN Global Compact: The Case of Visegrad Countries. *Journal of Risk and Financial Management*, *13*(3), 41. doi:10.3390/jrfm13030041

Chapter 9
Is the European Union a Pole of Corporate Social Responsibility?

ABSTRACT

This chapter focuses on the analysis of the efforts made by the European Union authorities to encourage companies in the process of promoting sustainable development and involvement in various CSR actions. On the one hand, at the EU level, many regulations provide the general framework for the voluntary development of CSR programs. On the other hand, public institutions are involved in meeting sustainable development objectives set at the European and international levels. The tools are numerous, having a higher degree of adaptability depending on the company size, activities, and origin of the capital. Over time, the concerns of European institutions have intensified and have targeted not only the social responsibility of companies but also of public authorities, which through specific instruments can impose certain conduct on companies. The companies paid particular attention to ensure the communication of the actions taken and the results obtained with different categories of stakeholders.

INTRODUCTION

Changing the paradigm of involving companies in activities with an impact on sustainable development is a complex, long-term process that is

DOI: 10.4018/978-1-7998-3988-0.ch009

supported by international institutions such as United Nations, International Labor Organization, World Trade Organization or the International Health Organization through specific tools such as guidelines, statements, communications. In these ways, the international organisations are trying to support companies for running CSR programs.

Various aspects of social development were addressed at the international level during meetings, being adopted specific statements or standards that can guide the actions of companies.

The Tripartite Declaration of Principles on Multinational Enterprises and Social Policy adopted in 1977 by the International Labor Organization was revised in 2000, in the light of the ILO Declaration on Fundamental Principles and Rights at Work adopted in 1998. This statement is notable for its comprehensive content, as it covers all aspects of social policy, such as industrial relations, employment, training and applies to all economic actors such as regardless of the form of organization (multinational corporations, governments, associations of employees and employers).

The Copenhagen Declaration on Social Development was adopted in 1995 at the World Summit for Social Development. The Copenhagen Declaration on Social Development was adopted. On this occasion, the positive effects of globalization on sustainable development such as the dissemination of cultural experiences and values were recognized, but also highlighted the negative consequences such as poverty, unemployment, social disintegration specific to adjustment processes. For these reasons, the Program of Action adopted, the signatory countries undertake "to promote respect for the fundamental rights of workers, including the prohibition of forced labor and minors, freedom of association and collective bargaining, equal pay for women and men for the same value, non-discrimination in employment, implementation of ILO conventions in the case of signatory countries so as to support sustainable economic development and growth ».

In 1998, the International Labor Organization Declaration on Fundamental Principles and Rights at Work was adopted, which recognized the international standards of labor: (1) freedom of association and effective recognition of the right to collective bargaining; (2) the elimination of any form of forced or compulsory labor, (3) the effective abolition of child labor; (4) elimination of discrimination in respect of employment and occupation.

Guidelines for Multinational Enterprises developed by the OECD in 2000 stand out by providing voluntary principles and standards for responsible behavior of transnational corporations in areas such as: employment, industrial relations, human rights, environment, competition, information dissemination, taxation, fighting corruption and protecting consumers. The voluntary adoption of these principles and standards ensures a positive impact of the activity of transnational corporations on the economic, social and environmental progress necessary to achieve the objectives of sustainable development. Multinational corporations must respect the rights of employees to be represented by trade unions and to engage in collective bargaining and to be involved in the effective abolition of child labor, the elimination of all forms of forced or compulsory labor, and the elimination of discrimination against employees.

The activity of the World Trade Organization (WTO) also targets the issue of the relationship between trade and social issues. Discussions on the relationship between the multilateral trading system and labor standards were held at the Marrakesh ministerial meeting in April 1994. At the WTO Ministerial Conference in December 1996, proposals were made to set up a Working Party to examine the link between international trade and working conditions, an initiative supported by developed countries but vehemently rejected by developing countries. Development. The reason for the refusal was based on the idea that developed countries are trying to promote certain protectionist measures by promoting labor standards. In the final statement, the signatory countries reject the use of labor standards for protectionist purposes, and the comparative advantage over wages in developing countries is not in question.

At the third WTO Ministerial Conference in November 1999 (in Seattle), the representatives of some developed countries requested the discussion of a new topic: trade and labor. The EU's position on this issue reflected the conclusions reached by the European Council at its October meeting. Given the desire of some WTO members to link labor standards to trade sanctions but also the sensitivity of developing countries to this issue, they have generated some failure of this conference.

The term CSR has been used in the literature since the 1960s, but at EU level, concerns about social responsibility are much more recent. Specific concerns related to CSR, namely the protection of the environment, can be detected at EU level since the 1970s, when the first action plan for the environment was launched in 1972. Subsequently, the European Union issued numerous directives in this field, thus becoming the creator a single supranational policy (Delbard, 2008; Matei, 2013).

The concept of sustainable development was officially endorsed by the EU in the 1992 through Maastricht treaty. Sustainable development has become a constant concern of European officials who are trying to find the tools and create the right methods so that the principles of sustainable development are adopted and applied not only by public institutions but also by companies. They seek to harmonize the interests of different categories of stakeholders on economic development, environmental protection and social inclusion. (Breitbarth et al., 2009; Matei et al., 2012; Roblek et al., 2020; Vukić et al., 2020).

Companies and institutions must be aware of the role they play in this complex process. For this reason, an important role is played by communicating the measures taken and the results obtained on various levels such as environmental protection or involvement in the development of local communities. Concrete measures have been taken at EU and Member State level to disclosure non-financial information, given its importance for various categories of stakeholders (Lenssen et al., 2008; Matei, 2013; Gigauri, 2015; Siminica & Sichigea2018; Voica &Stancu, 2021). Having regard to all these EU efforts to develop specific CSR regulations and to integrate these concerns into European policies and strategies, they transformed the EU in "the most vibrant region in the terms of progress in CSR" (Breitbarth et al., 2009).

THE MAIN CONCERNS AND ACHIEVEMENTS REGARDING CSR IN THE EU

The concerns of European officials regarding CSR are a logical extension of sustained efforts to promote sustainable development and reduce social exclusion. Thus, the first initiatives related to the field of social responsibility date from the 90s of the last century. In 1993, President Delors launched the fight against social exclusion, mobilizing European authorities but also holding companies accountable for this complex process. At the European Council in March 2000, European officials called on companies to be involved in various areas such as increasing the social inclusion of European citizens, lifelong learning, work organization, equal opportunities for men and women, sustainable development.

Social responsibility became a priority for the European Commission in 2001, when a specific document entitled Green book ***"Promoting a European framework for corporate social responsibility"*** was launched (COM (2001) 366). CSR is " a concept whereby companies integrate social and environmental concerns in their business operations and in their interaction with their stakeholders on a voluntary basis ". This definition is noted by emphasizing the voluntary nature of CSR and its intrinsic links with stakeholder models, thus implying a compromise between the interests of different categories of stakeholders of a company, more precisely between shareholders and non-shareholders (Delbard, 2008).

Even if CSR is voluntary, companies have no specific legal obligations in this regard, stakeholders such as employees, consumers or investors can generate active behavior of firms because their actions sanction or encourage economic actors to have a proactive attitude towards promoting the principles of sustainable development, initiating and developing of CRS programs in order to minimize the negative externalities they can generate. Specialized studies have demonstrated not only the importance of this real involvement but also the way in which the results obtained are communicated and the long-term relationship with stakeholders is managed (Garcia-Sanchez et al., 2016, Fuente et al., 2017).

The globalization of the world economy, the need to promote sustainable development, the intensification of competition and increase economic competitiveness have generated challenges and opportunities for companies. Thus, social responsibility can make a positive contribution to the strategic goal set at the 2000 Lisbon Summit, which is to make the EU "the most competitive and dynamic knowledge-based economy capable of sustainable economic growth that ensures more and more jobs and greater social inclusion ". (COM 366/2001, p. 3).

Following the publication of this book and the launch of public debates, the main positions of the different categories of stakeholders, the ways of involvement and the concrete actions of the EU to promote social responsibility at both regional and international level were identified. As expected, the opinions of different categories of stakeholders were numerous, given their different approaches and roles in promoting CSR (COM347 / 2002, p. 4).

The voluntary nature of the CSR actions is the main characteristic, being impossible to promote universal solutions considering the complex context in which the companies operate. Notable differences regarding the involvement of companies are due to the field of activity, the geographical area in which the companies operate, the capital structure - national / foreign / public / private (Letica, 2008; Steurer et al., 2012) .

Certain categories of stakeholders such as trade unions and civil society organizations draw attention to the limitations of CSR programs because the protection of the environment or the rights of employees and citizens are particularly complex phenomena that must have a legal framework to establish mandatory standards and measures. The voluntary nature of CSR actions does not always ensure a real involvement of companies, in some cases, CSR programs being only greenwashing or windowdressing strategies (Owen, 2005; Vollero et al, 2011; Bosun et al., 2014; Vollero at al., 2016).

In order to increase the effectiveness of these practices, the involvement of stakeholders in the promotion, development and evaluation of CSR programs is essential. The existence of mechanisms for measuring (accounting) the social and environmental impact of these programs is beneficial in order to ensure comparisons between entities that run similar or different programs.

A special category of stakeholders that have a major impact on the social involvement of companies are individual and institutional investors but also other entities on the financial market like stock exchanges or rating agencies (Matei et al., 2014; Verbeeten et al., 2016; Timbate, & Park, 2018).

Consumers also play an essential role in the process of shaping the behavior of companies in the sense that they can require them to provide as much information as possible on the conditions of production and marketing in terms of social and environmental aspects. Consumers can thus condone the less ethical or less responsible behavior of some companies by reducing the purchases of products or services sold by these entities (Pomering & Dolnicar, 2009; Öberseder et al., 2011; Gigaruri, 2012; Yu et al., 2018).

For a good promotion of CSR principles at European level, it is necessary to complement the measures taken at local, national and regional level. Moreover, the issue of CSR must be addressed in all areas of EU actions, being important not only the actions themselves but also triple bottom line reporting by companies that must present their social and environmental performance, including respect for human rights.

The European authorities must provide the framework for promoting the principles of social responsibility and support companies and public authorities in adopting socially responsible behavior. Through CSR Programs, companies help public authorities meet policy objectives on a voluntary basis. "CSR creates new reciprocal relations between public authorities and private enterprises" (Bredgaard, 2004, p. 4). For this reason, specialists believe that CSR is not just a new way of doing business by transnational coporations of small and medium enteprises but it is a new society governance model (Steurer. 2010).

By developing a European framework for promoting transparency, coherence and best CSR practices, but also by promoting a consensus on good practices for the evaluation of CSR programs, these ways of real involvement of companies can materialize:

- companies but also other entities such as public institutions or consumer associations that are interested in promoting SR actions on various levels can take concrete actions to meet the proposed objectives of promoting specific principles.
- Thus, it is necessary to initiate and develop constantly training activities for managers so that they acquire or improve their skills and competences in the field of CSR (these activities are necessary because the concept of CSR is not very promoted by universities through their educational offer, and anyway, it is necessary to update knowledge considering the evolution of CSR initiatives at regional and international level).
- Activities for disseminating information on good CSR practices, standards, benchmarking, monitoring, auditing, reporting and measurement (accounting).

In 2000, the **Charter of Fundamental Rights** was adopted, which establishes the rights and freedoms of European citizens, such as the right to education, the right to work and association, the right to normal working conditions, the right to social assistance and social security services; prohibits forced labor and slavery, inhuman treatment and torture, child labor, and promotes environmental and consumer protection. These provisions are in line with the Global Compact principles launched by the United Nations, in promoting socially responsible behavior in relation to various categories of stakeholders (Lenssen et al., 2006; Shaw, 2006; Matei, 2013; Brezoi, 2018).

The **Sustainable Development Strategy for Europe** adopted at the European Council in June 2001 in Gothenburg considers that environmental protection, social cohesion and economic growth are interdependent and essential for the development of European countries (Steurer & Hametner, 2013). The Commission Communication on Sustainable Development emphasizes public policies in the process of promoting the principles of sustainable development and CSR. Thus, public policies have "an important role to play in encouraging greater CSR and in establishing a framework to ensure the integration of social and environmental concerns into business. Companies should be encouraged to take a proactive approach to sustainable development both inside and outside the EU "(COM 366/2001, p. 5). Subsequently, national sustainable development strategies have been adopted at EU member state level. Despite the belonging of these countries to the large European family, the analysis of national strategies reveals certain negative aspects such as the lack of coherence regarding the set objectives and the indicators used to measure the progress made. According with Steurer and Hametner (2013, p.236), "environmental objectives and indicators are signifi cantly more coherent than social ones". In addition, the adoption of SD indicators also generates certain differences between countries because some of the member countries had the initiative to establish the set before adoption of the EU SDI framework in 2005.

Communication from the Commission to the Council, the European Parliament and the Economic and Social Committee: **Promoting core labor standards and improving social governance in the context of globalization** (COM 416/2001) brings in the center of preoccupations the social development and the observance of the fundamental rights as a basic objective for the European authorities. In this way, we are witnessing the intensification of attempts to support and promote the initiatives of institutions such as World Trade Organization or International Labor Organization that have developed various labor standards, but their impact is small.

The **White Paper of European Governance**, prepared in 2001, is distinguished by its approach to CSR. This paper is considered to have made a significant contribution to creating a favorable climate for entrepreneurship, thus being linked to the Commission's goal of creating an entrepreneurial, innovative and open"Enterprise Europe" (Vandekerckhove & Roland Commers,2005; Fairbrass, 2011).

In 2002, the European Commission published **Communication 347/2002 concerning Corporate Social Responsibility: A business contribution to Sustainable Development**. This communication is considered to be the presentation of the EU CSR promotion strategy. Given the new social and economic pressures that companies are subjected to, specialists have noticed numerous changes in the values, strategies and horizons of economic agents. It was observed that the development of successful businesses and the prosperity of shareholders is achieved not only by maximizing short-term profit, but also by a responsible orientation towards the social and environmental aspects that characterize the activity of any company. In this way, companies also contribute to the sustainable development of the economies in which they run their businesses and increasingly satisfy the interests of consumers who have become increasingly aware and informed about their rights. At European level, intense concerns about promoting public CSR policies are due to the desire of European officials to potentiate the positive effects and mitigate the negative effects of globalization on the European economy, the ultimate goal being sustainable development. In this sense, at EU level there is an attempt to build a strategy for the promotion of CSR among companies, starting from the basic principles of international agreements in the field, but respecting the principle of subsidiarity.

These concerns of European officials are determined by two considerations:

- CSR can also be a useful tool for other EU policies;
- The intense proliferation of CSR tools (management standards, labeling and certification schemes, reporting, etc.) can create confusion among consumer companies, investors and other stakeholders, which can ultimately lead to market distortions.

Therefore, the role of the European authorities is to facilitate the convergence of these instruments so as to ensure the proper functioning of the internal market. In addition, achieving this convergence leads to better results, increased transparency and credibility of CSR practices and tools.The main areas of action of the Commission are:

- Knowledge of the positive effects of CSR on business and society in Europe and in the world, and especially in developing countries;
- Development of exchanges of experience and good practices on CSR between companies;
- Promoting the development of socially responsible management skills;
- Encouraging the promotion of CSR among SMEs;
- Facilitating the convergence and transparency of CSR practices and tools (codes of conduct, management standards, labeling, presentation, reporting and auditing, socially responsible investments);
- Lunching a multi-stakeholder forum on CSR at EU level;
- Integration of CSR issues in European policies (employment and social affairs policy, company policy, environmental policy; consumer policy; public procurement policy, foreign policy, including development and trade policy, administrative policy).

Communication 82/2002 from the Commission to the European Parliament, the Council, the Economic and Social Committee and the Committee of the Regions: Towards a global partnership for sustainable development) emphasizes the need to strike a balance between the economic, social and environmental goals of European countries in order to ensure the present well-being, without affecting the possibilities of future generations to meet their needs.

Based on the concerns and sustained efforts of international organizations such as the WTO, the OECD or the ILO, the European authorities have taken various measures to:

- Exploiting globalization: trade for sustainable development;
- The fight against poverty and the promotion of social development;
- Sustainable management of natural and environmental resources;
- Improving the coherence of EU policies;
- Better governance at all levels;
- Financing sustainable development;

In addition, the European Social Agenda, also supported by the Nice European Council, emphasizes the role of corporate social responsibility in economic integration and the adaptation of working conditions in the new economy. The European Summit in Nice launched the idea of partnerships between companies, social partners, NGOs and local public authorities to manage social services to increase their social responsibility.

Communication 136/2006 from the Commission to the European Parliament, the Council and the European Economic and Social Committee *Implementing the partnership for growth and jobs: making Europe a pole of excellence on corporate social responsibility* recognizes the limited role of CSR in achieving sustainable development goals and the impossibility of substituting public policies for CR programs carried out by various companies However, the concrete ways in which CSR actions can contribute to achieving public policy objectives are mentioned. Thus, companies can promote various programs for:

- For the recruitment of more people from disadvantaged groups, thus achieving a better integration on the labor market and an increase of social inclusion;
- For the training of the workforce, which thus remains competitive in a global economy; there is also an increase in the employment rate, in the conditions of the aging population in Europe;
- For the promotion of certain non-toxic foods and chemicals or for the awareness of the population regarding the prevention of certain diseases, which contributes to the improvement of public health;
- For environmental protection or investments in eco-innovation, thus contributing to a more rigorous use of natural resources and to the protection of the environment;

- Improving the image of companies and entrepreneurs in the communities, thus contributing to the cultivation of a more favorable attitude towards entrepreneurship;
- For better respect for human rights, the environment and labor standards, especially in developing countries;
- To reduce poverty and achieve the Sustainable Development Goals.

Given the above, we can conclude that European officials consider social responsibility to be an important element of economic competitiveness. In the Communication from the European Commission for the **relaunch of the Lisbon Strategy** (2005), European officials make the following statement: "Voluntary initiatives by companies in the form of social responsibility practices can be an essential contribution to sustainable development, while strengthening the potential for innovation and competitiveness. of Europe ".

The principles of social responsibility shape not only the activity of private companies but also that of public authorities. In this regard, the efforts of European officials to develop a **Green Public Procurement Policy**, which has an impact not only on public authorities, but also on private companies as a result of the multiplier effects, are noteworthy. Every year, the European authorities record expenditure representing 16% of European GDP (COM 400/2008, p. 2), which is why it is considered that public procurement can significantly shape production and consumption. Moreover, the demand for green products from public authorities can lead to the expansion of the development of green technology and the market for green goods.

Through the policy of green public procurement, the European authorities thus align with the efforts and concerns recorded worldwide such as the OECD Recommendation on Green Public Procurement, the establishment of the Marrakech Task Force on Sustainable Procurement created after the Summit Johannesburg World Conference on Sustainable Development (2002), the adoption of sustainable procurement policies by developed countries (USA, Canada, Australia, Japan, South Korea) or developing countries (China, Thailand, Philippines).

At EU level, the potential of green public procurement was first highlighted by the European Commission in 2003, which, through the Integrated Product Policy, recommended that Member States adopt national EPA action plans. By the summer of 2010, national action plans had been adopted in 21 countries, while Bulgaria, Estonia, Greece, Ireland, Hungary and Romania were in the process of adopting these plans.

The concerns of European officials also resulted in the adoption of regulations:

- Directive 2004/17 / EC of the European Parliament and of the Council on public procurement procedures for entities in the energy, transport, water and postal services sectors;
- Directive 2004/18 / EC of the European Parliament and of the Council on the coordination of procedures for the award of public works contracts, public supply contracts and public sector contracts, which have brought some novelties, namely the inclusion of environmental requirements in the specifications techniques, the use of eco-labels; establishing social and environmental conditions for carrying out contracts;

Taking in account the limited effects found after the application of these regulations but also to the evolution of concerns regarding the involvement of companies and public authorities in promoting sustainable development, in February 2014, the Council of the European Union and the European Parliament adopted two directives in orde to simplify the public procurement procedures and to improve the results of their applicatiion. So, the new laws that which governs specific activities at European level are Directive 2014/24/EU on public procurement, and Directive 2014/25/EU on procurement by entities operating in the water, energy, transport and postal services sectors. Until April 2016, the EU countries had the obligation to transpose the new rules into national law Directive 2014/24/EU on public procurement, and

Currently, Green Public Procurement policy is an integral part of the Sustainable Development Strategy (2006), the Action Plan on Sustainable Consumption and Production and the Sustainable Industrial Policy.

Green Public Procurement policy is based on certain environmental criteria that must be met by goods and services purchased by public authorities. At the level of European countries, there are many criteria and approaches, but European officials are fighting to reconcile these criteria so as not to distort the European market, reduce administrative barriers for economic operators, and reap benefits from corporations that operates in several European countries and by SMEs that have a limited capacity to master public procurement procedures (Matei, 2013; Siminică et al., 2020).

The Green Public Procurement criteria were divided into two categories: non-binding basic criteria and non-binding environmental award criteria, which serve to stimulate the additional environmental performance of goods and services. The first criteria were introduced in 2008 for ten goods / services: graphic and copying paper, cleaning products and services; office IT equipment, construction, transportation, furniture, electricity; food and catering services; textiles, gardening products and services. Since 2010, criteria have been developed for other other categories of goods such as windows or mobile phones.

Green Public Procurement policy can generate many long-term beneficial effects that can contribute to the sustainable development of the European economy:

- By purchasing products from recyclable materials or printers that print on both sides, natural resources are saved;
- By excluding toxic substances from construction and renovation works, better working conditions for employees are ensured;
- By purchasing buses and cars with a low level of gas emissions, air pollution in cities is reduced;
- By purchasing organic food, eutrophication caused by inappropriate agricultural practices is reduced.

Given these positive effects on sustainable development and the multiplier effects on economic agents and consumers, in some European countries, for certain products, the Green Public Procurement policy is binding: Portugal and Germany for wood and LCC use, the Czech Republic for IT.

Starting from the concept of Green Public Procurement, at the level of the European Union, a new concept crystallized in time, namely **socially responsible acquisitions**. Thus, in 2001, the European Commission published Interpretative Communication 566/2001 on the legislation applicable to public procurement and the possibility of integrating social considerations in public procurement (interpretative communication of the Commission on the Community law applicable to public procurement and the possibilities for integrating social considerations into public procurement).

The term “social considerations” used in this Communication has a wide scope and implies respect for fundamental rights, the principles of equal treatment and non-discrimination, national and European legal regulations in the social field, but also preferential clauses (such as reintegration). people with disabilities or without a job).

Over time, the concerns of European officials to insert social considerations in the public procurement process have intensified and led to the emergence of a new concept: **socially responsible public procurement (SRPP)**. According to the official definition, " SRPP are public procurement operations that take into account one or more social aspects: employment opportunities, decent work, respect for social and labor rights, social inclusion (including people with disabilities), equal opportunities, accessibility, design for all, taking into account sustainability criteria, including issues related to ethical trade and a wider voluntary compliance with corporate social responsibility (CSR), while respecting the principles enshrined in the Treaty on the Functioning of the European Union (TFEU) and the procurement directives "

The inclusion of social considerations or aspects in the public procurement process involves a link between Single Market policy (public procurement policy is a component of Single Market policy) and social policy, which plays an important role in EU development. In addition to technical progress, social cohesion, protection and improvement of the quality of the environment are the pillars of sustainable development and the process of European integration.

The European authorities were also concerned about the need to publish information on the social involvement of corporations. In this sense, certain normative acts regarding the content of the reports made by the companies have been modified.

Thus, by Regulation no. 1606/2002, the European Commission amended its accounting directives (Modernization of accounting directives). Thus, through the management report, companies must make public information of a non-economic or non-financial nature, and each member country is responsible for developing the rules for incorporating this requirement into national law.

In addition, Directive 2003/51 / EC required non - financial reporting in the case of companies listed on a regulated capital market. "In order to extend the understanding of the company's development, performance or position, the analysis (in the annual report) should include both the financial results and, where appropriate, the results of the relevant non-financial key indicators, including information on environmental issues, and on employees ".

Given the progress made by large companies in non-financial reporting and the interest of different categories of stakeholders in the economic, social and environmental involvement of companies at EU level, The non-financial reporting Directive (2014/95/EU) was adopted. Through this law, large public interest entities with over 500 employees like listed companies, banks, and insurance companies are bound to disclose certain non-financial information. This directive has been late transposed into the law of the Member States, but the results not being spectacular so far. Given the diversity of companies that have to make such non-financial reports, Communication 2017/C 215/01 Guidelines on non-financial reporting (methodology for reporting non-financial information) was adopted in oder to offer to interested firms concrete **examples of Key Performance Indicators (KPI). This communication also has the role of ensuring a certain harmonization of the non-financial reporting made by the companies that have this obligation** (Markota Vukić et al., 2019).

REPORTING OF NON-FINANCIAL INFORMATION BY EUROPEAN COMPANIES

The involvement of companies in CSR activities is more and more intense, but considering the differences between companies in the field of activity, company size, capital origin, management's vision on the importance of CSR programs, (non) listing on the stock exchange, information provided to stakeholders not only different but are presented in very varied ways. Thus, the obligation to report non-financial aspects appeared, as well as the need to standardize the published information to ensure the comparability of data by stakeholders over time. New concepts like, non-financial reporting, sustainable reporting and integrated reporting, with CSR aspect appeared (Voica & Stancu, 2021).

At the international level, there are many standards, guidelines and reporting frameworks than can be used by companies to prepare a non-financial or integrated report. The best known are Global Reporting Initiative (GRI); Corporate Social Responsibility Report; Integrate report (IIRC); Communication on Progress (Global Compact); International Integrated Reporting Framework; Guidance on Corporate Responsibility Indicators in Annual Reports; KPIs for ESG.

In order to track the performances of the European companies in the field of CSR, we chose to use the database published by GRI for period 2007-2017 with the following specifications:

- The five sectors energy, chemicals, metal products, mining, and automotive with high social and environment were selected.
- The data for four continents - Asia, Europe, Latin America & the Caribbean and Northern America were selected (the analyse is not focused on Africa and Oceania because the CSR activities for companies from these regions are very modest).

- GRI has been chosen for this analysis because it is an independent organization based on Amsterdam, Netherlands.
- Sustainability Reporting Guidelines (SRG) are available as a free public good and they are continuously improved and revised (Voica & Stancu, 2018).
- The Sustainable Disclosure Database (SDD) of GRI are available on line and the submitted reports could be downloaded by stakeholders. In this way, the information asymmetry between companies and stakeholders are reduces and the trust is increased The public scrutinity is very important because the companies are oblige to improve their CSR practices and opportunistic managerial behavior is sanctioned by the consumers and implicitly reduced.
- GRI reporting provides an overview of the company's activities, each entity being required to report data for the entire set of indicators not being able to focus only on the positive aspects that would lead to the promotion of a distorted image among stakeholders (González et al., 2018).

Oil and gas companies have come to the attention of the press and consumers for several decades for several reasons. On the one hand, they were involved in various scandals regarding the constant pollution of the environment or by generating ecological disasters, and on the other hand by initiating a large press company through which they tried to wash the image among the stakeholders. In some cases, press campaigns have been clearly decoupled from the company's activity, being only a marketing strategy to improve the image, not being supported by concrete actions aimed at protecting the environment or improving working conditions in countries where oil fields are exploited. Moreover, in some cases, marketing strategies have aimed to rebrand companies and focus stakeholder attention on future activities and less on actions initiated in the past or currently carried out by oil companies. In addition, some of these companies have tried to adapt to the new trends imposed by the transition to the bioeconomy and have even invested in alternative energy sources. On the other hand, oil companies keep the front page of economic newspapers because more and more portfolio investors make public their divestment decisions from these companies, selling their shares and thus sanctioning the socially irresponsible activity of these companies. The behavior of companies in the energy sector is highly monitored by stakeholders given the negative impact that some of the activities carried out on the environment have. In addition, in some cases, CSR programs have only been used as greenwashing tools by which companies have sought to divert stakeholder attention from the real impact on the environment (Alazzani et al., 2013; Agudelo et al., 2020). Globally, Europe is surpassed by Asia (figure 1), where the most active countries are China and Japan.

Figure 1. The evolution of reports number for Energy companies
Source: Global Reporting Initiative

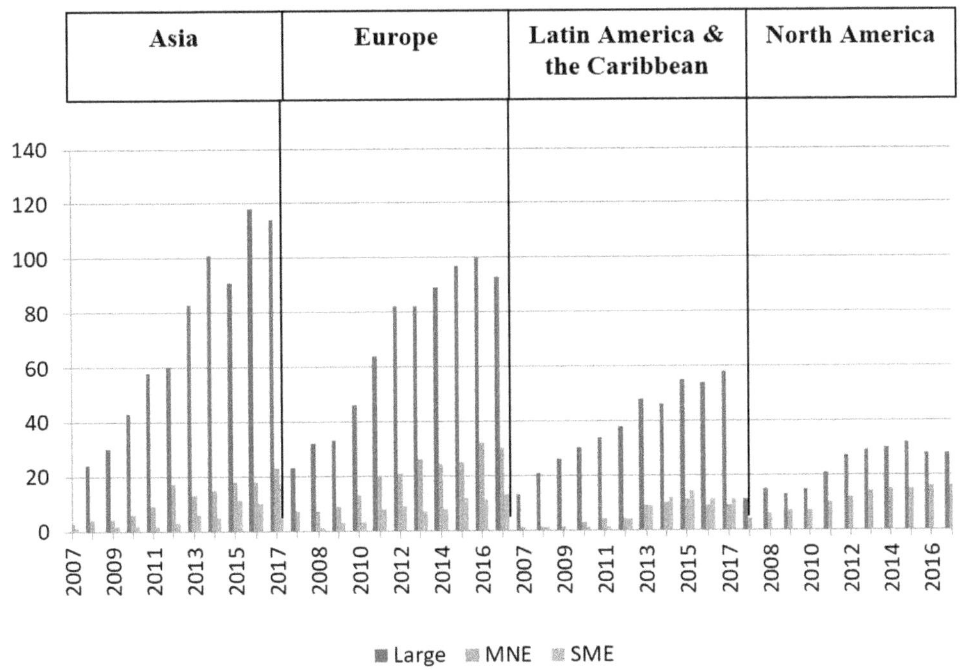

Given the relocation of heavily polluting production capacity in Asia, the number of sustainability reports published by companies is also considerably higher for the Asian continent (figure 2).

In the case of mining, large Asian companies rank first in terms of the number of sustainability reports published. The fact can be explained by the greater number of such companies on this continent, but also by their interest in having a well-founded image among stakeholders (figure 3).

The car industry was shaken by the Volkswagen scandal that showed the fragility of consumers in front of a transnational giant that only aims to maximize profits at any cost. This scandal has undermined the confidence of stakeholders in the automotive industry whose negative externalities are multiple and can manifest themselves in the long run, affecting the environment

Figure 2. The evolution of reports number for Chemicals companies
Source: Global Reporting Initiative

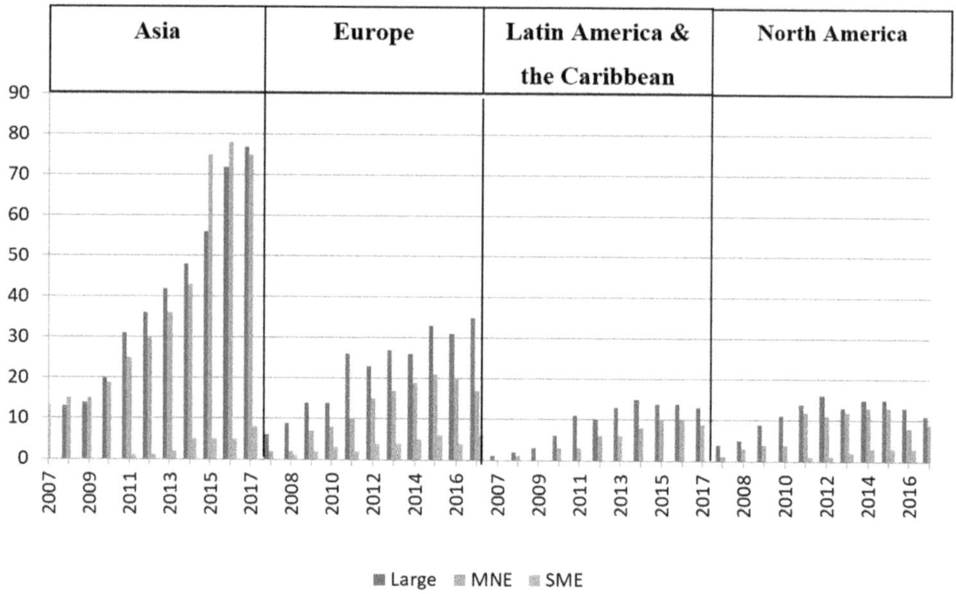

Figure 3. The evolution of reports number for Mining companies
Source: Global Reporting Initiative

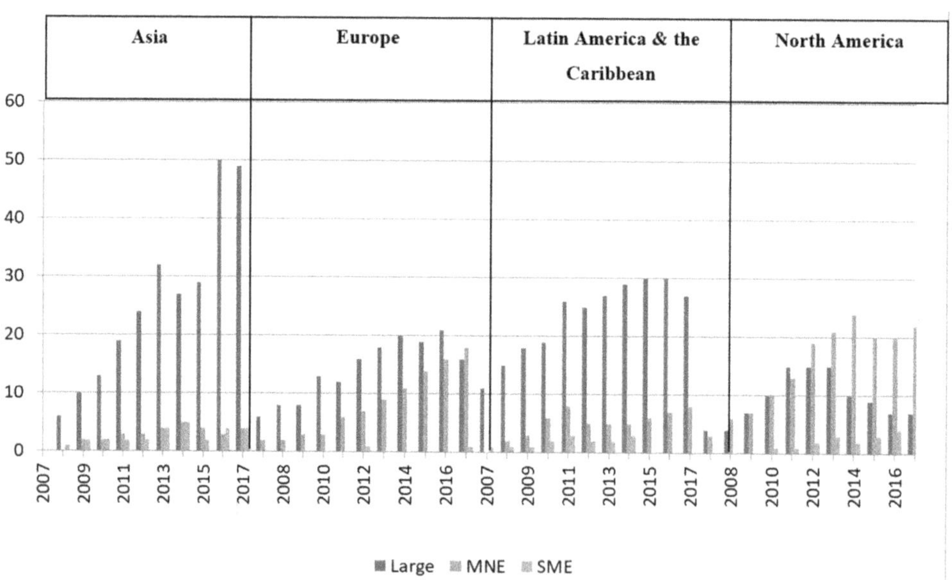

in various countries. Despite this scandal, after 2015 there is no substantial increase in the number of sustainability reports published by companies in the field worldwide and in Europe for large companies. This trend is available only for multinationals (figure 4) .

Figure 4. The evolution of reports number for Automotive companies
Source: Global Reporting Initiative

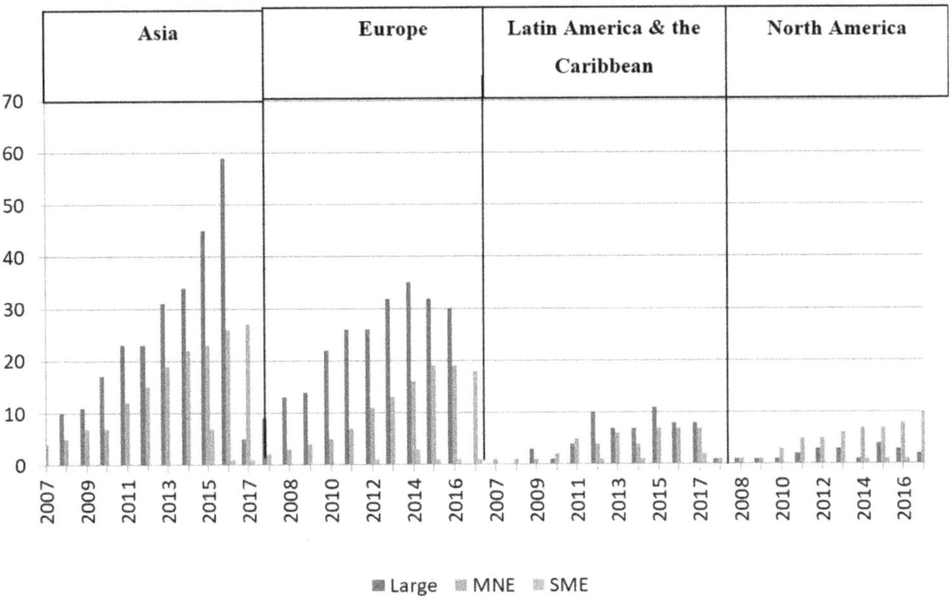

Metal industry is another economic sector that generates many negative externalities, which is why companies must initiate various measures to improve the image among stakeholders. The involvement of CSR in action and the publication of non-financial data are some of the initiatives that these companies are taking. The concrete results are different depending on the geographical area, the leader being Asia.

CONCLUSION

The European Union stands out at international level through its multiple initiatives for the elaboration of some legal regulations with obligatory character or with voluntary character for companies and public authorities.

These regulations either target strictly CSR or broader areas such as sustainable development, environmental protection. Despite the existence of these regulations, the analysis of statistical data published by GRI on sustainability reports places the European continent in second place in the world, after Asia.

The approach of the companies regarding the provision of non-financial information to the stakeholders is different depending on the field of activity, the existence of some legal regulations, the origin of the capital. From the point of view of the dissemination of information on regarding the environmental impact, the oil and gas companies are trying to improve their image among the stakeholders. At the international level, CSR reporting rates for the oil & gas sector are highest according to KPMG data released in the year 2017. Toward an average of 60%, the ratio for these companies is 81%. Most companies opted to choose to present CSR information in their annual financial report. Companies that decide to provide more complex information on CSR actions are usually doing so this by publishing a sustainability report (Calace, 2014; Sierra-Garcia et al., 2018). At the international level, the most widely used reporting form on CSR is the GRI standard (KPMG, 2017).

REFERENCES

Agudelo, M. A. L., Johannsdottir, L., & Davidsdottir, B. (2020). Drivers that motivate energy companies to be responsible. A systematic literature review of Corporate Social Responsibility in the energy sector. *Journal of Cleaner Production*, *247*, 119094. doi:10.1016/j.jclepro.2019.119094

Alazzani, A., & Wan-Hussin, W. N. (2013). Global Reporting Initiative's environmental reporting: A study of oil and gas companies. *Ecological Indicators*, *32*, 19–24. doi:10.1016/j.ecolind.2013.02.019

Bosun, P., Teodorescu, M., & Teodorescu, B. (2014). Corporate Social Responsibility–Collaborating for the Future. *International Journal of Education and Research*, *2*(3).

Bredgaard, T. (2004). Corporate social responsibility between public policy and enterprise policy. *Transfer: European Review of Labour and Research*, *10*(3), 372–392. doi:10.1177/102425890401000305

Breitbarth, T., Harris, P., & Aitken, R. (2009). Corporate social responsibility in the European Union: A new trade barrier? *Journal of Public Affairs: An International Journal*, *9*(4), 239–255. doi:10.1002/pa.333

Brezoi, A. G. (2018). Ethics and corporate social responsibility in the current geopolitical context. *Economic Insights - Trends and Challenges*, *7*, 45–52.

Calace, D. (n.d.). Disclosure in Non-Financial Reports as Strategic Leverage: can it Increase Firms' Value? *European Journal of Economics and Management*, 7.

Delbard, O. (2008). CSR legislation in France and the European regulatory paradox: An analysis of EU CSR policy and sustainability reporting practice. *Corporate Governance: International Journal of Business in Society*, *8*(4), 397–405. doi:10.1108/14720700810899149

Fairbrass, J. (2011). Exploring corporate social responsibility policy in the European Union: A discursive institutionalist analysis. *Journal of Common Market Studies*, *49*(5), 949–970. doi:10.1111/j.1468-5965.2010.02162.x

Fuente, J. A., García-Sanchez, I. M., & Lozano, M. B. (2017). The role of the board of directors in the adoption of GRI guidelines for the disclosure of CSR information. *Journal of Cleaner Production*, *141*, 737–750. doi:10.1016/j.jclepro.2016.09.155

Garcia-Sanchez, I. M., Cuadrado-Ballesteros, B., & Frias-Aceituno, J. V. (2016). Impact of the institutional macro context on the voluntary disclosure of CSR information. *Long Range Planning*, *49*(1), 15–35. doi:10.1016/j.lrp.2015.02.004

Gigauri, I. (2012). Attitudes of georgian consumers towards corporate social responsibility. *European Scientific Journal*, *8*(9).

Gigauri, I. (2015). Communication needs for corporate social responsibility in developing countries: The case of Georgia. *WORLD (Oakland, Calif.)*, *5*(2).

González, M., del Mar Alonso-Almeida, M., & Dominguez, D. (2018). Mapping global sustainability report scoring: A detailed analysis of Europe and Asia. *Quality & Quantity*, *52*(3), 1041–1055. doi:10.100711135-017-0502-y

Jung, J. C., & Sharon, E. (2019). The Volkswagen emissions scandal and its aftermath. *Global Business and Organizational Excellence*, *38*(4), 6–15. doi:10.1002/joe.21930

KPMG. (2017). The road ahead. *Survey of Corporate Responsibility Reporting 2017*. https://home.kpmg/uk/en/home/insights/2017/11/kpmg-international-survey-of-corporate-responsibility-reporting-2017.html

Lenssen, G., Arenas, D., Lacy, P., Pickard, S., & Delbard, O. (2008). CSR legislation in France and the European regulatory paradox: An analysis of EU CSR policy and sustainability reporting practice. *Corporate Governance: The International Journal of Business in Society*.

Lenssen, G., Gasparski, W., Rok, B., Lacy, P., & Eberhard-Harribey, L. (2006). Corporate social responsibility as a new paradigm in the European policy: how CSR comes to legitimate the European regulation process. *Corporate Governance: The International Journal of Business in Society*.

Letica, B. (2008, June). Three CSR models in new European Union member states and candidate countries. In *CSR PAPER 43.2008, proceedings of Third Core Conference: The potential of CSR to drive integration in an enlarged Europe* (pp. 19-20). Academic Press.

Markota Vukić, N., Omazić, M. A., & Aleksić, A. (2019). Corporate Social Responsibility Strategy and Reporting: Overview of Practice in Selected European Countries. *Interdisciplinary Description of Complex Systems: INDECS, 17*(2, 2-B), 355–367. doi:10.7906/indecs.17.2.11

Matei, M. (2013). *Responsabilitatea socială a corporaţiilor şi instituţiilor şi dezvoltarea durabilă a României*. Expert Publishing House.

Matei, M., Popescu, C., & Enescu, G. (2012). Promoting corporate social responsibility by public authorities in the European Union. In *The 18th International Business Information Management Association Conference, Istanbul, Turkey* (pp. 1998-2008). Academic Press.

Öberseder, M., Schlegelmilch, B. B., & Gruber, V. (2011). "Why don't consumers care about CSR?" A qualitative study exploring the role of CSR in consumption decisions. *Journal of Business Ethics, 104*(4), 449–460. doi:10.100710551-011-0925-7

Owen, D. (2005). CSR after Enron: A role for the academic accounting profession? *European Accounting Review, 14*(2), 395–404. doi:10.1080/09638180500126892

Pomering, A., & Dolnicar, S. (2009). Assessing the prerequisite of successful CSR implementation: Are consumers aware of CSR initiatives? *Journal of Business Ethics, 85*(2), 285–301. doi:10.100710551-008-9729-9

Roblek, V., Bach, M. P., Meško, M., & Kresal, F. (2020). Corporate social responsibility and challenges for corporate sustainability in first part of the 21st century. *Cambio. Rivista sulle Trasformazioni Sociali, 10*(19), 31-46.

Shaw, J. J. A. (2006). The European Constitution and CSR; Consensus or Conflict. *Social Responsibility Journal, 2*(2), 186–193. doi:10.1108/eb059265

Sierra-Garcia, L., Garcia-Benau, M., & Bollas-Araya, H. (2018). Empirical Analysis of Non-Financial Reporting by Spanish Companies. *Administrative Sciences, 8*(3), 29. doi:10.3390/admsci8030029

Siminică, M., Avram, M., Roxana, L. P., & Avram, L. (2020). The adoption of national green procurement plans from the perspective of circular economy. *Amfiteatru Economic, 22*(53), 15–27. doi:10.24818/EA/2020/53/15

Siminica, M., & Sichigea, M. (2018). Corporate Social Responsibility as a Voluntary Initiative But a Mandatory Non-financial Reporting Link Between the Social and Financial Performance of Romanian Companies. In *Current Issues in Corporate Social Responsibility* (pp. 77–96). Springer. doi:10.1007/978-3-319-70449-4_6

Steurer, R. (2010). The role of governments in corporate social responsibility: Characterising public policies on CSR in Europe. *Policy Sciences, 43*(1), 49–72. doi:10.100711077-009-9084-4

Steurer, R., & Hametner, M. (2013). Objectives and indicators in sustainable development strategies: Similarities and variances across Europe. *Sustainable Development, 21*(4), 224–241. doi:10.1002d.501

Steurer, R., Martinuzzi, A., & Margula, S. (2012). Public policies on CSR in Europe: Themes, instruments, and regional differences. *Corporate Social Responsibility and Environmental Management, 19*(4), 206–227. doi:10.1002/csr.264

Timbate, L., & Park, C. K. (2018). CSR performance, financial reporting, and investors' perception on financial reporting. *Sustainability, 10*(2), 522. doi:10.3390u10020522

Vandekerckhove, W., & Roland Commers, M. S. (2005). Beyond voluntary / mandatory juxtaposition. Towards a European framework on CSR as Network Governance. *Social Responsibility Journal, 1*(1/2), 98–103. doi:10.1108/eb045800

Verbeeten, F. H., Gamerschlag, R., & Möller, K. (2016). Are CSR disclosures relevant for investors? Empirical evidence from Germany. *Management Decision, 54*(6), 1359–1382. doi:10.1108/MD-08-2015-0345

Voica, M. C., & Stancu, A. (2021). Corporate Social Responsibility Reporting: Background, Evolution and Sustainability Promoter. *Sustainable Management for Managers and Engineers*, 109-155.

Vollero, A., Palazzo, M., Siano, A., & Elving, W. J. (2016). Avoiding the greenwashing trap: Between CSR communication and stakeholder engagement. *International Journal of Innovation and Sustainable Development, 10*(2), 120–140. doi:10.1504/IJISD.2016.075542

Vollero, A., Siano, A., Palazzo, M., & Elving, W. (2011). Corporate Communication and CSR; comparing Italian and Dutch energy companies on anti-greenwashing strategies. *CSR Communication conference 2011: The 1st international CSR Communication conference*.

Vukić, N. M., Omazić, M. A., Pejic-Bach, M., Aleksić, A., & Zoroja, J. (2020). Leadership for Sustainability: Connecting Corporate Responsibility Reporting and Strategy. In Leadership Styles, Innovation, and Social Entrepreneurship in the Era of Digitalization (pp. 44-72). IGI Global.

Yu, L., Tsai, S. B., Li, D., Teng, L., & Li, G. (2018). A Research of the Influence on the Consumer Behavior From CSR Information Embedded in the Process of Online Purchasing. In *Green Production Strategies for Sustainability* (pp. 117–134). IGI Global. doi:10.4018/978-1-5225-3537-9.ch007

Chapter 10
CSR Practices in the Emerging Economies of Asia

ABSTRACT

Corporate social responsibility is a management strategy implemented in companies throughout developing countries in Asia. In the forefront is China, which is now becoming a CSR global brand by impacting society and the environment. India is fast catching up to the race where business law forces business to invest in CSR practices. Pakistan and Bangladesh are now members of the global economy, and the industries in respective countries have realized that sustainability enhances their corporate image. The change in the emerging economies is from public awareness and accountability for corporate contribution to society. The chapter put forward the CSR practices by companies in Pakistan, India, Bangladesh, and China.

INTRODUCTION

CSR stands for corporate social responsibility, which is a management practice used by business enterprises, governments, and non-governmental organizations (NGOs) to combine planet (environment), profit (economic), and people (social) concerns in their operations. The combination is a balance between all three P's while keeping shareholders in mind. The management practice is more than the aid, patronage, or charity concept, which helps reduce poverty. The CSR activities is now a global phenomenon that is management practices by developed and developing countries; however, it differs due to

DOI: 10.4018/978-1-7998-3988-0.ch010

prevailing cultural, religious believes and practices in the respective countries. Some of the critical CSR activities involved "environmental management, eco-efficiency, responsible sourcing, stakeholder engagement, labor standards, and working conditions, employee and community relations, social equity, gender equality, human rights, good governance, anti-corruption measures, charity, educational funding, and medical assistance." Similarly, according to Epstein (2011) and Laura Musikanski (2020), CSR's practices are "Corporate responsibility (CR), sustainability, corporate social responsibility (CSR), sustainable development, triple bottom line, and environmental and social stewardship."

The CSR concept is as old as the industrial revolution in the 1800s. During the mid-1800s, there was a lot of hue and cry for labor conditions in the United States. The country reformers were concerned with the companies' human resource management (HRM) practices and the resulting social and economic problems. At the time, successful industrialist Andrew Carnegie in the steel industry became famous because of large donations for education and research. Following the footsteps, John D. Rockefeller also contributed half a billion US dollars to religious, educational, and scientific causes (THOMAS, 2019).

The term "Corporate Social Responsibility" is coined by Howard Bowen, an American economist, in his publication "Social Responsibilities of the Businessman" in 1953 (Bowen & Johnson, 1953). However, the concept was officially introduced by the "Committee for Economic Development" in 1971. The more evolved idea was implemented in 1980 by US companies catering to business practices' social and environmental interests. The academic researchers also come forth to write on the management practice; in 1991, Professor Donna J. Wood pen and proposed a CSR model to provide a framework for evaluating the effects and results of CSR programs implementation in business firms (see figure 1).

The same year Professor Archie B. Carroll researched and published his famous work "The Pyramid of Corporate Social Responsibility" on CSR implementation and its critical success factors (see figure 2). In the year 2000, the world witness CSR as a philosophy practiced by fortune 100 companies such as "Wells Fargo, Coca-Cola, Walt Disney, and Pfizer" (THOMAS, 2019).

Figure 1. Model for corporate identity and responsibility
(Wood, 2010)

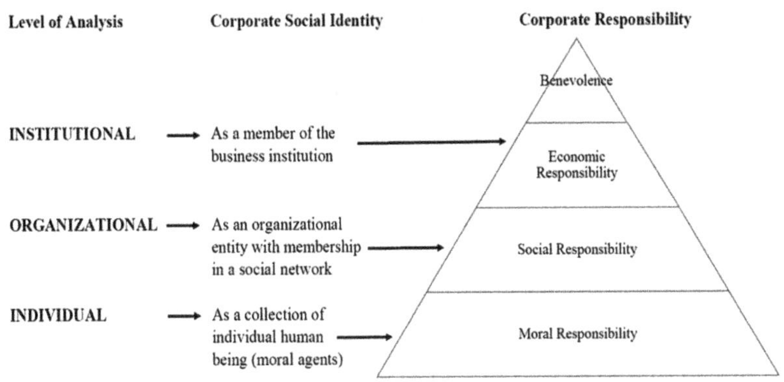

Figure 2. Corporate Social Responsibility Pyramid
(Carroll, 2016)

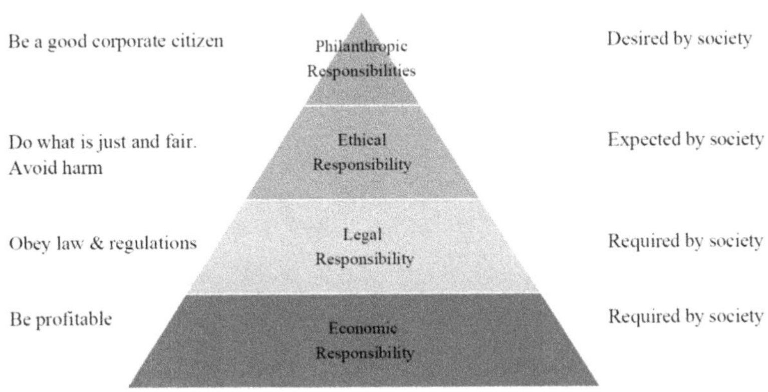

The "Triple Bottom Line or Triple P (people, planet, and profit)" concept is the basis of sustainability, and John Elkington coined the term in 1994. Triple Bottom line accounts for the factor of business activities by an enterprise that affects "economic, environmental and social impact" (see figure 3) (Dalibozhko & Krakovetskaya, 2018).

Figure 3. Triple Bottom Line concept
(Dalibozhko & Krakovetskaya, 2018)

Figure 4. United Nations 17 sustainable goals to transform the World
(UN, 2015)

Figure 5. CSR Pyramid for developing countries
(Visser, 2008)

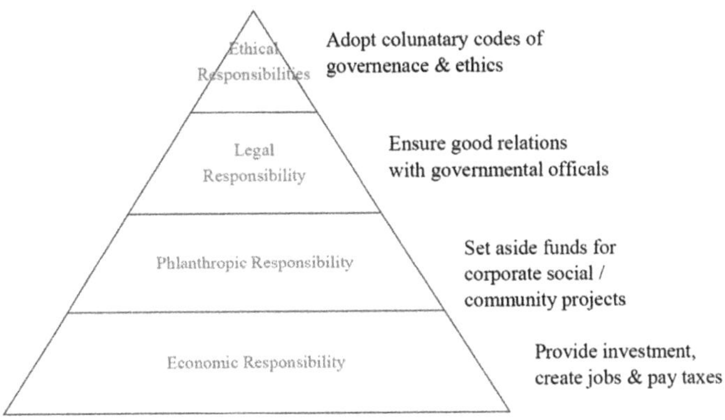

After much global appreciation for the strategic management concept, the United Nations (UN) also brings forward its development goals for 2016-30 to unify "economic growth, human development, environmental protection." In its 2015 summit, the UN identified seventeen CSR goals passed by 193 member countries covering a wide range of social, economic, and environmental development. Compared with the Millennium Development Goals, the UN SGDs need the collaboration of governments and business enterprises (Petrovskaya, 2017) (see figure 4).

CSR PRACTICES IN EMERGING ECONOMIES OF ASIA

Scholars have raised questions on whether the framework adopted in developed countries suits developing countries (Jamali, 2014). For CSR activities in developing countries, Visser (2008) proposed a hierarchy that suggests economic responsibility to be the pyramid's base (see figure 5). The concept is similar to Carroll's proposed pyramid; however, philanthropy is on second than ethical responsibility ensured by "legal and ethical responsibility" (Visser, 2008). The logic for philanthropist activities pushed legal and ethics on third and fourth respective priorities is due to prevailing economic conditions in developing countries: "poverty, unemployment, and shortage of foreign direct investment." The case is valid, especially in Asian developing countries like India, Pakistan, and Bangladesh, where unemployment and poverty are rampant.

The word philanthropy derives from the Greek words "Phillen or Love" and "Anthropos or Human." Many companies in Muslim countries adhere to the idea of generosity and practices in the form "Zakat" and "Sadqah," which are Arabic for charity (Jamali, 2014). The difference between the two is "Zakat" is obligatory for wealthy individuals. An amount of 2.5% is a levy on saving like precious metal (gold, silver, copper) or stashed cash currency. However, Sadqah is a discretionary charity that an individual Muslim can give any time of the year to help the poor or needy and society.

In his study, Visser (2008) argued that country cultural traditions and norms influence CSR, and in developing countries, religion is a significant factor in driving CSR activities. The survey conducted by Vives (2005) on 1,300 SMEs in Latin America is proof that religion is the motivation for CSR activities in a developing country. The context of Islam is essential, especially in CSR activities in Muslim developing countries in Asia, as it provides a framework for organizations to conduct their business. "Zakat" distribution has a positive impact on society and the economy. However, many companies confuse the whole concept of CSR as only paying "Zakat" to NGOs and social welfare institutions (Qasim et al., 2011). China's example can explain cultural influence: CSR activities focus on the Confucian cultural tradition that describes "benevolence, philanthropy, and humaneness" (Yin & Zhang, 2012).

Besides the religious and cultural influence on CSR activities, the political systems and governments also play a vital role in Asian developing countries (Dartey-Baah & Amponsah-Tawiah, 2011). The democratic reforms improved corporate management and infused ethics, a positive driver for business firm CSR activities (Jamali, 2014). India is a good example where government institutions shaped CSR efforts in enterprises to inculcate fundamental values by erecting business laws applicable to all; this influences top managers to embrace CSR practices. In 2014, India was the first country in Asia to make CSR activities compulsory by incorporating "section 135 of India's Companies Act." The laws dictate that a company has to spend 2% from the past three years average net profit for CSR activities.

To present CSR activities in Asian developing countries, below are activities segregated country wise:

CSR Practices in Pakistan

CSR in Pakistan came into the limelight in international media due to child labor in the sports manufacturing industry in Sialkot (Awan et al., 2012). The country witnesses the increase in domestic and international NGOs numbers, mostly working for CSR awareness (Yunis et al., 2017). Organizations like "Pakistan Centre for Philanthropy (PCP), United Nations Industrial Development Organization (UNIDO), United Nations Development Program (UNDP), International Labor Organization (ILO), and Responsible Business Initiative (RBI)" are working to promote CSR activities in the country. However, the concept is new, but many big brands in the country are working to improve the lives of fifty-five million people living below the poverty line (Muzaffar, 2020). The number can reduce If enterprises throughout the country play their part in giving back to the community. Below are examples of the brands which are contributing generously to CSR activities.

1. Coca-Cola CSR activities: The international brand in Pakistan is fully active in CSR practices. The brand has launched a campaign called "Bottle of Change," which raises funds for a welfare organization known as "The Edhi Foundation." Coco-Cola doubled the amount on top of the raised fund. Besides charity, the company also involves other CSR initiatives like entrepreneurship programs for women and education allowance for the country's needy.
2. JS Bank CSR Activities: JS Bank is the only bank compliant with the "green climate fund" and the country central bank's green banking guidelines. The bank's CSR activities envelop, finance 120 solar power projects in the country and promote education; it financed 30 schools. They encourage a paperless environment to contribute directly to Pakistan's ecosystem and reduce the foreign exchange burden on paper imports. In 2020, the bank supplied food and medicines in Sindh province during monsoon flooding, besides funding other relief programs. Further for environmental improvements, JS bank has joined hands with WWF to save mangrove plants in Baluchistan province coastal belt by planting hundred thousand sprouts. The plantation is the food source for dolphins and other coastal birds.
3. PSO CSR activities: Pakistan State Oil is one of the big oil companies in Pakistan. They are involved in initiatives like "education, healthcare, community building, women empowerment, special children welfare,

sports development, and relief activities." To promote education for the underprivileged in the country, the company has supported many schools. The company has also joined forces with health organizations to provide free health care facilities for the poor.

4. PTCL CSR activities: Pakistan Telecommunication Limited is the biggest telecom company that improves social and environmental problems. The company focuses on "health, education, environments, and several community projects." The company also planted trees to safeguard the environment. Educational funding for needy children aimed to make them better citizens. Employ activities like blood donations and retirement schemes, commendable CSR practices. Following are the focus CSR plan of the company:
    a. "PTCL Razakaar – A structured employee volunteer program through which employees act as ambassadors of the organization and participate in humanitarian activities on areas of need.
    b. Education
    c. Youth Development
    d. Health & Safety
    e. Environment
    f. Disaster Response
    g. Inclusion"
5. Engro Fertilizer and Engro Corp CSR activities: A big name in fertilizers and the Agri industry are involved in farmer welfare. The group collaborated with "System Productivity Innovative Rice Trainings (SPIRIT)" for training farmers in "resource conservation, water-saving, plant population management, and improved harvesting agricultural productivity." More than thirty-eight villages and twelve thousand farmers took part in improving the food supply chain.
6. Soya Supreme Oil CSR activities: An edible oil company in Pakistan, in collaboration with INDUS Hospital, started childhood awareness programs from 2018 to 2019.

CSR PRACTICES IN INDIA

India is one of Asia's most significant countries, with a staggering population of 1.38 Billion (Worldometer, 2020). The country is an emerging economy with a lot of FDIs and international companies coming for investment. As a CSR initiative, India's government in 2014 amended its business law by incorporating "section 135 of India's Companies Act." The regulation dictates that a company has to spend 2% of the past three years average on a specific net profit for CSR activities. Below is the list of the top 10 companies in regards to CSR activities (Fernandes, 2020):

1. Tata Chemicals: For years 2019-20, the company sanctioned was USD 2.9 million; however, it spends USD 5.12 million on CSR projects. The CSR activities are focus on the value of life and raising sustainable and integrated expansion in the company operational areas.
2. Infosys Ltd.: The group spent USD 48.8 million on different CSR practices. The main focus of the company is the reduction of carbon emissions. The company is using daylight in the office to go green.
3. Bharat Petroleum Corporation Ltd.: The company as a donation from salaries is USD 0.5 million. Further, they actively organized relief efforts for the COVID pandemic in July 2020. The team distributed COVID kits and educated four hundred families.
4. Mahindra & Mahindra Ltd.: The expenses on CSR activities are USD 12.7 million for 2018-2019. For underprivileged girls, education support USD 1.1 million.
5. ITC Ltd.: The company spent USD 41.6 million for CSR activities and donated USD 29 million. The relieved CSR activities for COVID spread around 25 states in India. The actions constituted food distribution and COVID kits.
6. Ambuja Cement Ltd.: The company collaborated with different organizations and NGOs, which spread around twelve states in India and has flourished the lives plus one million people.
7. Tata Motors: The company spent USD 3 million in CSR activities. Further for CSR activities, US 0.2 million for Karla flooding in 2018.
8. Vedanta Ltd.: The company spends USD 42 million on CSR, which is higher than last year's. The CSR activities changed the lives of three million people.
9. Hindalco Industries Ltd.: The company spends a staggering amount of UDD 4.63 million. The prescribed amount for CSR, in contrast, is far less than USD 4 million. The activities constitute schooling, health, sustainable living, structure development, and social reforms affecting one million people and seven hundred thirty villages. For education, an amount of USD 1.5 million spends further on CSR.
10. Toyota Kirloskar Motor India: The company, as CSR activities, invested in improving sanitation conditions. Six hundred fifty schools build in

the country. Further, they are working to produce cars with zero carbon emissions till the year 2050. The main focus for the company's CSR activities remains the environment. Zero carbon and water optimization during manufacturing.

Table 1. Bangladeshi corporates survey

Company Name	Paid-up Capital	Yearly Turnover
Apex Tannery	1,799,929	36,225,440
Apex Adelchi Footwear Ltd.	5,905,279	1,127,891,343
Bexomco Pharmaceuticals	29,735,184	93,213,653
Brac Bank	37,911,893	2,297,626,078
IDLC Finance	14,615,566	25,510,807
Summit Alliance Port Limited	4,657,611,905	56
Singer Bangladesh	4,637,770	66,626,133
Titas Gas Dist. Co. Ltd	11	809,628,367
Grameenphone Ltd.	159,477,973	1,051,848,352
Nestle Bangladesh	No annual report	No annual report
Babylon Group	351,246	1,547,183
Gemini Sea Foods Ltd.	236,211	12,730,404

(Sobhan, 2014)

BANGLADESH CSR ACTIVITIES

Bangladesh is an Asian developing country with an annual GDP growth rate of 5.2 and 6.8% in 2020-21 (ADB, 2020). The ready-made garment exports to western countries are the primary revenue source (Delautre & Abriata, 2018). The sector is still lacking CSR standards of other Asian developing countries, but much is being done over the past years to improve CSR initiatives. Bangladesh came in the limelight in international media due to the collapse of "The Rana Plaza" garment factory, with a death toll of one thousand and a hundred twenty-seven and more than twenty-five hundred injured (Yardley Jim, 2013). However, few other factory fire incidences between 2006 and 2009 killed four hundred and fourteen workers and firefighters (Campaign, 2012). As more foreign investors are coming to invest, CSR activities are picking pace in the country (Delautre & Abriata, 2018). They are still a long way to go in contrast to the other to their Asian league. According to Sobhan's (2014) survey on twelve corporations in Bangladesh (see table 1), are the company details and the numbers are in US dollar. The country is a partner in the global economy and is well aware of CSR initiatives needed to establish its environmental and social image. The apparel companies, as a member of associations as the "Bangladesh Garment Manufacturers and Exporters Association (BGMEA) and the Bangladesh Knitwear Manufacturers and Exporters Association (BKMEA)," do practice CSR as western customer demand it. Unlike India, there is no governmental pressure or policy in this regard.

Below are a few CSR activities done by Bangladeshi corporates:

1. Apex Adelchi Footwear Limited

The company is the top exporter of footwear from Bangladesh to western retail stores and invests in employees' health and welfare through a full-fledged medical center and a day-care center. The company is a member of the Business Social Compliance Initiative (BSCI) as a CSR initiative.

2. Apex Tannery Limited Company

Founded in 1976 with a turnover of US$ 30million annually. The company provides scholarships to worthy students and drinking water for the "Rayerbazar Boddhovumi slums."

3. IDLC Finance limited company

A leading leasing company has taken steps to reduce carbon emissions and actively campaigned for "Let's make a greener planet!" by tree plantation.

4. Grameenphone Limited Company

Bangladesh's largest mobile collaborates with the Government of "Bangladesh, WHO & UNICEF" since 2007 to create awareness for polio eradication. Also, jointly with USAID, the company provides critical lifesaving information to new and pregnant mothers.

CSR PRACTICES IN CHINA

China's image, with regards to CSR, has changed dramatically since 2000. From low-cost produce in the early 1990s to high-value technological products, it is now an Asian CSR brand. In the start, Chinese companies do not implement CSR as their core value, but since 2006 the country went through a turning point. The companies started to publish their CSR practices, and academia and NGOs propagated the best ways (The Collective, 2018). The Sichuan earthquake in May 2008 had a profound effect on the people to look at companies for contribution as donations for the catastrophe. Chinese companies donated a handsome RMB 1.6 billion, and those avoided were subject to online public annoyance. It was a turning point in the Chinese corporation's strategic thinking and has grown to this date. CSR has now evolved beyond simple charity, and companies have now aligned themselves with China's strategic development.

Below are some impactful examples of Chinese CSR examples:

1. Alibaba

The company is one of the biggest online shopping platforms where buyers and sellers meet. The company has engaged with four hundred seventy million participants for public welfare projects. The company donated a staggering amount of USD ninety million to help the needy of society.

2. Country Garden Holdings

The Guangzhou property developers are China's largest in their sector. Besides establishing a school, scholarships and training colleges and USD one hundred and thirteen million given in charity.

3. JD.COM

A B2C online company provided twenty-five thousand jobs and supported farmers by building one hundred three business incubators to run agri-business. The company's CSR also practices financial support to farmers in seventeen hundred counties for debt servicing. They also collaborated with L'OREAL's famous beauty brand to provide training and jobs for disabled people of the country.

4. Ant Financial

Ant Financial invested in energy conservation and carbon emission reduction, which led to low-carbon life for millions of people. They run a massive tree plantation in 2017 by planting eight million trees and reducing five thousand tons of carbon emissions per day.

CONCLUSION

Asian developing countries are still struggling with the concept of CSR in contrast to companies in developed countries. The ambiguity comes due to the cost benefits of CSR implementation. However, society's welfare is ignored at large, especially for countries like Bangladesh, focusing on cost reduction. Air Pollution is another significant concern that is very high in developing countries due to a lack of sustainable, responsible business practices by enterprises. However, large companies follow a steady code of conduct regarding CSR compared to SMEs, as they are sensitive about their image. The region's CSR trend is recent and will evolve as a business core value as they are becoming global and connecting with western markets. Governments have to play an essential role in this regard, and India is a good example. The academic role is vital to enforce CSR's importance in upcoming business managers and consumers in the region. The best example to follow is China, as it is becoming a global brand regarding CSR. The country is fully exploiting technology to achieve top-class CSR practices. Whereas top trending CSR activities are "environmental protection, poverty alleviation, healthcare, food safety, education." Also, the companies in China are seeking strategic partnerships to enhance and better sustainable image globally. The unignorably crucial factor due to poor CSR practices is its effect on the food supply chain. Developing countries rely on the agriculture sector to sustain food supply and job creation. All economic sectors have to become responsible to maintain the ecosystem to do business, reduce poverty, and improve living and health standards in the region.

REFERENCES

ADB. (2020). *Bangladesh: Economy*. Asian Development Bank. https://www.adb.org/countries/bangladesh/economy

Awan, A. W., Kamal, Y., Rafique, M., & Khan, S. (2012). Corporate social responsibility in Pakistan economy. *Business and Economic Review*, *2*(1), 1–31. doi:10.22547/BER/4.1.1

Bowen, H. R., & Johnson, F. E. (1953). *Social responsibility of the businessman*. Harper.

Campaign, C. C. (2012). *Hazardous workplaces: Making the Bangladesh Garment industry safe*. Academic Press.

Carroll, A. B. (1991). The pyramid of corporate social responsibility: Toward the moral management of organizational stakeholders. *Business Horizons*, *34*(4), 39–48. doi:10.1016/0007-6813(91)90005-G

Carroll, A. B. (2016). Carroll's pyramid of CSR: Taking another look. *International Journal of Corporate Social Responsibility*, *1*(1), 3. doi:10.118640991-016-0004-6

CSR in China: From Follower to Leader - Collective Responsibility. (2018). The Collective. https://www.coresponsibility.com/csr-china-follower-leader/

Dalibozhko, A., & Krakovetskaya, I. (2018). Youth entrepreneurial projects for the sustainable development of global community: evidence from Enactus program. *SHS Web of Conferences, 57*, 1009.

Dartey-Baah, K., & Amponsah-Tawiah, K. (2011). Exploring the limits of Western corporate social responsibility theories in Africa. *International Journal of Business and Social Science*, *2*(18).

Delautre, G., & Abriata, B. D. (2018). Corporate social responsibility: Exploring determinants and complementarities. *ILO Research Department Working Paper, 38*.

Epstein, J. (2011). *So You Call This CSR? Or One of Its Many Other Names?* Forbes. https://www.forbes.com/sites/csr/2011/07/28/so-you-call-this-csr-or-one-of-its-many-other-names/?sh=6cc3a7302d41

Fernandes, K. (2020, September 14). *Top 20 Indian Companies for CSR in 2019 - The CSR Journal*. The CSR Journal. https://thecsrjournal.in/top-indian-companies-for-csr-2019/

Jamali, D. (2014). CSR in developing countries through an institutional lens. In *Corporate social responsibility and sustainability: Emerging trends in developing economies*. Emerald Group Publishing Limited.

Muzaffar, A. (2020, May). *Corporate sector contribution in life of common man*. The Nation. https://nation.com.pk/18-May-2020/corporate-sector-contribution-in-life-of-common-man

Petrovskaya, N. E. (2017). The role of small business in employment: Evidence from the USA. *Finansovaya Analitika: Problemy i Resheniya= Financial Analytics. Science and Experience*, *10*(3), 343–356.

Qasim, Z., Muralidharan, P., & Ramaswamy, G. (2011). Corporate social responsibility and impact of CSR practices in the United Arab Emirates. *International Conference on Technology and Business Management*.

Sobhan, R. (2014). *Corporate social responsibility in Bangladesh: practice and perpetuity*. Safety and Rights Society.

Thomas. (2019, September). *A Brief History of Corporate Social Responsibility (CSR)*. Thomas Insights. https://www.thomasnet.com/insights/history-of-corporate-social-responsibility/

United Nations. (2015, September). *Envision 2030: 17 goals to transform the world for persons with disabilities*. https://www.un.org/development/desa/disabilities/envision2030.html

Visser, W. (2008). Corporate social responsibility in developing countries. In The Oxford handbook of corporate social responsibility. Academic Press.

Vives, A. (2005). *Social and environmental responsibility in small and medium enterprises in Latin America*. JSTOR.

Wood, D. J. (2010). Measuring corporate social performance: A review. *International Journal of Management Reviews*, *12*(1), 50–84.

Worldometer. (2020). *India Population (2020) - Worldometer*. https://www.worldometers.info/world-population/india-population/

Yardley, J. (2013). Report on Bangladesh Building Collapse Finds Widespread Blame - The New York Times. *The New York Times*. https://www.nytimes.com/2013/05/23/world/asia/report-on-bangladesh-building-collapse-finds-widespread-blame.html

Yin, J., & Zhang, Y. (2012). Institutional dynamics and corporate social responsibility (CSR) in an emerging country context: Evidence from China. *Journal of Business Ethics*, *111*(2), 301–316.

Yunis, M. S., Durrani, L., & Khan, A. (2017). Corporate social responsibility (CSR) in Pakistan: A critique of the literature and future research agenda. *Business and Economic Review*, *9*(1), 65–88.

Chapter 11
CSR Practices in Western Countries

ABSTRACT

Corporate social responsibility in Western countries has evolved to impact corporate governance, responsible manufacturing, and resource conservation. The citizens are more aware and vigilant for any discrepancy on the part of the corporations. The United States of America and the United Kingdom are considered the yardsticks for CSR practices in Western countries. Countries have enacted a law regulating companies to disclose their CSR practices. The companies also perform CSR practices due to enhancing their brand image and connecting with society. The magnitude of CSR practices depends on company size and financial muscle. However, for public CSR initiative and its reach depends more on the size of the donation.

INTRODUCTION

Corporate Social Responsibility is an integral part of the western corporate culture. The countries in the western hemisphere have brisked the CSR journey compared to their Asian counterpart. The corporates have a sense of responsibility to do justice for their imbalances due to their business process. It is partly due to the embedded culture and the legislatures and the land law, forcing corporates for CSR practices. Western countries constitute certain geographical regions based on customs, societal norms, technology, and religious belief. The geographical areas that present "Occident" are the

DOI: 10.4018/978-1-7998-3988-0.ch011

Americas and Europe; however, other factors combine two countries in the east that are Australia and New Zealand, also consider Western countries. Faith is also an essential identity as majorly countries have Christian populations. According to the World Population Review (2020), there are sixty-eight countries, mostly in Europe and the Americas, and eight out of the top 10 developed nations are from the same region. The political system in all western countries is democratic, and human rights and values are considered the top priority.

The West's CSR has been evolving since the 1950s: the famous American economist Howard Bowen published his book "Social Responsibilities of the Businessman" in 1953. The philosophy continues to grow, and in 1991, the CSR researcher Archie B Carroll published the famous CSR pyramid (see figure 1). The much followed Carroll's model by the corporation and academic researchers suggests that corporations be profitable while obeying the law and being ethically responsible for avoiding any harm. Finally, the corporates should be a good corporate citizens by conforming to philanthropic responsibilities.

Figure 1. Three Dimensional Carroll's Pyramid
(OpenStax CNX)

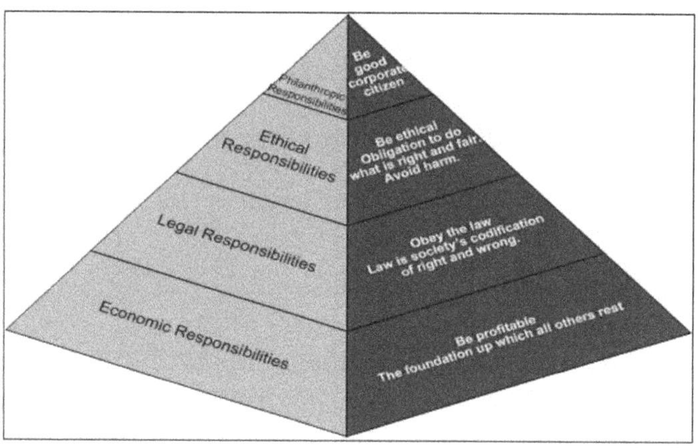

REGIONAL IMPACT ON CSR

The CSR practices in different countries differ due to values and attitudes in a business enterprise (Melovic et al., 2019). The industrial setting and country's culture strongly impact CSR practices (Aguilera et al., 2007;

Hay & Gray, 1974). The main reason is the behavior of top managers in the organization, which influences due to their country's culture (Hofstede, 2001) and organization (Schein, 1992) culture and their respective industry dynamics (Sirmon & Lane, 2004). Western countries are initiators of CSR and have influenced CSR practices, which are implemented differently in various business enterprises (Melovic et al., 2019). Many researchers believe that history, culture, traditions, and economy are the drivers for organizations and managers to perceive and implement CSR practices differently (Azmat & Zutshi, 2012; White, 2008). The CSR approach and methods in western countries differ from others due to below differences (Chen, 2016):

1. Western Citizen

The western citizen believes in self-development at a very early age and becomes independent. The governments are mainly welfare and support its citizen in this regard. It makes the children more independent, and they rely less on their parent's economic support. The environment shapes depending on their strength, which makes them enthusiasts and daring.

2. Education System

The education system bases on real-life experience, and teachers are more like coaches. The students are encouraged to be independent thinkers and also allows them to share their feeling and experiences. It inculcates soft power, which makes them better than their counterparts in other countries to appeal to others through their ideas. The culture promotes sports, outdoor recreations, and teamwork. At a very early age, they have freedom of expression, which gives them confidence. The phycological implications for the western education system on students as a society evolve to betterment.

3. Technology

Western countries are far ahead in technology. Over the years, governments and academia are continually stirring much-needed improvement as they allocate needed resources and human talents for the purpose. All significant inventions are shaping the twenty-first century invented in the west, and the trend continues. In all walks of life, western countries surpass others collectively. Aviation, military, medical, computers, and internet technologies are a few examples.

4. West Is Global Economic Power

The global economic systems control Western countries like the USA and the E.U. influence institutions like the IMF and the World bank. These institutions set international standards that other countries have to follow. The world currencies established for international trading are the U.S. and E.U. dollar. All major big corporations are in western countries and have a more significant contribution to the global economy. However, China is the only country that has surpassed all others, but the west stands tall collectively.

5. Political System

The democratic system prevails as a mechanism to govern the country and gives people the right to select what they think is appropriate. The legislation is done collectively but is a rigorous process, unlike other systems. However, democracy guarantees an individual citizen's rights from any religion, race, or creed. Western countries have separated state and church; thus, religion does not influence government working. However, many counter critics suggest that even with the separation influence of religion still exists. The western countries mostly following the Christian faith, which propagates the most extraordinary form of love between God and men is to help other people (Britannica, 2016). The propagation of charity for the poor is why many western countries fund developing and underdeveloped countries for medical and food supplies.

CSR PRACTICES IN WESTERN COUNTRIES

CSR is an integral part of the business in western countries, and its philosophy overrides all business strategies. The CSR in the west is not merely superficial charity events and donations for branding or media gimmick but also a business mission. The business organization can create differentiation through price and quality of the product and pay due attention to public relations and brand perception. Western consumers are critical about the products, and the sustainable business practice surrounds its production. Besides having a competitive advantage of having CSR, it also serves to hunt potential human resources for the company.

A relatable example is the "Discovery Education" collaboration with "3M" to run a mentorship program called "Young Scientist Challenge" during summers (Young Scientist Lab, 2020). The mentorship program targets students of 5th to 8th grade in the USA. The practices that corporates adopt are versatile in nature; an example of Western companies' CSR practices from 2010 to 2018 is in the table 1.

Table 1. CSR practices of Western corporates from 2010 to 2018

Year	Country	Company	CSR Practice
2018	USA	Abercrombie and Fitch	Health support for children
2017	France	Twitter	Support for press freedom
2016	USA	IBM	Provide computing for cancer projects
2015	France	Intermache Supermarket	Food waste management and its awareness
2012	Germany	Heinz and Ford	Educate and promote sustainability
2011	Canada	XEROX	Medical research and community welfare
2010	USA	Levi's	Supporting indigenous industry and communities

The most critical issue for western countries is global environmental pollution and its management. The pressure remains for all companies, even for those who outsource their manufacturing in developing countries. Apple, a U.S. cellular giant, has to faced embarrassment for keeping a good number of employees on the contractual contract in India (BBC News, 2014). Similarly, H&M, a Swedish fashion giant, faced similar media backlash when it did not pay fair labor wages in four sourcing countries (Reuters, 2018). In Germany, car manufacturers faced public pressure due to diesel engines' carbon emission, demanding a ban on their production. In Germany, BMW started its CSR activities revolving around greener production to produce environmentally-friendly engines. BMW claims that the car engines manufactured have reduced 40% carbon emission since 1990s and produce one hundred and forty six thousand electric cars to reduce further (BMW, 2020). The environmental-sensitive companies in western countries have high financial performance (Sharma, 2019).

The western corporates also use empathy and center their CSR activities by elevating marginalized communities. An example of people-powered CSR practice is a U.K. consortium of twenty-seven mining companies that donated an amount of USD 315 million for Covid-19 affected areas in Africa, the

Americas, and Australia (Clift & Court, 2020). Such CSR practices build public opinion in favor of corporates due to their compassionate corporate outlook. Western corporations utilize every medium to disclose their CSR practices, especially the reliance on social media. The ALS Association in 2013 started the "Ice Bucket Challenge," which got much public support. The campaign target is to raise funds for medical research. The ALS Association increased USD 2.8 million in 2013 and USD 100 million in 2014 after the challenge got viral on social media (Diamond, 2014).

Figure 2. Report on H&M's controversial advertisement
(Samantha West, 2018)

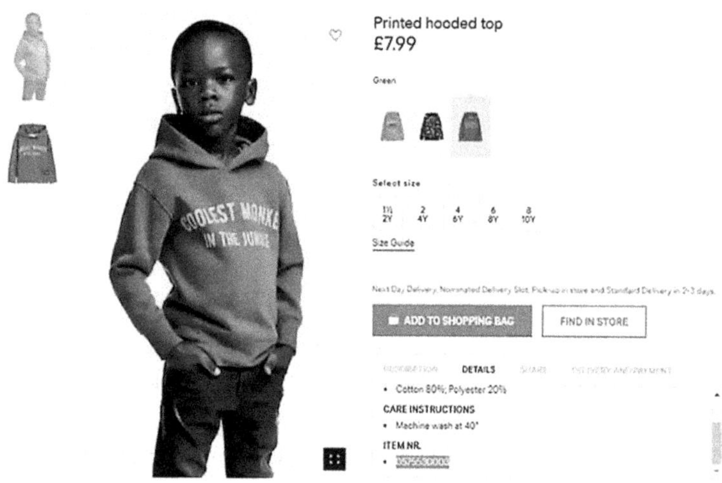

Clothing giant H&M apologized on Jan. 8 and removed this advertising image from its website.

The CSR practices and campaigns widely appraise in western countries and, if diligently done, could yield the desired benefit. High appreciation in the west's society is because of public awareness of CSR and collective consciousness on corporates' modus operandi. Thus, the consciousness translates to demand corporates in western countries to be ethically responsible towards all stakeholders in their society. The public vigilance and uproar on defaulting corporates are easy, affordable, and efficient due to social media and the internet. The Swedish retailer H&M (see fig) and soft drink Pepsi faced a similar backlash on social media when their marketing campaigns tinted racism. The citizen demanded a public apology by H&M (Olsen,

2018) and Pepsi (Smith, 2017); the companies have to remove the content and publicly apologized (see figure 2).

The legal implications for corporates failing on CSR have severe consequences in western countries. The lawsuits in case of carelessness in developing the product could end up in USD millions and billions. Regarding the environmental damages, Exxon Mobil has to sustain USD 3.2 billion for cleanups and restoration for oil spills in Alaska, the USA, in the year 1989 (HISTORY, 2018). In 2019, John & Johnson had to recall thousands of talcum bottles from shelves when the USA federal drug authority (FDA) found traces of asbestos in the sample. The multibillion-dollar pharma corporation has to pay billions of USD when the state jury found them guilty. The corporation still faces 20,000 talcum powder suits till 2020 (DRUG WATCH, 2020). Besides healthcare and environment, the western citizens and governments are sensitive about consumer data and its privacy. American social media giant FACEBOOK in 2018 has faced public and government scrutiny due to improper handling of consumer data (Abbruzzese & Boyce, 2018). Again, the social media giant came under fire: the Federal Trade Commission of USA (FTC) file sued against the corporation for illegally monopolizing social media. The FTC claims that FACEBOOK has strategically bought other social media companies like Instagram in 2012 and What's App in 2014 (Lordan, 2020).

The USA and Europe are role models for CSR practices worldwide. In Europe, the United Kingdom ranks on top. The corporation in the countries grasped the understanding that businesses have to engage with practices for society's wellbeing (Soh et al., 2014). The USA was the second-largest economy globally, with a GDP of USD twenty-one trillion in 2019 (BEA, 2020), and UK GDP stands at two trillion British pounds (Statista, 2020). CSR disclosure is not compulsory as per law in the USA; however, it regulates such disclosure in the U.K. (Bhatia & Makkar, 2019). A large number of companies in the USA disclose their CSR practices and their results to the public. There is minimal government interference in economic activities. However, societal demands, brand image, and shareholders; the disclosure becomes inevitable. Since 2000, U.K. appoints a minister for CSR and have many environmental reporting standards like "ACCA" (Association of Chartered Certified Accountants) and the formation of social and ecological research bodies as "BITC" (Business In The Community) and "ISEA" (Institute of Social and Ethical Accountability). The country has given due consideration to climate and in 2008 decreed the "Climate Change Act." The "Companies Act 2006" obligates corporations to provide CSR practices, and later in 2013, the law amended to disclose further information on greenhouse gas emissions by corporations. Below are examples of CSR practices in western countries:

1. Walt Disney

The USA entertainment giant commits to environmental and societal welfare. The company promoted volunteer services by donating free passes to a million people to exchange their work in charity programs. Every year, for 10,000 fatally sick children, the company, through its CSR program, fulfills their wishes in collaboration with "Make-A-Wish." The company is involved in wildlife and ecosystem protection since 1995. The total charity donations in the year 2019 stand at three hundred and thirty-eight million U.S. dollars. The company in environmental protection saved an area of three hundred fifteen million acres of land. The company, in terms of volunteer's donation per hour, donated six hundred thousand hours for welfare programs (Walt Disney, 2020) see figure 3

Figure 3. Disney Conservation on thewaltdisneycompany.com
(Disney Conservation, 2020)

2. Lego

Lego is a Danish company producing toys for children. In 2018, the company donated five hundred and twenty thousand LEGO toy sets. The company awarded one million USD for children affected by the Rohingya and Syrian wars. For environmental protection, the company is switching to plant-based plastics as raw material for their toys. Another effort in ecological protection is installing forty thousand solar panels and harnessing windmills for their factories, offices, and stores in Denmark (LEGO, 2020).

3. Natura Cosmetics

The western company hails from Brazil and produces cosmetic products. It is recognized to develop an environment-friendly economy for the amazon rainforest. The company collaborates with other indigenous businesses to use raw material from the rainforest for job creation. Natura is also a B Corp certified company, which is proof of its best CSR practices. The company's CSR practices revolved around forest conservation, waste management, environmental protection, and sustainable packaging for its products used globally (Natura, 2020).

4. Novo Nordisk

The Danish company ranks at the top in the pharmaceutical sector for its CSR practices. The most significant and commendable CSR practice is to produce economical and affordable life-saving insulin medicine. For environmental protection, they have invested in alternate energy in North Carolina in the USA to make operations sustainable from the year 2020. Further to use wind energy, they have collaborated with DONG energy for establishing wind farms (NOVO NORDISK, 2020). NOVO CSR practices exhibited in figure 4.

5. Microsoft

The U.S. software giant is CSR practices to empower underprivileged people globally by providing education, technology access, and rights protection. The company former CEO, Bill Gates, a known philanthropist, formed a separate NGO, Gates Foundation, to reduce global inequity. The foundation is also famous for polio disease eradication drives in developing and underdeveloped (Gates Foundation, 2020). The tech giant CSR practices supported twelve million youth in fifty-four countries by educating them in computer science. For minorities, the company donated three billion USD in 2018 as business assistance (Microsoft, 2020) see figure 5.

Figure 4. NOVO NORDISK CSR campaign on chronic diseases (NOVO NORDISK, 2020)

Figure 5. Microsoft disclosure for CSR practices (Microsoft, 2020)

6. Google

Another U.S. tech giant's CSR practices consider the workplace a serious matter. However, its media and public backlash due to its employee sacking questioning its diversity strategy are famously known as the anti-diversity memo scandal (Oakes, 2017). The CSR practices balanced, and the company came across safely through the rough ocean. The company propagates to provide equal opportunity offers multiple perks to all employees. It is trying to facilitate and hire people who served in the military, identifies as LGBTQ, or disable for office working environment. For environmental protection and deforestation, Google tracks farmlands and allows countries to use the data to protect lands (Goolge, 2020).

7. Dell Technologies

The famous U.S. desktop manufacturers have CSR practices that demand environmental preservation. It used fifty thousand U.S. tons of sustainable materials and recovered one million U.S. tons of used electronics in Dell's product. The company commits to globally spread STEM (Science, Technology, Engineering, and Mathematics) for education. Further, the company also provides solar-powered classrooms for girls. DELL provides Dell Genomic Data Analysis Platform to detect cancer and its treatment (Dell Technologies, 2020; Wood, 2020).

8. ING Group

The ING is a financial group of The Netherlands. The group provides financial services in retail sectors and is active in 40 countries worldwide. The group collaborates with UNICEF to impact the lives of one and half million children since 2005. The company claims to target one billion adolescents between the ages of 10-19 years. The company is vigilant of its carbon footprint and commits to reduce 80% carbon by the year 2022 and achieve a 90% reduction by the year 2030. For energy conservation, ING group CSR targets reduce 65% energy by 2030 compared to 2014. Water conservation targets are 26% till the year 2022 (Sustainability I ING, 2020).

9. Enel Group

The Enel Group is an Italian business that commits to three areas: sustainability, innovation, and available power. The CSR practices revolved around all three areas. The company uses renewable sources to produce clean energy, and the idea is to keep all operations of the power plant green. The company's CSR practices propagate "open innovation" to facilitate a cultural change for using mother earth resources. Open innovation seeks collaboration with academia, partners, customers, and employees to handle transitional energy challenges (Enel Group, 2020).

10. Algonquin Power and Utilities Group

The Canadian group ranks 10 of "Corporate Knights Global 100" for sustainability in the year 2020. For gender equality, the company is recognized by "Bloomberg Gender-Index." The company issues green bonds for investment in renewable energy. Algonquin Power CSR practices exhibited in figure 6.

Figure 6. CSR practices for the improvement of socio-economic factors (Algonquin, 2020)

11. Osram

The Dutch lighting company produces semiconductors, LEDs, and sensors for the automotive industry. The CSR practices envelop governance, environment, and society. The company has provided a hotline, "Tell Osram" for all employees and partners to inform of any compliance violations to tackle corruption. The company ensures CSR practices on every level of the company's supply chain. A balanced scorecard use for procurement activities. Qualified suppliers have to disclose CSR practices on queries and audits by external auditors. To provide consistent quality, the company each year qualifies for ISO 9001 management systems and IATF 16949. Other certification for CSR includes ISO 14001, ISO 45001, and ISO 50001. OSRAM CSR practices exhibited in figure 7.

Figure 7. CSR practices focusing on governance, environment, and society (OSRAM, 2020)

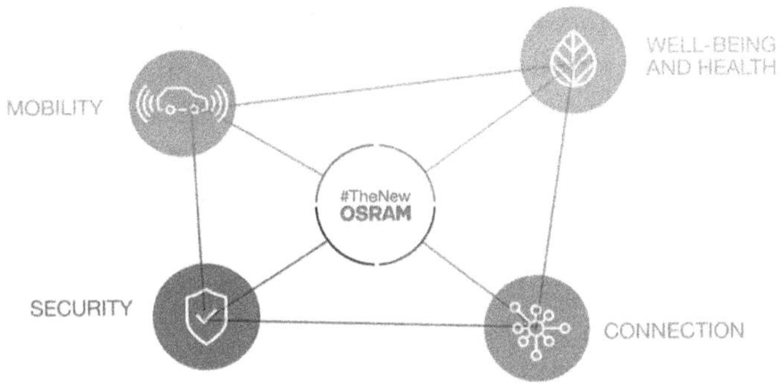

CSR PRACTICES OVERVIEW

An overview of CSR practices by western countries is shown in table 2.

Table 2. CSR practices by other western companies

Companies	CSR practices
Intel	CSR practices involve environmental protection for water conservation, which saved over sixty-four billion gallons of water.
Apple	CSR practices in corporate governance: in 2018 by hiring underrepresented members of the society.
Bosch	CSR practices involve assisting students to develop prosthetic hands to donate to the disabled individual.
Michelin	CSR practices to create awareness about tire treads and safety in children.
Canon	CSR practices involve collaboration with The Arbor Day Foundation since 2009 to plant over four hundred thousand trees.
Estee Lauder	CSR practices led to form an internal team called "The Responsible Sourcing Working Group" for supplier sustainability.
CISCO	CSR practices inculcated digital and entrepreneurial skills in two million students.
SONY	The company's CSR practices involve developing a 4K surgical microscope and free learning programs for the general public.
TOMS	The company donated sixty million shoes as CSR practices for children around the world.

(Fundura, 2020)

CONCLUSION

Due to their high per capita income, the CSR practices in Western countries involve more profound activities in societal impact than only charity to reduce poverty compared to companies in Asia. Every citizen in western countries connects to social media, enabling more vigilance on corporations and their business activities. CSR practices have realized many benefits and have transform corporations to impact society positively. The corporates are more aware of conserving the earth's resources and improve their operations; it could cost brand image and decrease revenue. The consumer buying decision in western countries bases on brand CSR practices. Western brands use CSR practices to connect with communities in their respective countries. The West's CSR practices do not depend on generous amounts but focus on corporations' initiatives and efforts. The small and medium companies in the West for CSR activities majorly target the community and environment in their vicinity, while big groups with financial muscle have a global reach. The CSR practices involve free education, environmental protection, economic development, women empowerment, equal work opportunity, disaster relief, and arts and culture promotion. As Ralph Waldo Emerson, "we do not inherit the earth from our ancestors; we borrow it from our children."

REFERENCES

Abbruzzese, J., & Boyce, J. (2018). *Facebook's 2018 timeline: Scandals, hearings and security bugs*. NBC News. https://www.nbcnews.com/tech/tech-news/facebook-s-2018-timeline-scandals-hearings-security-bugs-n952796

Aguilera, R. V., Rupp, D. E., Williams, C. A., & Ganapathi, J. (2007). Putting the S back in corporate social responsibility: A multilevel theory of social change in organizations. *Academy of Management Review*, *32*(3), 836–863. doi:10.5465/amr.2007.25275678

Algonquin. (2020). *Algonquin Power & Utilities Corp*. https://Algonquinpower. Com/Sustainability/. https://algonquinpower.com/sustainability/

Apple "failing to protect Chinese factory workers". (2014). BBC News. https://www.bbc.com/news/business-30532463

Azmat, F., & Zutshi, A. (2012). Influence of home-country and regulatory environment on CSR perceptions: The case of Sri Lankan immigrant entrepreneurs. *Thunderbird International Business Review*, *54*(1), 15–27. doi:10.1002/tie.21435

BEA. (2020). *Gross Domestic Product, Fourth Quarter and Year 2019 (Advance Estimate) | U.S. Bureau of Economic Analysis (BEA).* Bea.Gov. https://www.bea.gov/news/2020/gross-domestic-product-fourth-quarter-and-year-2019-advance-estimate

Bhatia, A., & Makkar, B. (2019). Csr disclosure in developing and developed countries: A comparative study. *Journal of Global Responsibility*, *11*(1), 1–26. doi:10.1108/JGR-04-2019-0043

BMW. (2020). *Sustainability at the BMW group*. BMW Group.

Bowen, H. R. (2013). *Social responsibilities of the businessman*. University of Iowa Press. doi:10.2307/j.ctt20q1w8f

Charity Britannica. (2016, September). *Encyclopedia Britannica*. https://www.britannica.com/topic/charity-Christian-concept

Chen, P.-W. (2016). *The factor lead differences Between Western and Eastern*. https://www.arcgis.com/apps/Cascade/index.html?appid=efda627156b84814ac19216dbe3ef3df

Clift, K., & Court, A. (2020, March). *COVID-19: How companies are responding*. World Economic Forum. https://www.weforum.org/agenda/2020/03/how-are-companies-responding-to-the-coronavirus-crisis-d15bed6137/

Corporate Social Responsibility and sustainable development in the global environment - Business Fundamentals - OpenStax CNX. (n.d.). Retrieved December 20, 2020, from https://cnx.org/contents/1ttgPM0x@4.3:rchi6FGQ@5/Corporate-Social-Responsibility-and-sustainable-development-in-the-global-environment

Dell Technologies. (2020). *Progress Made Real*. Dell Technologies. https://corporate.delltechnologies.com/en-us/social-impact.htm

Diamond, D. (2014). *The ALS Ice Bucket Challenge Has Raised $100 Million—And Counting*. Forbes. Com.

Drug Watch. (2020). *Johnson & Johnson – Products, Recalls, Lawsuits & Scandals*. Drughwatch.Com. https://www.drugwatch.com/manufacturers/johnson-and-johnson/

Enel Group. (2020). *Our commitment*. Https://Www.Enel.Com/Company/Our-Commitment. https://www.enel.com/company/our-commitment

Exxon Valdez Oil Spill. (2018). https://www.history.com/topics/1980s/exxon-valdez-oil-spill

Gates Foundation. (2020). *Foundation Fact Sheet - Bill & Melinda Gates Foundation*. https://www.gatesfoundation.org/Who-We-Are/General-Information/Foundation-Factsheet

Google. (2020). *Google Sustainability*. https://sustainability.google/.

Hay, R., & Gray, E. (1974). Social responsibilities of business managers. *Academy of Management Journal*, *17*(1), 135–143.

H&M accused of failing to ensure fair wages for global factory workers. (2018). *Reuters*. https://www.reuters.com/article/us-workers-garment-abuse-idUSKCN1M41GR

Hofstede, G. (2001). *Culture's consequences: Comparing values, behaviors, institutions and organizations across nations*. Sage publications.

LEGO. (2020). *Sustainability - About us - LEGO.com US*. https://www.lego.com/en-us/aboutus/sustainability/

Lordan, B. (2020, December). *FTC Sues Facebook for Illegal Monopolization | Federal Trade Commission*. Federal Trade Commission. https://www.ftc.gov/news-events/press-releases/2020/12/ftc-sues-facebook-illegal-monopolization

Melovic, B., Milovic, N., Backovic-Vulic, T., Dudic, B., & Bajzik, P. (2019). Attitudes and Perceptions of Employees toward Corporate Social Responsibility in Western Balkan Countries: Importance and Relevance for Sustainable Development. *Sustainability*, *11*(23), 6763. doi:10.3390u11236763

Microsoft. (2020). *Microsoft Corporate Social Responsibility - Microsoft CSR*. Microsoft. https://www.microsoft.com/en-us/corporate-responsibility

Natura. (2020). *Natura - Sustainable development*. https://www.naturabrasil.fr/fr-fr/nos-valeurs/developpement-durable

Novo Nordisk. (2020). *Sustainable business*. Https://Www.Novonordisk.Com/Sustainable-Business.Html. https://www.novonordisk.com/sustainable-business.html

Oakes, O. (2017). *Google engineer sacked over anti-diversity memo*. https://www.prweek.com/article/1441509/google-engineer-sacked-anti-diversity-memo

Olsen, J. M. (2018). After'monkey hoodie'scandal, H&M hires diversity leader. *USA Today*.

OSRAM. (2020). *Sustainability at OSRAM – OSRAM Group Website*. Https://Www.Osram-Group.Com/En/Sustainability. https://www.osram-group.com/en/sustainability

Schein, E. H. (1992). *Organizational culture and leadership. Jossey-Bass.*

Sharma, E. (2019). A review of corporate social responsibility in developed and developing nations. *Corporate Social Responsibility and Environmental Management*, *26*(4), 712–720. doi:10.1002/csr.1739

Sirmon, D. G., & Lane, P. J. (2004). A model of cultural differences and international alliance performance. *Journal of International Business Studies*, *35*(4), 306–319. doi:10.1057/palgrave.jibs.8400089

Smith, A. (2017, April). *Pepsi Pulls Controversial Kendall Jenner Ad After Outcry*. NBC News. https://www.nbcnews.com/news/nbcblk/pepsi-ad-kendall-jenner-echoes-black-lives-matter-sparks-anger-n742811

Soh, C., Kim, H. J., & Whang, T. (2014). Corporate social responsibility (CSR) implementation in South Korea: Lessons from American and British CSR policies. *Journal of International and Area Studies*, 99–118.

Statista. (2020). *UK: GDP in pounds 2000-2018*. https://www.statista.com/statistics/281744/gdp-of-the-united-kingdom/

Sustainability. (2020). *ING*. https://www.ing.com/Sustainability.htm

Walt Disney. (2020). *Social Responsibility*. The Walt Disney Company. https://thewaltdisneycompany.com/social-responsibility/

West, S. (2018, January). *H&M faced backlash over its 'monkey' sweatshirt ad. It isn't the company's only controversy.* The Washington Post. https://www.washingtonpost.com/news/arts-and-entertainment/wp/2018/01/19/hm-faced-backlash-over-its-monkey-sweatshirt-ad-it-isnt-the-companys-only-controversy/

Western Countries 2020. (2020). *World Population Review.* https://worldpopulationreview.com/country-rankings/western-countries

White, A. L. (2008). *Culture matters: The soul of CSR in emerging economies.* Business for Social Responsibility.

Wood, M. (2020). *The World's Most Socially Responsible Companies.* Fundera. https://www.fundera.com/blog/corporate-social-responsibility

Young Scientist Lab. (2020). *3M.* https://www.youngscientistlab.com/challenge/about

Chapter 12
Socioeconomic Benefits of CSR

ABSTRACT

Businesses exist for the sole purpose of earning profit. The activities performed during business operations affects society and the economy. The effects depend on the resources used and the type of activity performed by the business organization. Due to public awareness and the United Nations 2030 sustainable vision, the society demands the organization act as a responsible corporate citizen. To ensure its responsibility, organizations strategize CSR initiatives and practices. The CSR practices compensate organizational, operational activities through which it earns premiums by consuming resources. The practices thus remove any doubt of its exploitation of resources. CSR practices and initiatives help to portrays the human side of the corporation. Companies, by their CSR practices, benefit the effected communities, which are affected by their business activities. Society uses the socioeconomic lens to gauge the impact of the company's CSR practice.

INTRODUCTION

Socioeconomic is a broad concept that envelops the interaction of society and economics. The traditional economic view states that business corporations exist to earn profits for stakeholders. The idea does not take into account the consequences of corporate actions. After the second world war, the world saw an increase in demand as the western lifestyle spread worldwide. The other reason for the high demand is the increase in population. The population boomed due to medical science advancements and improved birth rates; the

DOI: 10.4018/978-1-7998-3988-0.ch012

percentage remains high in developing countries. Globalization started after the second world war as countries united on a platform known as the United Nations. The countries in the west and east became part of supply chains to satisfy global consumption demands. Economies prosper life standard improved.

The growing demand mounts pressure on corporations to increase production and better manufacturing and processing efficiencies. It increases pressure for higher raw materials and product demand. The raw material comprises the earth's minerals, elements, rocks, water, and agriproducts mixture. Many of the materials are non-renewable in nature and are finite in quantity. The more products produced will result in the depletion of natural resources. Also, the value-adding raw material for consumption has particular impacts on the environment and economy globally. The most pronounced effect of the processing and consumption of raw materials is pollution. The pollution is present in the air, land, rivers, and sea. The contamination causes severity to all forms of life on earth, and science has proved its ill effects. It all translates to affect human beings and the environment needed for its habitat.

The economic fallout is another dimension that should not ignore during production. The cost of extraction and excavation is high and uses a lot of financial resources. The other significant cost is the health-cost of labor and the people in society. Further, the economic cost to eradicate pollution also adds to the toll. With all these ill-effects of high consumption and production due to globalization, economic disparity has grown. For instance, the western countries, due to high purchase power, are pushing growing economies to reduce production costs. The labor mainly absorbs the pressure in the developing economies. The disparity in income in the economies is due to the high supply of labor and low labor efficiency rate compared to their counterpart in the western countries. Health-related costs and death rates remain high as industries emit high pollution, mainly in Asian developing countries. Besides pollution, wealth in developing countries is more shrinking to fewer hands. Many SMEs in developing countries view organizational activities with traditional economic views, focusing on earning profits and improving their bottom line. They lack the respect of other stakeholders in which their organization exists.

SOCIETY ACTIONS AND UNITED NATIONS SUSTAINABILITY PLANS

Societies worldwide are becoming aware of the organizational consequences and effects of their activities on the environment. History remains evident of such implications, which haunts nations in the future. The most appropriate example is the British East India Company, which in the 1800s robbed the Indian sub-continent of its riches during the process (Britannica, 2020; Dalrymple, 2015). Societies in the west became aware of their rights and started asking corporations motives and held them accountable. The exploitation of western corporations still exists in underdeveloped countries in Africa and Asia. However, to avoid media backlash, corporations invest in public relations. The poor conditions, especially in the mining industry, prevail with poor labor standards health conditions. United Nations in 2015 adopted seventeen sustainable plans for the year 2030 for all countries to follow (see figure 1).

Figure 1. United Nations 17 sustainable goals to transform the World (United Nations, 2015)

However, many countries started sustainable strategies earlier. In the west, European Union launched its sustainability program in Gothenburg year 2001 and renewed it in 2006 (Eurostat, 2009). Later in 2013-14, India amended its business laws for implementing sustainability. After U.N. sustainable (2015) goals agreed by the general assembly, many consortiums like ASEAN

(Association of Southeast Asian Nations) and commonwealth nations started working for vision 2030. Regions like the Middle East and Africa collaborated with U.S. environmental protection agency to trot towards the sustainable goals 2030 set by U.N.

The U.N. sustainable goals set a momentum for every country, and it translates to societies via education institutions by incorporating subjects of corporate governance and environmental protection. Social media is an important driver to spread the importance of sustainability and its effect on our mother planet. The public awareness created in the process is transforming societies into more responsible citizens of the world. The same viewpoint transcends to organizations, but the momentum is slow and needs government and regulator authorities' attention in developing countries. The governments feel shy about intervening in business activities as this might slow the economic pace, which is a dire need of developing countries. Many such countries do not have the financial muscle to support organizations for sustainable goals, significantly affecting the environment. The organizations are only motivated to act up sustainable goals by providing initiatives by governments. Pakistan's green economy initiative encourages corporations by tax rebates and other incentives (Waheed, 2019).

SOCIOECONOMIC BENEFITS

CSR practices' socioeconomic benefits are two folds, one impacts the environment, and the other is economical. Hence, the benefits brought forward from the seventeen U.N. sustainable goals for 2030 (United Nations, 2015). Responsible corporates are helping societies to achieve the goals by applying the CSR practices, which yields the benefits that are as under:

1. Quality Education

Education is pivotal and an essential driver for societies to become better. It provides consciousness for people to grow and make their life better (Joseph, 2012). The CSR practices around the globe are helping deserving communities to strive for quality education. According to Fernandes (2020), Indian corporations have invested huge sums as CSR initiatives for education support. Below in table 1 presented is the data of Indian corporations for the educational endeavor.

Table 1. CSR practices for education incentives in India

Organization	CSR Practice
Reliance Industries	**USD 71.6 million:** The practice impacted providing education to two hundred thousand children in the country. Also, the practice provided scholarships to twelve thousand plus students for graduation in the field of their choice.
NTPC	**USD. 18 million:** The practices provide seven thousand and three hundred secondary schools to graduate level.
Wipro	**USD 17 million:** The practices support schools and colleges for I.T. technical support. Also, the company supports the needy student with scholarships
Infosys	**USD 13 Million:** The practice initiates to reduce the number of dropout students. The dropouts are mainly because of a lack of family income. The company also collaborates with "Avanti Fellows," supporting forty thousand students for the past eight years to provide quality education.
Mahanadi Coalfields Limited	**USD 9.4 million:** CSR practices support female education.
Tata Steel	**USD 9 million:** The CSR practice is responsible for launching one thousand school projects since 2015. The impact of the initiative helped eight thousand children to get a quality education.
Hindustan Zinc	**USD 7 Million:** The CSR practice impacts sixty thousand children in the country. Also, the mining company in the operating vicinity provides a full scholarship to girls for education purposes.
HDFC Bank	**USD 6.5 million:** The bank CSR practice provides quality education to eighteen thousand children
Mahindra and Mahindra	**USD 5.5 million:** The CSR practice to support education is thirty years old. The company provides vocational training and scholarships. The practice impacts a total of nineteen thousand students girls to receive a quality education.

2. Gender Equality

Gender equality is a notion that suggests females get equal opportunity in every walk of life. According to INED (2020) statistics, the female population is approximately equal to men globally; the ratio stands at 102 men and 100 female. Over the years, females have faced discrimination in organizations. The USA, which has the adjective of a developed country, does have a salary disparity between men and women. The men's salary is 19% higher than its gender counterpart (Payscale, 2020). The other discrepancy they face is for the job opportunity. One of the reasons is that the organization keeps in mind the maternity leaves they would seek during pregnancy (Elting Liz, 2018).

Gender inequality, if reduced, can benefit society in many ways. Inequality gives rise to violence against females, which occurs due to society condoning the behavior. The violence is due to male relationships based on aggression and no respect for their counterparts. To mitigate such societal horrors, the promotion of gender equality is inevitable. An able female can contribute in every walk of life if given equal opportunity, mostly since the impact remains high in the economy. The female contribution can increase a country's GDPs and support economic development (Klasen, 2018). In some developing countries, females having tertiary education do not become part of economic activities due to gender inequality in society. The CSR practices for gender equality ensures that female candidate seeking job or employee of the company gets an equal opportunity like their male counterparts. Females could support their families for a better livelihood. The increase in family income would help children to get quality education and health facilities. In developing and underdeveloped countries, the CSR practice for gender equality would make females independent and stand for their rights in any injustice in society and live happily (United Nations, 2020).

3. Clean Water and Sanitation

Clean water and sanitation are essential for a better life and to reduce any health-related problems. Due to the non-availability of clean water and miss managed sanitation, the rampant grave health issue is diarrhea (WHO, 2017). According to WHO (2020), diarrhea ranks at eight globally for the leading cause of death and ranks third for communicable disease in 2019 (see figure 2).

The trend has increased since 2017; the most common victim of the disease are the children under age 5 (see figure 3: age-wise and year-wise death chart globally) (WHO, 2017).

The most affected regions from the disease are developing countries, and one of the significant causes is no accessibility to clean water (Troeger et al., 2018). Besides deaths, the unproductivity in USD is two hundred and sixty billion every year (UNF, 2017). Clean water and sanitation are not only a threat to life but also burdens the economy.

Figure 2. Leading reason for global death in the year 2019
(WHO, 2020)

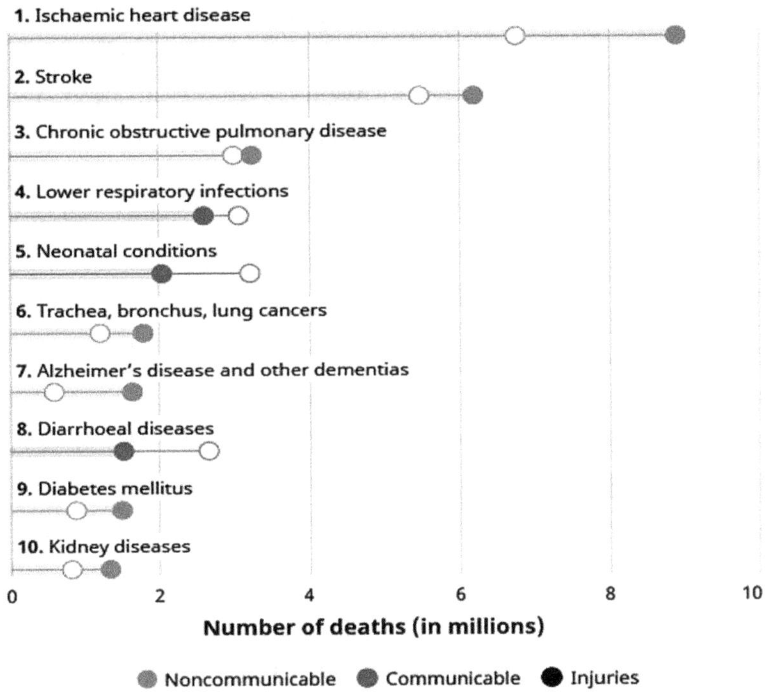

Figure 3. Diarrhea deaths by age since 1990
(IHME, 2017)

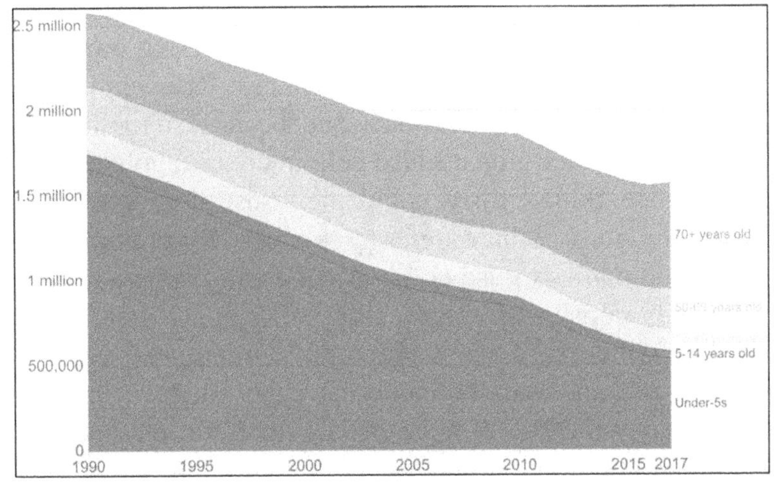

Many manufacturing organizations are either bound by government regulatory bodies or customers for compliance. ISO 14001 (2015) is an environmental management compliances guide companies for waste management. By following ISO 14001, organizations remain compliant to avoid discharge any affluents harming water resources in their operational area. Due to CSR practices, companies are always looking for a modern method in which water usage minimizes. Besides water consumption, many companies provide clean water facilities in their operational vicinity in developing and underdeveloped countries by installing water filter plants. The initiative makes available clean water to drink and wash for hygiene purposes. The CSR also provides sanitation facilities for deserving communities. The sanitation facilities ensure to reduce any related health problem. ITC limited build nine thousand household toilets and twenty-four thousand sanitary units in fourteen states in India. Both CSR practices of clean water and sanitation from companies help the masses to ensure a healthy life and less burden on health care systems.

4. Affordable and Clean Energy

Energy is an essential aspect of our modern lives in the 21st century. All technology around us needs electricity as energy. Energy is crucial in every walk of life; access is vital for students to get an education and start jobs. It is essential to run hospitals and appliances for medical assistance. Energy plays a pivotal role in humanity as it faces many challenges and transformations in the 21st century. The primary source of producing energy is hydropower, fossil fuel, and nuclear fuel. The methods are expensive in cost, and besides hydropower, the latter emits pollution. The benefits of renewable energy are many, but the most prominent is reducing greenhouse gas emissions in the environment, which is a significant cause of increased temperature globally. It helps reduce the burden on countries exchequer because of fossil fuel imports. The new renewable power projects also help in creating jobs for society.

The CSR practices initiated drive companies to use more renewable sources for affordable and zero pollution energy sources. Solar and wind energy used by many companies to use cheaper and clean energy. Also, products designed for daily consumption are energy efficient. Prime examples are air conditioners, which use for maintaining room temperature. The energy consumption is high, and now companies have designed the appliance using inverter technology, which is 70% more efficient than conventional technology

(Changhong RUBA, 2020). The utility companies in developing countries also create awareness by their CSR initiatives to reduce waste. Solar, wind farms, and sea currents are the latest trends to produce affordable and clean energy (World Nuclear Association, 2020). Hydropower is initially very expensive. The projects take a longer time to complete.

5. Reduced Inequalities

Social class differences have existed since the early ages of civilization. A group of few have all, and the rest many have none. Some inequalities arise due to family lineage and social class; however, the right to education, social status, and to earn wealth should not be denied (United Nations, 2015). Many companies have CSR practices that provide an opportunity to the disabled, persecuted communities, from all races and creed, and destitute of society. Educational supports and scholarships by companies reduce inequalities by inculcating the skill set required in the current era. Also, companies make sure that all employees get equal opportunities and none remains discriminated against through their corporate governance. Reduced inequality also entails modern slavery, a term used to exploit developing countries and communities to buy goods at low rates to sell in developed countries (Wool And The Gang, 2020).

6. Responsible Consumption and Production

Responsible consumption and production is an idea to separate economic growth from ecological degradation and efficient use of resources to promote sustainability. The rate of consumption globally is higher in contrast to the percentage of available planet's capacity, and to dire the situation, the wastages and pollution increases during the process. The whole idea depends on using resources efficiently and effectively for economic gains. The ecological and environmental degradation is kept minimum to avoid pollution during the complete life cycle. The responsible consumption starts at the initialization phase while designing the product, which will enable sustainable produce for consumers following the disposal of waste and recycling of products.

The researchers, academians, and corporations are paying much attention in this direction. "Cradle to Cradle" and "Circular economy" are good examples of such initiatives. Much of the virgin products consume high energy and depletes raw material (Recycle Nation, 2020). Societies worldwide are striving to reduce natural resource consumption by avoiding wastage in the production process and consumption. To make responsible consumer companies for their CSR practices, encourage recycling, reuse, and discourage irresponsible consumption by advertisements and marketing campaigns. The manufacturing process reinvented to reduce the usage consumption of natural raw material; an example is the amount of water used in textile. In the same industry, researchers invent new fibers extracted by processing used plastics to make yarn and cloths (Nolan, 2019). Drip irrigation is another technique in the agri-sector to minimize the usage and wastage of water. For internal purposes, as CSR practices, many companies use signboards in washrooms and toilets to remind users to avoid water wastage. In offices, signboards are visible to remind employees to switch off any unwanted light source, computers, or appliances to save energy for consumption. The governments are becoming instrumental in propagating citizen to be responsible consumption and regulating corporations to be responsible producer and produce sustainable products.

Figure 4. Benefits for climate action
(CCA Coalition, 2021)

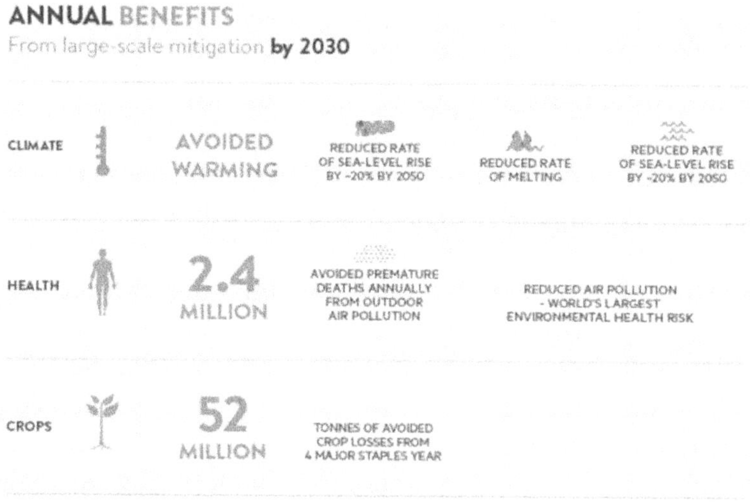

7. Climate Action

Climate action needs global attention; it has adverse socioeconomic effects. The delay in mitigating CO2 emissions and pollution increases global warming, higher sea levels, risk in food supply chain disruption, and deteriorating public health. Climate action efforts would drastically improve the health sector's situation, food supply chain, and, most importantly, global weather (see figure 4 for benefits). According to Mountford et al. (2018), an estimated USD 3 trillion value economic benefit can realize by 2030 due to climate action.

CSR practices by corporations for climate action are essential branding and marketing strategy. Many corporations disclose their initiatives to reduce greenhouse gas emissions and carbon footprint because of their CSR practices. The industry encompasses all infrastructure: offices or manufacturing facilities. Reduction in energy usage is another CSR practice that positively affects climate and is considered a significant action by society. As discussed earlier, renewable energy use also significantly impacts the world climate as it reduces global temperature. Companies worldwide are upgrading obsolete production systems to minimize wastage; this is now possible because of CSR practices and improved cost-efficiency. Companies are also relying upon greener infrastructure by using much of the daylight; the infrastructure constructs to utilize sunlight for long hours, thus reducing energy consumption.

Corporations for climate actions implement the green supply chain concept, where sustainable suppliers become partners to impact climate. The supply chain ecological footprint helps increase the positive impact on the ecosystem. Another commendable step due to CSR practice is digitization by many organizations, which positively affects the environment. Paperless documentation decreases the rate of deforestation. It also avoids the waste management corporations have to do as regulation, especially in countries and regions where the waste management is regulated by law: like in the United Kingdom. Climate action has been taken very seriously by developed countries; however, corporations in developing and underdeveloped countries still lack in this direction. CSR practices by corporations in particular economies need improvement as such practices to implement needs government support and incentives.

8. Life Below Water

The U.N. sets fourteen targets sustainable initiatives for "Life Below Water" (Global Goals, 2020). The targets cover all aspects ranging from marine life to ecosystem protection. Corporations' CSR practices ensure that no effluents from business activities harm the marine ecosystem and marine life. The track of carbon footprint by corporations provides to reduce ocean acidification. Nutrient pollutions is also a big problem as it reduces the oxygen level in the sea. The main contributor to nutrient pollution is nitrogen and phosphorus, used as fertilizers in the agri-industry (EPA, 2020). Researchers and corporations are trying to find new methods to increase productivity by organic farming and thus less reliance on the two chemicals, which causes harm to marine life. The latest technique is also incorporated in modern agriculture to reduce drainages in China for rice paddy (Zhang et al., 2011). The commendable CSR practices include corporate vigilance about the effluents, waste management systems, and usage of chemicals which do not harm marine life (Toprak & Anis, 2017).

9. Partnership for Sustainable Goals

CSR practices for partnering to achieve sustainable goals have enabled the corporation and government to collaborate for better ways and sustainable goals. Examples of business enterprises and NGOs are now a reality. Public and private collaborations are also taking place to achieve sustainability. Sustainable development Goals Fund (SDGF, 2020) is the collaboration of public and private partnerships. Business leaders worldwide work as an advisory board to achieve the goals set by the United Nations. The partnership helps in the capacity building and distribution of wealth. Similar examples are of hospitals in collaboration with World Health Organizations are evident of such associations. In Pakistan, national programs like malaria, tuberculosis, and HIV manage by a partnership between the government, hospitals, and NGOs: the project funded by the World Bank, UNDP, WHO, and the Government of Pakistan (Ahmed & Nisar, 2010)

Figure 5. A Pakistani e-commerce website to provide food for the needy (Tohfay.com, 2020).

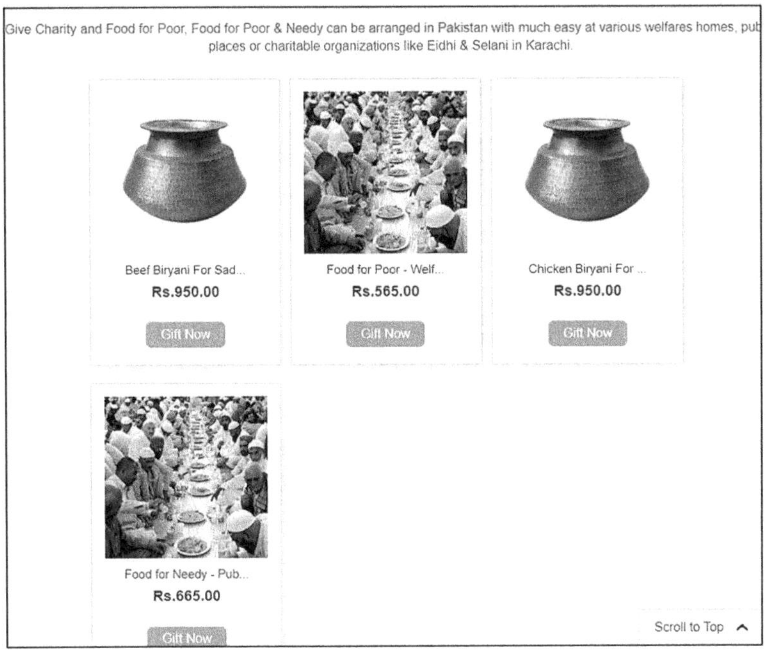

10. No Poverty and Zero Hunger

In developing and underdeveloped countries, poverty and hunger are issues faced by deprived communities. The government of particular countries lacks funds and financial muscle to overcome the problem. The problem also exists due to a low food supply chain and lack of opportunities to uplift masses above the poverty line standardized by countries. The poverty line calculates the cost of adult sustenance of all essential items in a particular country; in Pakistan, it is USD 1.90 earning per day (Kenton, 2020). The corporations in developing and underdeveloped country's CSR practices target poverty reduction and zero hunger initiatives. Companies like Xerox, Toms, and Microsoft (Bill & Amanda Gates) have CSR practices contributing to poverty reduction for underprivileged communities worldwide (Dogmazer, 2018). Tata Steel, an Indian steel giant, has been providing resources needed by villages in India. The resources include fertilizers, pesticides, water wells, and pumps for agriculture support (Prasad & Kumar, 2013). The contributions help the community's destitute, as provided resources and funds help to earn a livelihood. It reduces the burden on the economy and also helps in job creation.

The companies are also actively participating in Zero hunger through CSR initiatives. The "Dehli Food banking" is a step initiated by Response-Net in India. The Foodbank is responsible for feeding seventeen thousand children across thirteen states in the country. Companies ask the customer for donations as CSR practice; the company provides services to feed the community's needy. Toofay.com is an e-commerce company in Pakistan that has dedicated a full page for the purpose, and the prices are mention in Pakistani Rupee (see figure 5).

NGOs and welfare organizations are also actively participating for the purpose. "Chipa Welfare Association" is a charity organization that provides food for labor and needy people in Pakistan's major cities. Companies in Pakistan have volunteer programs run under CSR practices for the corporate employees to donate a day salary for such initiatives. An example is the Agha Khan University Hospital, and Unilever Pakistan donated two million Pak rupees (OICCI, 2020). Many such donations collect with employee's approval for national causes and calamities.

CONCLUSION

Corporations worldwide have practices that have impacts positively on socioeconomic. It creates a positive image and customer loyalty. CSR practices, along with corporate governance, would allow companies to connect with society. CSR is a strategic decision, and businesses should decide on the approach diligently. Money spends on CSR practices should not only satisfy regulations but should create sustainability. Smart companies are prudent in CSR disclosure as it betters their brand image in society. An analysis is essential; CSR practices must create value for society and the business. The value created for the community will have socioeconomic benefits, while companies will realize a lower cost of business, efficiency, revenue, brand image, and customer loyalty. The contributions made by companies will help the world achieve the U.N. sustainable goals of 2030.

REFERENCES

Ahmed, F., & Nisar, N. (2010). Public-private partnership scenario in the health care system of Pakistan. *EMHJ-Eastern Mediterranean Health Journal*, *16*(8), 910–912. doi:10.26719/2010.16.8.910 PMID:21469575

Britannica. (2020). *East India Company | Definition, History, & Facts*. Britannica. https://www.britannica.com/topic/East-India-Company

Changhong Ruba. (2020). *1.5 Ton - Heat & Cool, DC inverter - SDH-18OW - Air Conditioner*. https://www.changhongruba.com.pk/product/15-ton-heat-cool-dc-inverter-sdh-18ow-air-conditioner

Climate & Clean Air Coalition. (2021). Why we need to act now. *Climate & Clean Air Coalition*. https://www.ccacoalition.org/en/content/why-we-need-act-now

Dalrymple, W. (2015). *The East India Company: The original corporate raiders*. The Guardian. https://www.theguardian.com/world/2015/mar/04/east-india-company-original-corporate-raiders

Dogmazer, O. (2018). *Examples of the Private Sector Fighting Poverty*. Borgen Project. https://borgenproject.org/private-sector-fighting-poverty-examples/

Elting, L. (2018). Why Pregnancy Discrimination Still Matters. *Forbes*. https://www.forbes.com/sites/lizelting/2018/10/30/why-pregnancy-discrimination-still-matters/?sh=5115fb2163c1

EPA. (2020). *Sources and Solutions | Nutrient Pollution*. USA EPA. https://www.epa.gov/nutrientpollution/sources-and-solutions

eurostat. (2009). *Sustainable development in the European Union - 2009 monitoring report on the EU sustainable development strategy - Products Statistical Books - Eurostat*. https://ec.europa.eu/eurostat/web/products-statistical-books/-/KS-78-09-865

Fernandes, K. (2020). Companies Funding CSR In Education. *The CSR Journal*. https://thecsrjournal.in/top-10-companies-funding-csr-education/

Global Goals. (2020). *Goal 14: Life Below Water*. The Global Goals. https://www.globalgoals.org/14-life-below-water

INED. (2020). *Are there more men or more women in the world? - FAQs - Demographic fact sheets - Ined - Institut national d'études démographiques*. INED. https://www.ined.fr/en/everything_about_population/demographic-facts-sheets/faq/more-men-or-women-in-the-world/

Institute for Health Metrics and Evaluation. (2019). Global Burden of Disease Collaborative Network. Global Burden of Disease Study 2016 (GBD 2016) Results. Institute for Health Metrics and Evaluation.

ISO. (2020). *ISO - ISO 14000 family — Environmental management*. ISO Org. https://www.iso.org/iso-14001-environmental-management.html

Joseph, J. (2012). How the schooling environment shapes the consciousness of scholars towards peace and war. *Procedia: Social and Behavioral Sciences*, *55*, 697–706.

Kenton, W. (2020). *International Poverty Line Definition*. Investopedia.Com. https://www.investopedia.com/terms/i/international-poverty-line.asp

Klasen, S. (2018). The Impact of Gender Inequality on Economic Performance in Developing Countries. *Annual Review of Resource Economics*, *10*(1), 279–298. https://doi.org/10.1146/annurev-resource-100517-023429

Mountford, H., Corfee-Morlot, J., McGregor, M., Banaji, F., Bhattacharya, A., Brand, J., Colenbrander, S., & Stern, N. (2018). *Unlocking the inclusive growth story of the 21st Century: accelerating climate action in urgent times*. Academic Press.

Nolan, G. (2019). *Wool and the Gang launch eco-yarn made from recycled plastic bottles - British Plastics and Rubber*. British Plastics Co UK. https://www.britishplastics.co.uk/materials/wool-and-the-gang-launch-eco-yarn-made-from-recycled-plastic/

OICCI. (2020). *Combining the Power of Social Responsibility Corporate Social Responsibility Report 2018-19*. OICCI.Org. https://www.oicci.org/wp-content/uploads/2020/07/OICCI-CSR-18-19.pdf

Payscale. (2020). *Gender Pay Gap Statistics for 2020*. Payscale.Com. https://www.payscale.com/data/gender-pay-gap

Prasad, A., & Kumar, S. (2013). Poverty Alleviation through Corporate Social Responsibility Policy: An Ethnographic Study of Tata Steel Initiatives in a Jamshedpur Village. *Jharkhand Journal of Development and Management Studies*, *11*(2), 5297–5323.

Recycle Nation. (2020). *Virgin Materials – RecycleNation*. Https://Recyclenation.Com/. https://recyclenation.com/green-glossary/virgin-materials/

SDGF. (2020). *Public private partnerships*. Sustainable Development Goals Fund. https://www.sdgfund.org/public-private-partnerships

Tohfay.com. (2020). *Tohfay.com | Charity and Food for Poor*. Tohfay.Com Food for Poor. https://www.tohfay.com/food-for-poor-c-1200.html

Toprak, T., & Anis, P. (2017). Textile industry's environmental effects and approaching cleaner production and sustainability, an overview. *J Textile Eng Fashion Technol*, *2*(4), 429–442.

Troeger, C., Blacker, B. F., Khalil, I. A., Rao, P. C., Cao, S., Zimsen, S. R. M., Albertson, S. B., Stanaway, J. D., Deshpande, A., & Abebe, Z. (2018). Estimates of the global, regional, and national morbidity, mortality, and aetiologies of diarrhoea in 195 countries: A systematic analysis for the Global Burden of Disease Study 2016. *The Lancet. Infectious Diseases*, *18*(11), 1211–1228.

UNF. (2017). *Tapping the Benefits of Clean Water, Sanitation, and Hygiene*. United Nations Foundation. https://unfoundation.org/blog/post/tapping-benefits-clean-water-sanitation-hygiene-achieve-sustainable-development-goals/

United Nation. (2015). *Concepts of Inequality Development Issues No. 1*. United Nation. https://www.un.org/en/development/desa/policy/wess/wess_dev_issues/dsp_policy_01.pdf

United Nations. (2015, September). *Envision 2030: 17 goals to transform the world for persons with disabilities*. https://www.un.org/development/desa/disabilities/envision2030.html

United Nations. (2020). *Gender Equality*. United Nations. https://www.un.org/en/sections/issues-depth/gender-equality/

Waheed, A. (2019). *National Responsibility Framework for Sustainable Development: Responsible Business Framework integrating SDGs*. Responsible Business Initiative.

WHO. (2017). *Diarrhoeal disease*. World Health Organization. https://www.who.int/news-room/fact-sheets/detail/diarrhoeal-disease

WHO. (2020, December). *The top 10 causes of death*. World Health Organization. https://www.who.int/news-room/fact-sheets/detail/the-top-10-causes-of-death

Wool And The Gang. (2020). *Modern Slavery Statement – Wool and the Gang*. Wool And The Gang. https://woolandtheganghelp.zendesk.com/hc/en-us/articles/360019979854

World Nuclear Association. (2020). Estimation de la mortalité aviaire canadienne attribuable aux collisions et aux pertes directes d'habitat associées à l'éolien. *Avian Conservation & Ecology*, *8*(2). https://doi.org/10.5751/ACE-00609-080210

Zhang, Z., Yao, J., Wang, Z., Xu, X., Lin, X., Czapar, G. F., & Zhang, J. (2011). Improving water management practices to reduce nutrient export from rice paddy fields. *Environmental Technology*, *32*(2), 197–209. https://doi.org/10.1080/09593330.2010.494689

Chapter 13
CSR Practices in European Countries

ABSTRACT

European companies are front runners for their CSR practices. The companies are transparent and remain consistent with achieving the 17 UN SDGs. The European society remains responsible and aware of its responsibility towards people and the planet. The CSR practices were started by European companies as early as the 1800s. The companies became more aware of the advent of industrialization, and the progress took giant leaps since the 1980s. The European government, business enterprises, and the public are well prepared to achieve the 17 UN SDGs compared to other countries. Besides progressing well in their region, European institutions and organizations also help others achieve the same by guiding and becoming role models. International Organization of Standards (ISO) and Business Social Compliance Initiative (BSCI) are European initiatives to provide compliances and systems for business organizations to achieve sustainability and social accountability (SA8000).

INTRODUCTION AND HISTORY

Continent Europe holds significant importance in the discussion of CSR practices. Europe has played a substantial role in evolving CSR practices worldwide. The idea of corporations acting as corporate citizen goes back to the middle ages (Latapí Agudelo et al., 2019). The England monarchy

DOI: 10.4018/978-1-7998-3988-0.ch013

expanded the concept to use the corporations for societal development (Chaffee, 2017). As England's rule and business corporations grew in the eighteenth-century, corporations' ideas as agents of societal development migrated to America. The Victorian philanthropist, which was the outcome of Christian teachings, started to focus on the labor class by creating welfare schemes in Europe and America. According to Heald (1970), in London year 1844, an organization was formed by the name "Young Men's Christian Association" (YMCA) to propagate and inculcate Christian values in business activities for social wellbeing.

The idea evolved, and organizations used welfare to retain the workforce (Carroll, 2008). The whole momentum led to famous Macy's USA philanthropy, the philanthropist businessman funds orphanage in 1875. The activity is considered the first of its kind in the USA as the corporations started to record CSR activities. The philanthropy and social welfare idea in the 1900s transformed into a balancing act between organization stakeholders and profit-making. The managers in the organization started interacting with the external environment to perform socioeconomic responsibilities. In the 1960s, researchers began focusing on organizational philanthropy and social welfare and giving practical implications and advantages. The CSR idea was to revolutionize by Bowen (1953) as he claimed that large corporations have a profound impact on society and all stakeholders in the organization. Many scholars like Eells (1956) and Selekman (1959) also argued that big corporations have a positive role in reducing poverty.

In 1981, Europeans were the first to establish a commission on environmental development known as the "European Commission's Environmental Directorate." The Norwegian Prime Minister "Gro Harlem Brundtland" chaired the commission. In 1987 the commission published its first report, "Our Common Future," which defined environmental sustainability. The Brundtland commission truly paved the way for CSR in Europe. The CSR idea in Europe took another leap in contrast to other countries by forming European Environment Agency in 1990. The European Commission promoted CSR through the "European Business Declaration," In 1995, twenty organizations adopted the viewpoint to counter social exclusion and unemployment (Europe, 2018). "European Business Declaration" transmuted to "European Business Network for Social Cohesion," later renamed to "Corporate Social Responsibility Europe" (Europe, 2018). The CSR Europe pushed the CSR agenda throughout the continent by collaborating with European business leaders.

SUSTAINABLE DEVELOPMENT IN EUROPE SINCE 2000

In 2002, the European Commission introduced a Green Paper to establish "Promoting a European framework for Corporate Social Responsibility." The established framework helped to combat the socio-environmental problems of the new era. The effort shaped the European strategy to CSR, and it served as stimuli for CSR campaigns by European Commission. The commission carried out extensive discussion during 2001 and 2004 to relevant answers to write a policy for Europe. The meetings took place in Brussels, Helsinki, and Venice, and the agendas in the discussion: "what is CSR, why CSR, and how to promote and implement CSR."

The European Commission launched a road map for business enterprises to implement sustainability in the year 2005. The diligent cooperation by European countries resulted in consensus on CSR promotion and implementation in Europe. The European Commission held a public discussion on its renewed CSR strategy for European Union in 2014. The public expressed confidence in the commission's CSR efforts. The European Commission in 2015 consulted all stakeholders forum for their opinion on CSR. The stakeholder's meeting also expressed its confidence and believed that the commission has a pivotal role in promoting CSR and sustainability in European businesses and its strategies (European Commission, 2015). The European countries were well prepared and ahead of their time implementing sustainability and CSR practices in firms. The business culture in Europe is very optimistic about implementing CSRs to achieve European Commission sustainable development goals that are in accord with UN seventeen SDGs (see figure 1).

Besides Europe is a flag-barer for sustainability and CSR practices, the continent is also helping other countries to achieve the same. The International Organization of Standards (ISO) is an organization from Europe based in Switzerland that created CSR guidelines through management, quality, and environmental compliances (ISO 9001 and ISO 14001) (ISO, 2020). The compliance certifications are helping business corporations around the globe to achieve sustainability and corporate social responsibility. In 2005, the idea further evolved because the collaboration among two countries (Brazil and Sweden) and business stakeholders resulted in ISO 26000. The ISO 26000 specifically design provides sustainability guidelines for businesses, organizations, and corporations (see figure 2 for ISO 26000) (ISO 26000, 2021).

Figure 1. Recommendations to European Commission
(CSR Europe, 2020)

CSR PRACTICES IN EUROPE

The European corporations collaborated to form an organizational network called "CSR Europe." The organization in 2015 introduced an initiative called "Enterprise 2020 Manifesto." The objective of this initiative is to achieve sustainability according to UN SDGs. The created network's effectiveness can ascertain by the number of its collaborating members and partners, which has reached ten thousand (CSR Europe, 2021). The "Enterprise 2020 Manifesto" entails creating five sustainable values. The first value is to promote and create societal impact through best business practices. The second value of the manifesto targets to create members satisfaction to sustain the whole CSR idea. The third and fourth value that the manifesto strives to achieve is enterprises' financial stability and employee and organizational capacity development. Finally, the fifth value it targets to achieve is to assess the impact of business activities on society objectively to determine further improvement. There are forty corporate members of "CSR Europe" and below thirty-five multinational corporations (see table 1).

Figure 2. ISO 26000 seven core objectives
(ISO 26000, 2010)

Table 1. Corporate members of "Europe CSR"

ArcelorMittal	BASF	BBVA	Bridge Stone	Cemex
Coco-Cola EU	Enel	Engie	Epson	Ferrero
Hellenic Petroleum	Here	Hitachi	Huawei	IBERDROLA
IBM	Gruppo Bancario	ITOCHU	Johnson & Johnson	Mc Cain
MOODY'S	Orange	Pirelli	Samsung	Sdworx
Sodexo	Solvay	State Street	Takeda	Teleperformance
Titan	Total	Toyota	Unipol Sai	Volkswagen

(CSR Europe, 2021)

The pragmatism of the European Commission, business corporations, and multinationals working in the continent paved the way for Europe to stand out as a role model in CSR for the world to follow. To learn more about CSR practices in Europe, below are ten corporations from the forty corporate member list of "Europe CSR" organization. The selected five business enterprises with their CSR practices positively affect the environment, the community, and shareholders' interests.

Figure 3. Ten sustainability development goals
(Corporate Arcelormittal, 2021)

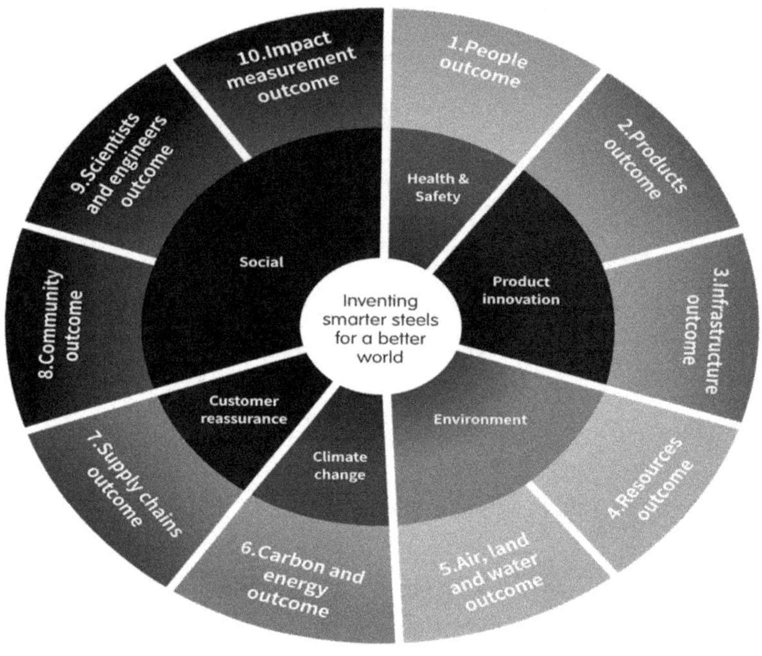

1. ArcelorMittal CSR Practice

The biggest steel manufacturers in Europe, the Americas, and Africa strive for best practices to remain sustainable and exercise CSR practices to better society. The company put forward ten sustainable goals to share sustainable development (see figure 3). The goals set by the company are cohesive, covering all spheres of people, profit, and planet. The company's CSR practices cover health and safety to impact people. The product innovation in the company focuses on the product produce and the constructed infrastructure of the company. The CSR policy covering the environment puts effort to use raw material responsibly without polluting air and water during steel production. To reverse climate change, the company monitors carbon emissions during production while using safe and clean energy sources for its energy consumption. Customer satisfaction also remains the company's CSR practice by having a green supply chain. Lastly, the CSR practices for social wellbeing have three objectives. To help communities, scientists, and engineers by funding and investing in improving its operations. Social wellbeing also measures the impacts due to its business operations and CSR practices. The company claims to reduce 30% carbon emission by 2030 and will become carbon neutral by 2050. For this purpose, the company is investing fifteen to twenty-five billion Euro Dollar smart carbon technology (see figure 4 for the euro roadmap)

Figure 4. Climate action Europe
(Corporate Arcelormittal, 2021)

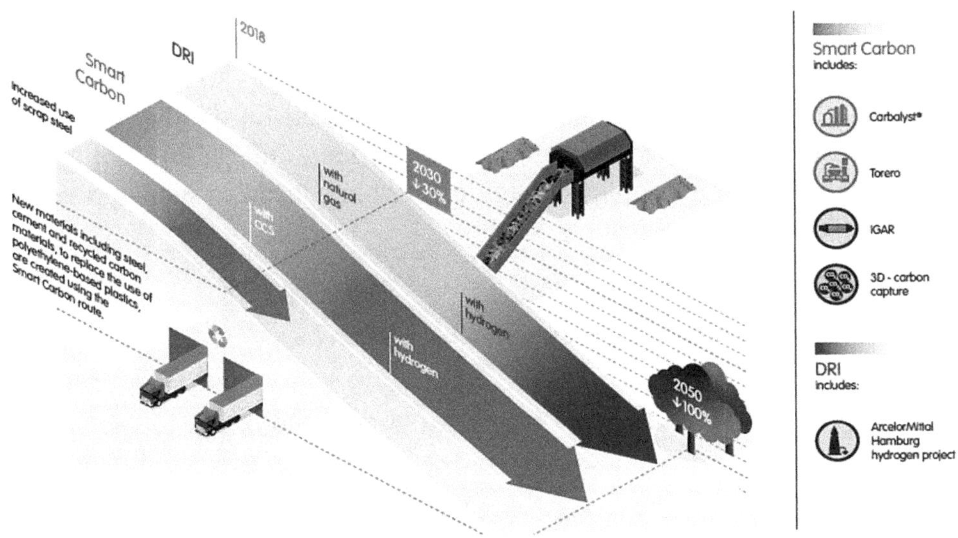

2. BASF CSR Practices

BASF is a chemical company founded in 1865 in Germany. They produce many chemicals and famous for making textile dyes for textiles and nonorganic chemicals. The company claims to target the economy, environment, and society. In the early days of its inception, the company only focused on its labor and employees for CSR practices; however, in 1920, the company implemented CSR practices to reach communities by attracting cultural enthusiasts. BASF finally, in 1993, started its first CSR project to support school students by funding to providing school laboratories. To this date, the company supports such projects in thirty counties worldwide. The company has been investing in protecting the environment since the 1960s. BASF started reporting its emissions in 1968 when such a concept was unknown to the rest of the world or required by government regulators. In 1974, BASF began its first water treatment plant, the most extensive in Europe. To reduce air pollution the company, build a heat insulator called Neopor™ in 1998. BASF always remains responsible as producer and consumer of resources.

3. BBVA CSR Practices

The BBVA is a global financial institution from Spain and has operations in Europe and the Americas. The financial institution CSR practices articulated by four company policy, which entails the positive impact on the environment, respecting the people's rights and dignity, investment in communities, and bringing social change in society. The bank also claims to adhere to UN SDGs and has pledged to invest one hundred billion Eurodollars in green finance. The bank spends one hundred and thirteen million Eurodollars to support eleven million people (see figure 5 for bank invest in social program and beneficiaries).

Figure 5. Investment in social programs and beneficiaries
(BBVA, 2021)

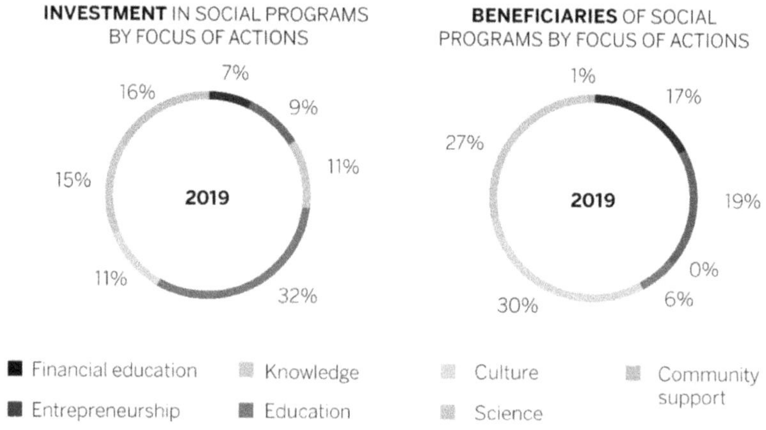

Through its BBVA Foundation, the bank supports five strategic areas covering the environment, medicine, science and technology, economy, and safety. Besides the BVA foundation, it also owns a non-profit organization, BBVA finance foundation, to support society's needy and vulnerable.

4. Enel CSR Practices

Enel is an Italian national electricity producer founded in 1962. The power company launched USD one and half billion dollar SDG-linked bonds to support the UN SDGs to invite private investors for their SDG initiatives in the US market in 2019. In the same year in Europe company issued two and half billion Euro Dollar SDG-linked bond. The company CSR practices measures through four goals: climate action, clean energy, industry innovation, and sustainability for cities and communities (see figure 6).

Figure 6. Enel four objectives driving the company's CSR practices
(Enel, 2021)

The company claims that SDG 13 is the biggest challenge. As a CSR practice, the company commits to reduce 80% greenhouse gases per kWh (kilowatt-hour) by 2030. Further, the company's CSR practice claims to decarbonize by 2050 completely. The CSR practice for SDG 17 development is to invest approximately seventeen billion Eurodollar in renewable and affordable energy. The company is investing sixteen billion Eurodollar in modernizing its infrastructure for sustainable development in three years. To target SDG 11, the company will build seven hundred and eighty thousand vehicle charging points by 2023 to educate the public to use energy more responsibly.

5. Hellenic Petroleum

The southeast European petroleum company was founded in 1998. The Greek petroleum company commits to achieving UN SDGs by its CSR practices. The company remains aggressive to complete all the goals. According to Hellenic Petroleum (2019), published sustainability report has achieved two out of seventeen UN SDGs.

The published report reveals as per company CSR's practice and policy, it spends seven million Eurodollar as an initiative to society. CSR practice's direct contribution amounted to six million Eurodollar in Greece while five hundred and fifty thousand Eurodollar will spend outside Greece as CSR practice. To eradicate any risk of corruption, the company has digitally transformed for transparency. As CSR practice to benefit employee, the company pays thirty-four million Eurodollar.

CONCLUSION

CSR practices in Europe stand as a role model for the world to follow. Because of their culture and governmental regulations, the European countries are more committed to achieving seventeen UN SDGs. Businesses are open and transparent about their CSR initiatives. The European Commission has played a vital role in propagating and creating a culture where companies are committed and feel responsible for impacting positively. Better people's lives, protect the environment, and make the planet sustainable for future generations. The Europeans CSR is beyond philanthropy and charity but working on proper sustainability development. The region's CSR practice will achieve decarbonization and neutral carbon emission until 2050 in their business operations and manufacturing.

REFERENCES

BBVA. (2021). Sustainability and Responsible Banking Model. *Información Corporativa | BBVA*. https://www.bbva.com/en/corporate-information/#responsible-banking-model

Bowen, H. R. (2013). *Social responsibilities of the businessman*. University of Iowa Press. doi:10.2307/j.ctt20q1w8f

Carroll, A. B. (2008). A history of corporate social responsibility: Concepts and practices. The Oxford Handbook of Corporate Social Responsibility, 19–46.

Chaffee, E. C. (2017). The origins of corporate social responsibility. *U. Cin. L. Rev.*, *85*, 353.

Corporate Arcelormittal. (2021). *Sustainability*. Corporate Arcelormittal. https://corporate.arcelormittal.com/sustainability

CSR Europe. (2018). *CSR Europe-20 years of business-policy interaction driving the CSR movement*. Author.

CSR Europe. (2020, February). *The EU Green Deal, A Timeline for Action — CSR Europe*. https://www.csreurope.org/newsbundle-articles/the-eu-green-deal-a-timeline-for-action

CSR Europe. (2021). *Our Network — CSR Europe*. https://www.csreurope.org/our-network-1

Eells, R. S. F. (1956). *Corporation giving in a free society*. Harper.

Enel. (2021). *Working with United Nations and building a sustainable business model*. Enel Company. https://www.enel.com/company/our-commitment/sdg-onu

European Commission. (2015). *Non-financial reporting*. European Commission. https://ec.europa.eu/info/business-economy-euro/company-reporting-and-auditing/company-reporting/non-financial-reporting_en

Heald, M. (1970). *The social responsibilities of business: Company and community 1900-1960*. Transaction Publishers.

Hellenic Petroleum. (2019). *Sustainable Development & Corporate Responsibility Report 2019*. Hellenic Petroleum. https://sustainabilityreport2019.helpe.gr/en/#sustainability-standards-and-verification

ISO. (2010). *ISO - Social responsibility - 7 core subjects of ISO 26000*. https://www.iso.org/publication/PUB100259.html

ISO. (2020). *History of ISO 26000 - ISO 26000*. ISO. https://iso26000.info/history-of-iso-26000/

ISO 26000. (2021). *ISO - ISO 26000 — Social responsibility*. ISO. https://www.iso.org/iso-26000-social-responsibility.html

Latapí Agudelo, M. A., Jóhannsdóttir, L., & Davídsdóttir, B. (2019). A literature review of the history and evolution of corporate social responsibility. *International Journal of Corporate Social Responsibility*, *4*(1), 1. doi:10.118640991-018-0039-y

Selekman, B. M. (1959). *A moral philosophy for management*. Academic Press.

Chapter 14
CSR Trends and Future

ABSTRACT

The future CSR challenges for business firms depend on the country's economy and cultural values. Firms must improvise to implement CSR practices accordingly. Corporations in developing and underdeveloped countries need to evolve their CSR practices from mild to strong sustainable-based views. The challenge is to adopt the correct degree of tradeoffs between the three capitals (planet, people, and profit). To survive and thrive, organizations should leave the traditional economic view, which remains sensitive about the bottom line. Societies are evolving more rapidly due to technological advancements in communication and the internet. The people are more critical to how organizations are conducting their businesses. News from any part of the world becomes global instantly with a click of a button. Vigilance is high from internal and external stakeholders of the company. CSR and its practices have a crucial role in all organizational functions in this dynamic and connected world.

INTRODUCTION

Corporate social responsibility has become an integral part of many western corporations, and gradual integration is observed in Asian corporations. The U.N. sustainable goals are the direction for the corporation to move forward. The corporation's CSR practices depend on the socio-economic structure of the country. Moving forward in the future, corporations face tuff challenges. The challenges range from selecting the best CSR practices for competitive

DOI: 10.4018/978-1-7998-3988-0.ch014

advantage and corporate message through the strategy. The Brundtland report is a milestone for sustainable development. It was published in 1987 and is considered a valid academic source to define sustainability (Tsalis et al., 2020).

According to (Sviluppo et al., 1987), sustainable development means a business firm meets its business activities' needs without affecting future generations' ability to do the same. It poses a future challenge for business firms to remain responsible throughout the process. The sustainable definition evolved further in the 1990s by incorporating stakeholders and identifying the human and natural resources as a prime objective to protect for the future. The evolving sustainability report adequately presents in the shape of U.N. seventeen sustainable goals for the year 2030. The U.N. sustainable goals might miss due to the growing population, especially in Asia (developing and underdeveloped) countries (Populations Matter, 2021). Besides challenges which undermine the whole sustainable effort globally, there exist CSR selection challenges which business faces. As stated in earlier chapters, location, culture, and economy are essential variables in selecting best-suited CSR practices by the corporations. However, the balance needs to be maintained to make tough choices by the business firm. The future challenges faced are both internal and external in nature. Comprising on both internal and external factor, below are important future challenges which firms faces to implement CSR practices.

CSR REPORTING

CSR practices mainly depend on human resource engagement to provide a congenial working environment for positive output. The CSR practices towards society's betterment are via direct interaction by supporting food drives, training, and employee volunteerism. Accompanying with environmental protection, a business firm tends to create challenging and soft values. The hard value created will result in cost reduction, for example, a paperless organization with cloud computing. In contrast, soft values entail luring new skilled human resources for organization progress.

Besides employees, organizations have to keep in view the interest of stakeholders and investors whose prime target is to earn a profit. The firm continually balances the cost of CSR practices and their bottom line. Further, organizations' daunting task is that CSR practices should create the right corporate message and match and contribute to the U.N. 2030 agenda. The firm publishes reports of all CSR activities and exercises for stakeholder consumption. United Kingdom has regulated a report format for firms to disclose CSR practices. In other parts of the world, the firm chooses to reveal only certain aspects of its CSR practices, such as environmental protection, philanthropy, or triple bottom line approach. The challenge for reporting CSR practices is equally painstaking for the internal environment compared to the external environment. The report serves as a dialogue between corporates and stakeholders and is accountable for assessing corporate social responsibility for sustainable development in all domains. The information helps build trust between the firm and stakeholders; any false report could tarnish the firm reputation. It helps create a competitive advantage as reporting provides the firm with a strategic position to bargain with different stakeholders. The firms can exploit progressive tax relieves by governments to support sustainability initiatives. The CSR practices and sustainability developments in the report can help progression in the business process. It gives a present-day picture and sets the tone for the future direction. With this, the firms better understand its strength and weakness for a future strategy for sustainability and CSR practices. Companies use creative methods to report CSR activities; mainly, the reports are available on the company's website for public review. Coca Cola (2020) published its CSR and sustainability practices on its website, giving a full update of the year 2019 to all stakeholders (see figure 1)

Firms by reporting also safeguard themselves from compliance breaches, which can be costly for the firm. The reporting of CSR practices would remain a future challenge for business firms; it should keep the corporate message alive while keeping all stakeholders' interests to earn profit and keep all unwanted costs at a minimum.

STRATEGY CHALLENGES

The strategy and model selection is also a significant challenge for firms around the globe. The academicians and researchers have advocated for the triple bottom line (planet, profit, and people) approach (see figure 2). It is possible by classifying the process into two categories. The first is a mild sustainability view where profit, planet, and people are tradeoff (Gimenez et al., 2012).

Figure 1. Coca-Cola overview in the company report
(Coca Cola, 2020)

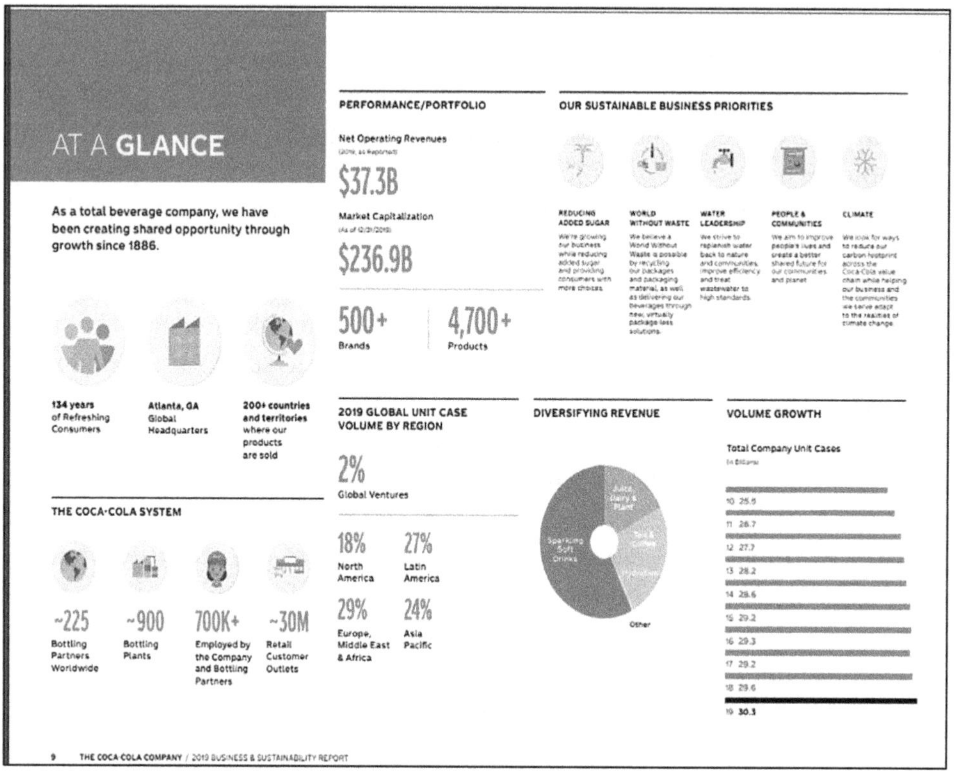

The second propagates firms with a robust triple-bottom-line sustainability-based view; the assumption bases on capital theory (Ekins et al., 2003). The firms can only tradeoff within the three capitals, and the rationale is to preserve the scarce resource for future generations (Nikolaou et al., 2019; Nikolaou & Tsalis, 2018). Western and Asian countries have to select a CSR model that fits in their business and culture dynamics. The selection can be in phases starting from mild to robust sustainability model, keeping in view the U.N. seventeen sustainable development goals (SDGs) and government regulation in their country. The firms should overcome this challenge to select their CSR practices by considering the one -sixty-nine sustainability targets in U.N. SDGs (Le Blanc, 2015; Salvia et al., 2019). The manufacturing enterprises can incorporate the SDGs in their supply chain stages by implementing compliance on suppliers for waste disposal and designing products responsible for production and consumption.

Figure 2. Triple bottom line purposed model for firms sustainability targets (Lyngaas, 2016)

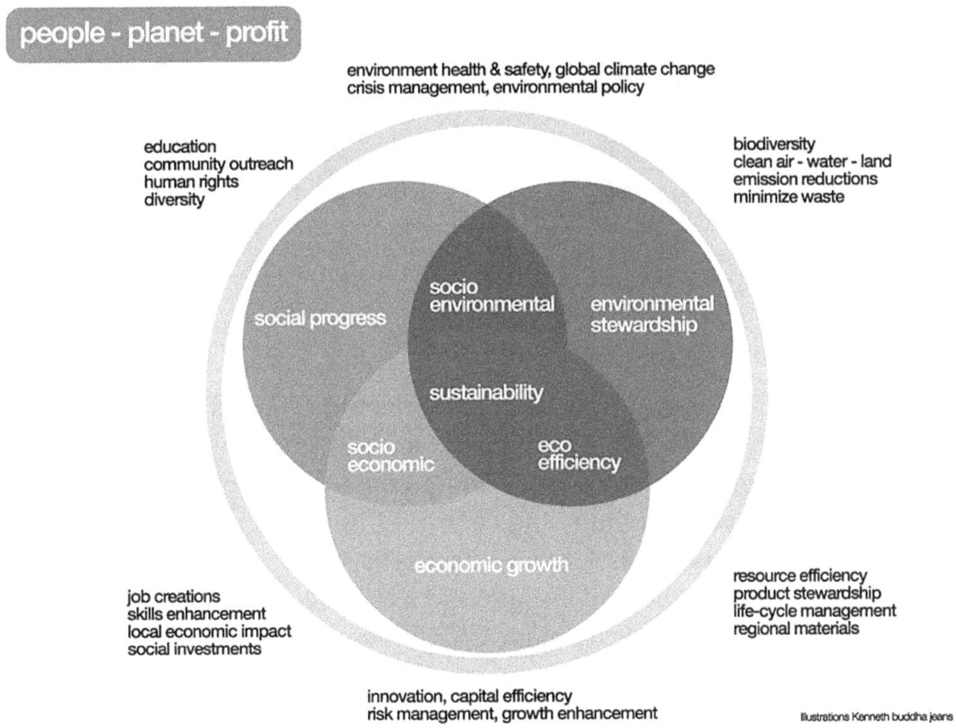

CSR PROPAGATION CHALLENGE

The propagation of CSR by firms in developing and underdeveloped countries is also a big challenge. CSR and sustainable projects are viewed by the traditional economic view, as discussed in the earlier chapters. It highlights the importance of sustainability and CSR; the idea should instill in all stakeholders through academia via schools and colleges. The concept should introduce in study curriculum and educational programs in developing and underdeveloped countries. The impregnated idea will fixate, and upcoming managers will think and act accordingly (de Paula Arruda Filho, 2017). Educational institutions are instrumental in shaping values to create an environment congenial for societal ethics. Business schools are essential to propagate CSR practices' value and importance by developing interdisciplinary approaches (Annan-Diab & Molinari, 2017) (see figure 3).

Figure 3. Adaptation of education to create a sustainable state
(Kioupi & Voulvoulis, 2019)

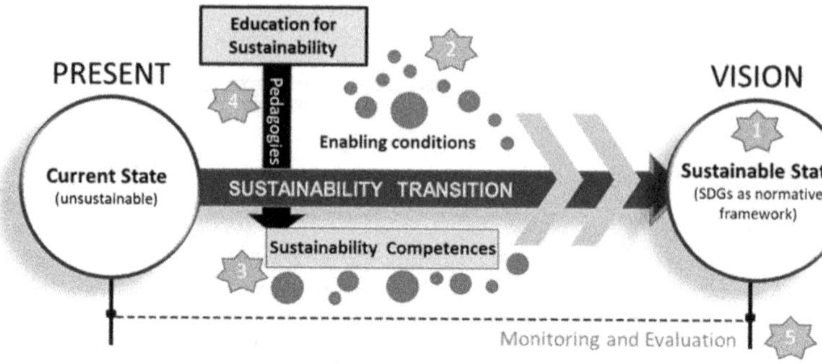

The framework adopted by Kioupi & Voulvoulis (2019) signifies how the current state transforms into a sustainable form by enabling conditions and competencies through developing training courses. The overall process of transformation must be monitor and control for improvement and increased efficiency. To effectively implement a liaison between academia, businesses and government are inevitable. The government's education regulation would enforce educational institutes to make CSR and sustainability a part of course work taught to students.

SOCIOECONOMIC PARADIGMS

The socio-economic paradigms will be the overriding force for CSR practice, which is a challenge and would be viewed differently throughout the world due to economic conditions. The CSR practices have evolved to fill the gaps in corporate governance (Barkemeyer, 2011). The holes created by businesses ranging from ecological protection, human and labor rights to equality and corporate corruption. Labor rights have been viewed differently due to socio-economic paradigms. Many western companies using developing countries as a production source would force suppliers for a limited working shift. On the contrary, the labor-hour restrictions deter extra income. Child labor is also a sensitive topic in the west and around the globe (see figure 4 media backlash on Nike).

Figure 4. Presentation on sustainability and child labor
(Paolo Taticchi, 2018)

However, it is somehow ignored for underdeveloped and developing countries because the economy cannot support families below the poverty line to provide essential items like food and clothes. The children under the age of 18 years help to provide essentials for family sustenance. Such CSR practices, in particular countries, would further increase poverty. According to Hussain-Khaliq (2004), child labor restriction in the football industry in Pakistan faced difficulty due to the same reason. Business enterprises can overcome the challenge of supporting child labor by providing self-development opportunities, protecting their rights, and safeguarding from any harassment in the workplace (Nichols, 1993). Lastly, women's empowerment and equality are perceived differently in different parts of the world. Female in Muslim communities would like to avoid working with male counterparts as the religion restricts and segregation is needed. Firms must overcome this challenge by keeping the community and society's sanctity before implementing any CSR practice.

DECREASING THE ENTROPY

The consumer demand is insatiable hunger, which is ever-growing in developed and western countries. The growing consumer demand increases entropy, leading toward market instability and irresponsible consumption and production. The clothing industry is a good example; according to Księżak (2016), spending on clothing is USD one trillion annually and is growing since 2000. The developing countries are responsible for three-fourths of the world's total export (Gardetti & orres, 2017). The western style is more fashion-conscious and needs rethinking (see figure 5).

Figure 5. The wastages of fast fashion
(Rasheed Maryam, 2019)

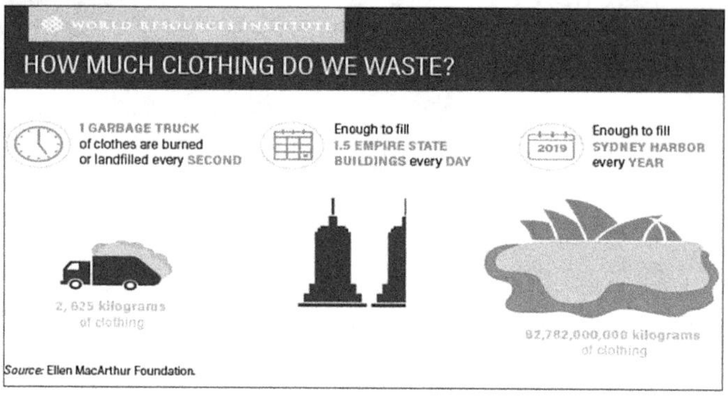

The circular economy is an answer to the problem. The challenge for the companies is to educate their consumer to reuse products to avoid consumer waste. The insatiable demand by consumers is increasing carbon footprint globally. For many developing countries, apparel and textile are crucial economic engines and provide jobs (de Abreu, 2015).

The fashion and clothing industry is one of the most significant contributors to waste at all supply chain stages (Zeller, 2012). The high demand and economic benefit lure developing countries to ignore a lot of sustainable goals. Western brands are buying from the third world while ignoring supplier CSR activities related to labor rights and working conditions. However, they remain sensitive to chemicals and raw material used, which can negatively impact consumers in their respective countries (see figure 6).

It is the biggest challenge for businesses that remain irresponsible about the supplier's CSR practices. The mining industry in different sectors, which are excavating raw material from third world countries, also remains insensitive about supplier CSR activities. The challenges for low-value items brands remain from both the market side and the supply side. The CSR practices for such firms should educate consumers to be responsible consumers and work with suppliers to improve CSR practices. The firms in developed and western countries have to improve costs to make room for suppliers to improve their working conditions. The challenge lies in changing the fashion consumption patterns and recalibration of the fast fashion concept, contributing to environmental pollutions.

Figure 6. Educating on impacts of apparel industry on the environment (Sardone Antonia, 2020)

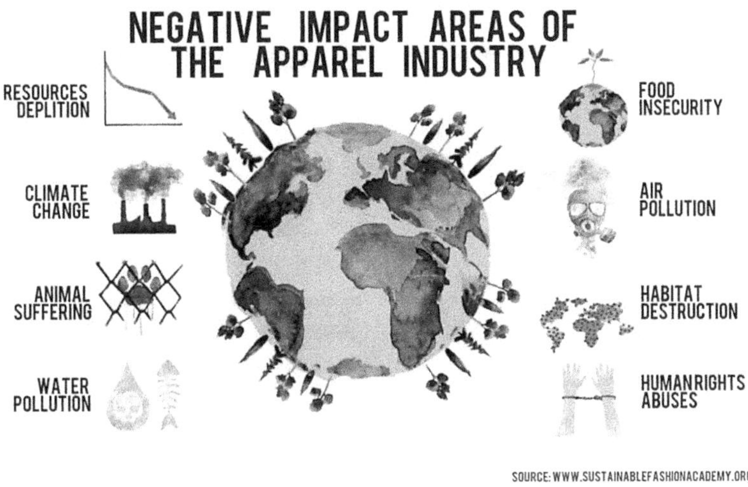

TECHNOLOGICAL CHALLENGES

The companies in developing and underdeveloped countries face a grave challenge of technological change, resulting in labor reduction as machines and robots will replace human resources. The industry 4.0 regime is taking over, which challenges CSR practices regarding and SGD's goal for zero hunger and poverty reduction. With machines and robots in production lines, quality and efficiency increase. For some industry where quality and efficiency is of utmost important industry 4.0 is inevitable. The evolving technology from industry 1.0 to 4.0 reduces labor usage during production (see figure 7).

As time passes, more and more jobs replace by machines and robots. Computing power has enhanced, and artificial intelligence is taking over. Western companies are keen to move forward and stepping up the pace. The disruptive technologies in manufacturing harm human resources, as many companies did not prepare accordingly (Handayani et al., 2020). Manyika et al. (2017) published a report in Mckinsey Global Institute that explains that due to industrial 4.0, approximately eight hundred million people will lose their jobs by the year 2030. The challenge for companies worldwide needs an out of box solution to counter the situation, and CSR has to play a crucial role while companies implement disruptive technologies to increase efficiency and effectiveness.

Figure 7. Depicting the evolution of the industry from 1.0 to 4.0 (Hamoudy, 2020)

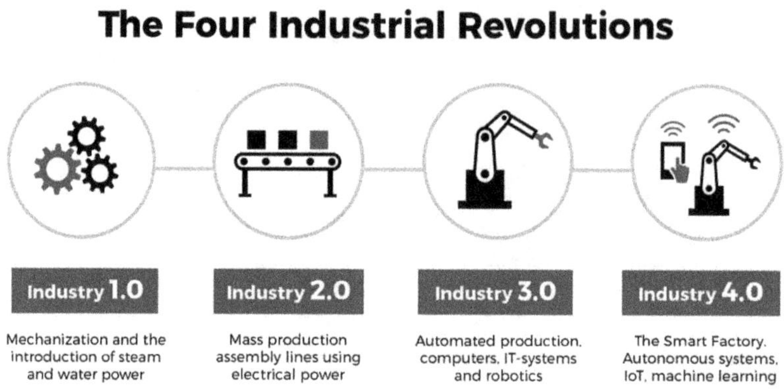

CONCLUSION

The future for CSR comes with many surprises to business enterprises. The firms strive to distinguish themselves as corporate citizens while making tradeoffs between resources to suit their environment better. Society is now aware and demands organizations to play their part for socio-economic betterment. The CSR practice should think out of the box for competitive advantage and communicating the right message. Academia is now most needed; knowledge management worldwide will bring innovative ideas for strategic managers to implement. The researchers must design disruptive technologies to avoid their negative impact on jobs in western countries. Through their CSR practices, companies should prepare for the future and train human resources to improvise accordingly. The chances are high that the world might miss its target for U.N. SDGs as the population increases in developing and underdeveloped countries. Government regulation is needed to check if corporate CSR practices contribute to providing sustainability and progressive taxing is an essential tool that can motivate firms in the right direction.

REFERENCES

Annan-Diab, F., & Molinari, C. (2017). Interdisciplinarity: Practical approach to advancing education for sustainability and for the Sustainable Development Goals. *International Journal of Management Education*, *15*(2), 73–83. doi:10.1016/j.ijme.2017.03.006

Barkemeyer, R. (2011). Corporate perceptions of sustainability challenges in developed and developing countries: Constituting a CSR divide? *Social Responsibility Journal*, *7*(2), 257–281. doi:10.1108/17471111111141521

Coca Cola. (2020, April). *Business and Sustainability Report 2019*. Coca-Cola Company. https://www.coca-colacompany.com/reports/business-sustainability-report-2019

de Abreu, M. C. S. (2015). Perspectives, drivers, and a roadmap for corporate social responsibility in the textile and clothing industry. In *Roadmap to sustainable textiles and clothing* (pp. 1–21). Springer. doi:10.1007/978-981-287-164-0_1

de Paula Arruda Filho, N. (2017). The agenda 2030 for responsible management education: An applied methodology. *International Journal of Management Education*, *15*(2), 183–191. doi:10.1016/j.ijme.2017.02.010

Ekins, P., Simon, S., Deutsch, L., Folke, C., & De Groot, R. (2003). A framework for the practical application of the concepts of critical natural capital and strong sustainability. *Ecological Economics*, *44*(2–3), 165–185. doi:10.1016/S0921-8009(02)00272-0

Gardetti, M. A., & Torres, A. L. (2017). *Sustainability in fashion and textiles: values, design, production and consumption*. Routledge. doi:10.4324/9781351277600

Gimenez, C., Sierra, V., & Rodon, J. (2012). Sustainable operations: Their impact on the triple bottom line. *International Journal of Production Economics*, *140*(1), 149–159. doi:10.1016/j.ijpe.2012.01.035

Hamoudy, A. (2020, August). *Industry 4.0 and how smart sensors make the difference*. https://www.spectralengines.com/articles/industry-4-0-and-how-smart-sensors-make-the-difference

Handayani, M., Baridwan, Z., & Irianto, G. (2020). Transformation Corporate Social Responsibility Towards Industrial Revolution 4.0: Strategy and Challenges. *Brawijaya International Conference on Multidisciplinary Sciences and Technology (BICMST 2020)*, 45–49.

Hussain-Khaliq, S. (2004). Eliminating child labour from the Sialkot soccer ball industry: Two industry-led approaches. *Journal of Corporate Citizenship*, *13*(13), 101–107. doi:10.9774/GLEAF.4700.2004.sp.00012

Kioupi, V., & Voulvoulis, N. (2019). Education for sustainable development: A systemic framework for connecting the SDGs to educational outcomes. *Sustainability*, *11*(21), 6104. doi:10.3390u11216104

Księżak, P. (2016). The CSR challenges in the clothing industry. *Journal of Corporate Responsibility and Leadership*, *3*(2), 51–65. doi:10.12775/JCRL.2016.008

Le Blanc, D. (2015). Towards integration at last? The sustainable development goals as a network of targets. *Sustainable Development*, *23*(3), 176–187. doi:10.1002d.1582

Lyngaas, K. (2016). *Triple bottom line - Sustainable & Refashioned Design by Buddha Jeans Sustainable & Refashioned Design by Buddha Jeans*. https://buddhajeans.com/encyclopedia/the-triple-bottom-line/

Manyika, J., Lund, S., Chui, M., Bughin, J., Woetzel, J., Batra, P., Ko, R., & Sanghvi, S. (2017). *Jobs lost, jobs gained: What the future of work will mean for jobs, skills, and wages.* McKinsey Global Institute.

Nichols, M. (1993). Third-world families at work: Child labor or child care? *Harvard Business Review*, *71*(1), 12.

Nikolaou, I. E., & Tsalis, T. (2018). A framework to evaluate eco-and social-labels for designing a sustainability consumption label to measure strong sustainability impact of firms/products. *Journal of Cleaner Production*, *182*, 105–113. doi:10.1016/j.jclepro.2018.02.042

Nikolaou, I. E., Tsalis, T. A., & Evangelinos, K. I. (2019). A framework to measure corporate sustainability performance: A strong sustainability-based view of firm. *Sustainable Production and Consumption*, *18*, 1–18. doi:10.1016/j.spc.2018.10.004

Paolo Taticchi. (2018). *An Introduction to Modern Corporate Sustainability.* https://www.google.com/search?q=An+Introduction+to+Modern+Corporate+Sustainability.+Paolo+Taticchi%2C+February+20th+2018&oq=An+Introduction+to+Modern+Corporate+Sustainability.+Paolo+Taticchi%2C+February+20th+2018&aqs=chrome.69i57j69i60.277j0j9&sourceid=chrome&ie=UTF-8

Populations Matter. (2021). *Population and the Sustainable Development Goals*. https://populationmatters.org/sdgs

Rasheed Maryam. (2019). *Overdressed & Overstressed | The Impact of Fast Fashion on Global Sustainability*. https://sustainablesquare.com/impact-of-fast-fashion/

Salvia, A. L., Leal Filho, W., Brandli, L. L., & Griebeler, J. S. (2019). Assessing research trends related to Sustainable Development Goals: Local and global issues. *Journal of Cleaner Production*, *208*, 841–849. doi:10.1016/j.jclepro.2018.09.242

Sardone, A. (2020, September). *Fashion Innovation Archives - University of Fashion Blog*. https://www.universityoffashion.com/blog/category/fashion-innovation/

Sviluppo, C. (1987). *Our common future*. Peterson's.

Tsalis, T. A., Malamateniou, K. E., Koulouriotis, D., & Nikolaou, I. E. (2020). New challenges for corporate sustainability reporting: United Nations' 2030 Agenda for sustainable development and the sustainable development goals. *Corporate Social Responsibility and Environmental Management*.

Zeller, C. (2012). *Self-regulation and labour standards: an exemplary study investigating the emergence and strenghening of self-regulation regimes in the apparel industry*. Academic Press.

About the Contributors

Syed Abdul Rehman Khan is a professor of Supply Chain and Logistics Management. Dr. Khan achieved his CSCP—Certified Supply Chain Professional certificate from the U.S.A. and completed his postdoctoral fellowship from Tsinghua University. Since 2020, Dr. Khan has been affiliated with Xuzhou University of Technology. He has more than nine years' core experience in supply chain and logistics at industrial and academic levels. Prof. Khan has attended several international conferences and has been invited as a keynote speaker in different countries. He has published 100+ scientific research papers in different well-renowned international journals and conferences. Also, Dr. Khan has achieved several research projects and scientific innovation awards.

Zhang Yu is affiliated with Chang'an University, China. Her research interest is reverse logistics, end-of-life vehicles, recycling techniques, and green practices in the corporate sector. She has published 25 research papers in different international journals and conferences. Also, she is an author of three books related to supply chain and business management.

Mirela Panait currently holds the position of PhD Professor at Faculty of Economic Sciences, Petroleum-Gas University of Ploiesti (Romania). She is also scientific researcher at Institute of National Economy from Romanian Academy. Her work experience derives from and includes teaching courses and seminaries; research activities; participating in scientific conferences. Regarding research activities, these are represented by publishing seven books and over 100 scientific papers in the field of interest: corporate social responsibility, sustainable development, foreign direct investment and financial market. She has published articles in leading international journals, including Land Use Policy, Energies, Sustainability and PlosOne. She is a reviewer for journals and conferences like Sustainability, Energies, Journal of

Risk and Financial Management. She is also guest editor or associate editor for prestigious journals from MDPI group or IGI Global publishing house.

Laeeq Razzak Janjua is currently working in financial sector as subject matter expert (SME) in financial intelligence unit (FIU). He has completed his research internship from Poznań University of Economics and Business as external candidate of DSE program. His research interests are sustainable development, financial economic, green finance, and financial crimes. He has published more than 10 research papers in different international journals.

Adeel Shah is a senior lecturer (Supply Chain and logistic Department) at the Institute of Business Management. Expert and researcher in Textile and Apparel Operations, supply chain management, and green Supply Chain. He has worked in the Textile and Apparel industry, managing operations and supply chain before academics and research involvement. He is actively involved in consultancy and capstone supply chain projects for various industries.

Index

G

I

O

P

R

S

www.ingramcontent.com/pod-product-compliance
Lightning Source LLC
LaVergne TN
LVHW081328300926
849161LV00008B/1907
* 9 7 8 1 7 9 9 8 3 9 8 8 0 *